AF840272

Human Rights, Culture, and the Rule of Law

This new book sets out to examine the relationship between culture and respect for human rights. It departs from the oft-made assumption that culture is closely linked to ideas about community. Instead, it reveals culture as a quality possessed by the individual with a serious impact on her ability to enjoy the rights and freedoms as recognised in international human rights law in meaningful and effective ways. This understanding serves to redirect attention towards a range of issues that have long been marginalised, but which warrant a central place in human rights research and on the international human rights agenda.

Special attention is given to the circumstances induced by cultural differences between people and the laws by which they are expected to live. These differences constitute a source of human distancing and alienation from, as well as conflict and disagreement with, the laws and legal systems in force. The circumstances are created by differing tools, know-how, and skills ('cultural equipment'), diverse settlements on matters that are ultimately indifferent from the standpoint of cosmopolitan moral law (*adiaphora*), and conflicts having their source in conflicting doctrines—ethical, religious, and philosophical—addressing deep questions about the ultimate purpose of human life ('comprehensive doctrines').

Each of the circumstances shifts the focus onto issues of critical importance to the aim of securing effective and adequate protection of individual freedom as societies become increasingly diversified in cultural terms. These issues are: access to laws and public institutions; exemption from legal obligations for reasons of conscience; fair resolution of conflicts having their source in differing ethical, religious and philosophical outlooks; and excuse for breach of law in case of involuntary ignorance.

Volume 6 in the series Human Rights Law in Perspective

Human Rights Law in Perspective
General Editor: Colin Harvey

The language of human rights figures prominently in legal and political debates at the national, regional and international levels. In the UK the Human Rights Act 1998 has generated considerable interest in the law of human rights. It will continue to provoke much debate in the legal community and the search for original insights and new materials will intensify.

The aim of this series is to provide a forum for scholarly reflection on all aspects of the law of human rights. The series will encourage work which engages with the theoretical, comparative and international dimensions of human rights law. The primary aim is to publish over time books which offer an insight into human rights law in its contextual setting. The objective is to promote an understanding of the nature and impact of human rights law. The series is inclusive, in the sense that all perspectives in legal scholarship are welcome. It will incorporate the work of new and established scholars.

Human Rights Law in Perspective is not confined to consideration of the UK. It will strive to reflect comparative, regional and international perspectives. Work which focuses on human rights law in other states will therefore be included in this series. The intention is to offer an inclusive intellectual home for significant scholarly contributions to human rights law.

Volume 1 Importing the Law in Post-Communist Transitions *Catherine Dupré*

Volume 2 The Development of the Positive Obligations Under the European Convention on Human Rights by the European Court of Human Rights *Alastair Mowbray*

Volume 3 Human Rights Brought Home: Socio-Legal Studies of Human Rights in the National Context *edited by Simon Halliday and Patrick Schmidt*

Volume 4 Corporations and Transnational Human Rights Litigation *Sarah Joseph*

Volume 5 Human Rights in the Community *edited by Colin Harvey*

Human Rights, Culture, and the Rule of Law

Jessica Almqvist

•HART•
PUBLISHING

OXFORD AND PORTLAND, OREGON
2005

Published in North America (US and Canada) by
Hart Publishing
c/o International Specialized Book Services
920 NE 58th Avenue, Suite 300
Portland, Oregon
97213-3786
USA
www.isbs.com

© Jessica Almqvist 2005

Jessica Almqvist has asserted her right under the Copyright, Designs and Patents Act 1988, to be identified as the author of this work.

Hart Publishing is a specialist legal publisher based in Oxford, England. To order further copies of this book or to request a list of other publications please write to:

Hart Publishing, Salters Boatyard, Folly Bridge, Abingdon Rd, Oxford, OX1 4LB
Telephone: +44 (0)1865 245533 Fax: +44 (0) 1865 794882
email: mail@hartpub.co.uk
WEBSITE: http//:www.hartpub.co.uk

British Library Cataloguing in Publication Data
Data Available

ISBN 1-84113-506-2 (hardback)

Typeset by Compuscript Ltd, Ireland
Printed and bound in Great Britain by
TJ International, Padstow, Cornwall

To Carlos

Series Editor's Preface

This work focuses on the concept of culture and its place in human rights law. The suggestion in this book is that the idea of a right to culture has not been subjected to sufficiently rigorous scrutiny and some inherited positions need to be questioned. The author argues that the dominant approach in human rights law links culture mainly to communities and the development of a right to cultural identity. She questions this and contends that culture is a property which belongs to each individual. The argument springs from the author's belief that human rights are tied closely to notions of individual freedom. She is concerned that the overriding purpose of human rights law might be eroded as a result of adopting a flawed conception of cultural rights. The study is a welcome contribution to the debate on the relationship between cultural diversity and human rights law.

Colin Harvey
Belfast
August 2005

Acknowledgements

This book is a revised version of my doctoral thesis defended at the European University Institute, Florence (May 2002). Several people have been crucial to the completion of this study. Needless to say, I am especially indebted to my supervisors Philip Alston and Jeremy Waldron for their outstanding guidance and invaluable comments on how to improve my arguments. My research has also profited greatly from seminars and discussions with Leslie Green, Massimo La Torre, Steven Lukes, Philip Pettit, Thomas Pogge, Joseph Raz, and Neil Walker as well as students and friends at UC Berkeley (1994–1995), European University Institute (1996–2001) and Columbia University (1998–1999), among them, Claudia Attucci, Patrizia Nanz, Edmee Tuyl, and Katharina Spiess. Special thanks for very useful comments by Neil Walker and Peter Jones who, in addition to my supervisors, took part in the examination of my doctoral thesis. Thanks also to the Swedish Research Council and the European University Institute for their financial support as well as to the Project on International Courts and Tribunals, the Center of International Cooperation, New York University, especially Cesare Romano, for moral support in the final stages of this book.

Lastly, without the love, encouragement, and support from my family, especially my parents Leif and Karin, my son Sebastian and, above all, my husband Carlos, this book might never have been completed. Therefore, I dedicate this book to Carlos.

New York, July 2004

Table of Contents

1

Introduction

THE ISSUES

THE PRESENT STUDY sets out to examine the relationship between culture and respect for human rights. It departs from the oft-made assumption that culture is closely linked to ideas about community. Instead, it reveals culture as a quality possessed by the individual with a serious impact on her ability to enjoy the rights and freedoms as recognised in international human rights law in meaningful and effective ways. This understanding serves to redirect attention towards a range of issues that have long been marginalised, but which warrant a central place in human rights research and on the international human rights agenda.

Special attention is accorded to the circumstances induced by cultural differences between people and the laws by which they are expected to live. These differences constitute a source of human distancing and alienation from, as well as conflict and disagreement with, the laws and legal systems in force. The present study focuses on the circumstances created by differing tools, know-how, and skills ('cultural equipment'), diverse settlements on matters that are viewed as ultimately indifferent from the standpoint of cosmopolitan moral law (*adiaphora*), and conflicts having their source in conflicting doctrines—ethical, religious, and philosophical—addressing deep questions about the ultimate purpose of human life ('comprehensive doctrines').

Each of the circumstances shifts the focus onto issues of critical importance to the aim of securing effective and adequate protection of individual freedom as societies become increasingly diversified in cultural terms. These issues are:

- access to laws and public institutions;
- exemption from legal obligations for reasons of conscience;
- fair resolution of conflicts having their source in differing ethical, religious and philosophical outlooks; and
- excuse for breach of law in case of involuntary ignorance.

The problems associated with each of these issues are acute in many multicultural societies. Nevertheless, the current human rights approach to culture does not engage with them. In favouring an understanding of culture as primarily linked to ideas about community and as warranting the universal affirmation of a right of a minority to protect its cultural identity, the current human rights approach avoids addressing critical questions about law and policy associated with the reality of cultural difference as a source of disagreement, conflict, ignorance, and alienation. Still, the circumstances induced by cultural differences are likely to intensify in the years ahead as a result of an ever increasing human mobility across the globe and the need to strengthen multilateral frameworks of cooperation across cultural divides and variations. These developments urge the advancement of an alternative human rights approach to culture.

LIMITATIONS

The present study is limited in three important respects. First of all, it does not address the possibility of using the arguments developed throughout the book in support of self-determination rights and their practical institutional implications. These issues are particularly pertinent for multinational states or organisations such as the European Union that purport to govern a society composed of a broad range of national and other cultures. This is not to say that a concern with what is defined in this book as 'suitable' cultural equipment, the difficulties involved in acquiring such equipment, and the general importance people tend to give to the specific content of their particular equipment to resolve ordinary life issues, cannot be used to support demands for self-determination and self-government. Nevertheless, the present study uses a static framework. This is so because the primary objective of this study is to develop a set of arguments about the different reasons for which we ought to care about people's specific cultural backgrounds and attachments, and to demonstrate that all our reasons for doing so are not only consistent with, but required by virtue of a commitment to ensuring a minimum provision of respect for individual freedom, and that such respect does not necessarily require the recognition of collective rights. In other words, it does not discuss the adequacy of a state or state-like (such as the European Union) institutional framework as such.

A second limitation is its assumption about the state as a potential violator of human rights in the absence of any consideration of cultural difference among its inhabitants in its law-making and law-applying activities. It claims that a human rights concern with culture generates obligations on the part of the state to secure the conditions that ensure the effective and adequate enjoyment of individual freedom. Thus, it does not discuss whether non-state actors, including corporations, non-governmental organisations, and international organisations, such as the United Nations or the World Bank, are similarly obligated to consider cultural difference among their beneficiaries in the development and implementation of programmes, projects, and policies by virtue of a commitment to individual freedom. Once again, the arguments advanced in this book do not rule out a consideration of other actors besides states and their obligations to consider the immediate impact of culture on one's ability to enjoy that freedom. Nevertheless, the state is the main institutional actor whose culture is in question as societies become more diverse; it is the most straightforward case of cultural dominance since it has the coercive powers of law at its disposal to retain that dominance.

A third limitation is its focus on *liberal* theories of justice and liberal democratic societies. One reason for this is that it is commonly assumed that such theories, and the societies for which they have been designed, are consistent with respect for human rights. Indeed, it is not unusual to see liberal theories of justice as providing the correct measures of what it means for the state to respect those rights in its law-making and law-applying activities. As this study seeks to demonstrate, however, their ignorance of cultural difference wrongfully legitimises laws and policies which seriously undermine the possibility of individual freedom for everybody. Another reason for this focus has to do with a more general argument about the need to link a theory of human rights with a theory of justice that takes seriously the need to recognise the difficulties involved in human rights implementation. Liberal theories highlight the need for national legislatures and judiciaries to consider a range of factors in the process of implementing human rights, including the need for common regulations, conflict-resolution, and the protection of other values besides those associated with culture-oriented concerns, such as public health, safety, and order. A human rights approach to culture must recognise the difficulties involved in balancing a range of various culture-oriented concerns with other pertinent human rights concerns.

OUTLINE OF CHAPTERS

The second chapter provides an inventory of notions of culture that have been introduced and recognised in international human rights law. A careful examination of international human rights law reveals an understanding of culture as referring to something which everybody has a right to participate in; however, it is also understood as posing obstacles or barriers to the equal enjoyment of international human rights as well as harbouring practices of violence in contravention of these rights. Nevertheless, as this chapter indicates, the recognised notions of culture and their complex impact on human rights remain largely unexplored by international human rights institutions. More significantly, this question has been overshadowed by the resurgence of identity politics and the growing belief that talk of culture essentially urges the sustained recognition of a right to cultural identity.

The third chapter advances a critique of the current human rights approach for its failure to present a comprehensive framework that is capable of addressing and responding to the many issues related to culture arising in contemporary deliberations about rights and justice. It is suggested that attitudes of avoidance, idealism, simplicity and, more recently, particularism, which have become characteristic of a human rights approach, are not conducive to advancing our understanding of the complex role and significance of culture from the standpoint of human rights.

The fourth chapter articulates the contours of a conceptual and evaluative framework that places the notion of the cultural dimension of the individual and its relationship to the aim of ensuring the effective and adequate enjoyment of individual freedom at the centre of human rights research. To this end, it distinguishes between skills, norms, and ideological outlook, and explains the various ways in which each of these cultural aspects are of direct relevance for clarifying what is required in terms of conduct by the main public institutions (legislatures, courts, administrative agencies, etc) assigned to secure international human rights in a Rule of Law context. The four subsequent chapters of the book then develop this theme in greater detail.

The fifth chapter is devoted to the notion of cultural equipment as it captures the sense in which the individual possession of culture-specific skills, tools, and know-how affects the enjoyment of human rights and freedoms. The analysis begins with an explanation of what cultural equipment consists of, how it is acquired, and its central role in human action. Thereafter attention is directed to the critical importance of having cultural equipment suitable to one's place of residence in order to access laws and public institutions, to play a role in political life, to participate in the economy, and to secure a fair share of income and wealth.

The analysis undertaken in the sixth chapter seeks to complement the argument about cultural equipment in its focus on the role and significance of cultural norms and rules on human action. It introduces the notion of *adiaphora* to explain what sorts of human affairs are typically governed by cultural norms (dress, diet, prayer, child-rearing) and to emphasise their supposed moral irrelevance from the standpoint of cosmopolitan moral law. This understanding of the relationship between culture and morality is contrasted with the reality of conscientious engagements on precisely these matters and an argument about the need to be responsive to, and, if possible, accommodate such engagements into the fabric of law.

The seventh chapter, in contrast, is centred on conflicts and disagreements having their source in diverse opinions on how to behave on matters of *adiaphora*. It alerts us to the fact of conflicting ethical, philosophical, and religious doctrines comprising rules and norms regulating human conduct in the field of *adiaphora* and believed to apply universally and categorically. It is suggested that the disagreements that are generated by a diversity of such doctrines cannot be resolved by way of cultural accommodations, but direct attention to the need for authority and democratic participation in their resolution.

The eighth chapter addresses the way in which law-applying institutions (courts and administrative agencies) may encounter problems of culture and how to best respond to them. To this end, it develops a claim about the need to excuse acts and omissions contrary to law in case of involuntary ignorance resulting from deficient cultural equipment.

The ninth and final chapter discusses the need for an international human rights agenda on culture that does not suffer from the shortcomings inherent in the predominant formulation of the right to culture as a right to enjoy one's own culture, but which takes seriously the critical importance of being able to access the culture of the broader society as well. It also makes a number of concrete recommendations about the core content of such a human rights agenda on the basis of the arguments developed throughout the book.

2

The Proliferation of Culture in International Human Rights Law

TALK OF CULTURE in human rights and diplomatic circles emerged phoenix-like at the beginning of the 1990s in reaction to three rather different events: the ethnic revivals in post-communist politics with their corollary demands for national independence and self-determination,[1] the partial success of indigenous people in establishing their own distinct human rights agenda,[2] as well as the criticism of the claim about the universal validity of human rights advanced by the 'Asian Tigers' in the World Conference on Human Rights in Vienna in 1993 and reflected—at least to some extent—in its concluding document.[3] Their criticisms found partial support in the proclaimed need to consider difference in cultural heritage once in the business of implementing human rights and advocated by the

[1] See especially the UN Declaration of the Rights of Persons Belonging to National or Ethnic, Religious or Linguistic Minorities, GA Res 47/135, Dec 18 1992; UN GAOR, 47th Sess, Supp No 49, at 210, UN Doc A/47/49 (1992); Council of Europe Framework Convention for the Protection of National Minorities, Nov 10 1994, Europ TS 157; and Document of the Copenhagen Meeting of the Conference on the Human Dimension of the CSCE, 29 July 1990, Art 32, reprinted in (1990) 29 *International Legal Materials* 1305.

[2] HR Berman, 'Introductory Note. United Nations Commission on Human Rights Sub-Commission on Prevention of Discrimination and Protection of Minorities: Draft United Nations Declaration on the Rights of Indigenous Peoples' (1995) 34 *International Legal Materials* 541.

[3] Vienna Declaration and Programme of Action, United Nations World Conference on Human Rights, 25 June 1993, UNDoc A/CONF 157/23. Para 5 of the Vienna Declaration reads in full: 'All human rights are universal, indivisible and interdependent and interrelated. The international community must treat human rights globally in a fair and equal manner, on the same footing, and with the same emphasis. While the significance of national and regional particularities and various historical, cultural and religious backgrounds must be borne in mind, it is the duty of States, regardless of their political, economic and cultural systems, to promote and protect all human rights and fundamental freedoms.'

preparatory meetings in Africa,[4] Latin America and the Caribbean,[5] Asia,[6] and Islamic countries.[7]

While these events evidently boosted a sense of urgency to give culture a firm place in human rights research, it must be noted that the issue of culture was not novel, but had surfaced already at the time of the adoption of the Universal Declaration of Human Rights in 1948.[8] At that time, however, the cultural critique came from academic circles and was most forcefully expressed in the 'American Anthropological Statement' submitted to the drafters of the Declaration. The American anthropologists regarded it as imperative that the following principles would be taken into account:

1. the individual realises his personality through his culture, hence respect for individual differences entails a respect for cultural differences;
2. respect for differences between cultures is validated by the scientific fact that no technique of qualitatively evaluating cultures has been discovered; and
3. standards and values are relative to the culture from which they derive so that any attempt to formulate postulates that grow out of the beliefs or moral codes of one culture must to that extent detract from the applicability of any Declaration of Human Rights to mankind as a whole.[9]

Considering the immediate purpose of the Declaration to condemn, once and for all, the outrageous atrocities that took place during the Second World War, the somewhat abstract and lofty propositions about the tie between individual human beings and particular cultures listed in the anthropologists' statement did not receive much attention. The final inclusion of a provision

[4] Tunis Declaration on Human Rights, Regional Meeting of Africa of the World Conference on Human Rights, 6 November 1992, UN Doc A/CONF 157/AFRM/14–A CONF 157/PC/57, 24 November 1992.

[5] San José Declaration on Human Rights, Regional Meeting for Latin America and the Caribbean of the World Conference on Human Rights, 22 January 1993, UN Doc A/CONF 157/ LACRM/15–A/CONF 157/PC/58, 11 February 1993.

[6] Bangkok Declaration on Human Rights, Regional Meeting for Asia of the World Conference on Human Rights, 2 April 1993, UN Doc A/CONF 157/ASRM/8–A/CONF 157/ PC/59, 7 April 1993.

[7] Cairo Declaration on Human Rights in Islam, Aug 5, 1990, Organisation of the Islamic Conference, UN GAOR, World Conference on Human Rights, 4th Sess, Agenda Item 5, UN Doc A/CONFR 157/PC/62/Add 18 (1993).

[8] See eg MA Glendon, *A World Made New*: *Eleanor Roosevelt and the Universal Declaration of Human Rights* (New York, Random House, 2001), 221 ff.

[9] American Anthropological Association, 'Statement on Human Rights' (1947) 49 *American Anthropologist* 539.

on culture was motivated by a proclaimed importance of individual participation in the cultural life of the community (Article 17(1)).[10]

Since the adoption of the Universal Declaration of Human Rights, a number of culture-related interests and concerns have been introduced and incorporated into the fabric of international human rights law. There is no international legal (or quasi-legal) instrument devoted to culture alone. Instead, the term 'culture' crops up in a broad range of international documents (conventions, declarations, reports, etc) indicating the potentially far-reaching significance of culture in different fields of human rights, including cultural rights, self-determination rights, and the right to development as well as the rights of women, children, national minorities, indigenous peoples, and migrants.

THE RIGHT TO CULTURAL PARTICIPATION

The idea of a right to culture as an individual right to take part in cultural life which was recognised for the first time in the Universal Declaration of Human Rights has been reaffirmed several times in international instruments, including the International Covenant on Economic, Social and Cultural Rights (1966) (ICESCR)[11] as a right to take part in cultural life;[12] the Convention on the Elimination of All Forms of Racial Discrimination (1989)[13] as a right to equal enjoyment and participation in cultural activities (Article 5(e)(*vi*)); and the Convention on the Rights of the Child (1990)[14] as a right of children to participate freely in cultural life and the arts (Article 31).[15]

[10] Universal Declaration of Human Rights, 10 December 1948, Art 17(1), GA Res 217 (III), UN GAOR, 3rd Sess, Supp No 16, UN Doc/A/810. Article 17(1) reads in full: 'Everyone has the right to freely participate in the cultural life of the community, to enjoy the arts and to share in scientific advancement and its benefits.'

[11] International Covenant on Economic, Social and Cultural Rights, 16 December 1966, Art 1, GA Res 2200A(XXI), 21 UN GAOR, 21st Sess, Supp No 16, at 49, UN Doc A/6316 (1966) [hereinafter ICESCR].

[12] ICESCR, Art 15 reads in full: '1. The States Parties to the present Covenant recognize the right of everyone: (a) To take part in cultural life; (b) To enjoy the benefits of scientific progress and its applications; (c) To benefit from the protection of the moral and material interests resulting from any scientific, literary or artistic production of which he is the author. 2. The steps to be taken by the States Parties to the present Covenant undertake to respect the freedom indispensable for scientific research and creative activity. 4. The States Parties to the present Covenant recognize the benefits to be derived from the encouragement and development of international contracts and cooperation in the scientific and cultural fields.'

[13] International Convention on the Elimination of All Forms of Racial Discrimination, 21 December 1965, opened for signature 7 March 1966, 660 UNTS 195 (entered into force on 4 January 1969).

[14] Convention on the Rights of the Child, 20 November 1989, Art 31, 1577 UNTS 44, 49 (entered into force on 2 September 1990).

[15] Convention on the Rights of the Child, Art 31 reads in full: '1. States Parties recognize the right of the child to rest and leisure, to engage in play and recreational activities appropriate to the age of the child and to participate freely in cultural life and the arts. 2. States Parties shall respect and promote the right of the child to participate fully in cultural and artistic life and shall encourage the provision of appropriate and equal opportunities for cultural, artistic, recreational and leisure activity.'

Furthermore, the right is specifically mentioned in several regional instruments, namely the American Declaration of the Rights and Duties of Man (1948)[16] and the Additional Protocol to the American Convention on Human Rights (1994).[17] Also the African Charter on Human and Peoples' Rights (1981) affirms that every individual may freely take part in the life of his community (Article 17(2)),[18] and the right is specifically mentioned in the African Charter on the Rights and Welfare of the Child (1990) as a right of the African child to participate freely in cultural life.[19] In addition, the Draft Protocol to the African Charter on the Rights of Women in Africa (2000) pronounces that women shall have the right to live in a positive cultural context and to participate at all levels in the determination of cultural policies.[20]

In view of its historical significance and its multiple affirmations in international human rights law, it is surprising how little interest has been given to the meaning of the right to cultural participation in comparison with other cultural rights. For example, when commenting on Article 15(1)(a) of the

[16] American Declaration on the Rights and Duties of Man, Art 8(1), OAS Resolution XXX, Final Act of the Ninth International Conference of American States, 48 (Mar 30–May 2, 1948). Art XIII reads in full: '1. Every person has the right to take part in the cultural life of the community, to enjoy the arts, and to participate in the benefits that result from intellectual progress, especially scientific discoveries; 2. He likewise has the right to the protection of his moral and material interests as he regards his inventions or any literary, scientific or artistic works of which he is the author.'

[17] Additional Protocol to the American Convention on Human Rights in the Area of Economic, social and Cultural Rights, 'Protocol of San Salvador', 17 November 1988, Art 14(1)(a), OAS Treaty Series 69, (1989) 28 *International Legal Materials* 156, corrections at (1989) 28 *International Legal Materials* 73, 1341 and (1989) 28 *International Legal Materials* 156, 573, 1341, OAS Treaty Series No 69 (1989) (entered into force: 16 November 1999). Art 14 reads in full: '1. The States Parties to this Protocol recognize the right of everyone: (a) To take part in the cultural and artistic life of the community; (b) To enjoy the benefits of scientific and technological progress; (c) To benefit from the protection of moral and material interests deriving from any scientific, literary or artistic production of which he is the author. 2. The steps to be taken by the States Parties to this Protocol to ensure the full exercise of this right shall include those necessary for the conservation, development and dissemination of science, culture and art. 3. The States Parties to this Protocol undertake to respect the freedom indispensable for scientific research and creative activity. 4. The States Parties to this Protocol recognize the benefits to be derived from the encouragement and development of international cooperation and relations in the fields of science, arts and culture, and accordingly agree to foster greater international cooperation in these fields.'

[18] African Charter on Human and Peoples' Rights, Jun 27, 1981, (1982) 21 *International Legal Materials* 58, 60, Art 17. Art 17 reads in full: '1. Every individual shall have the right to education; 2. Every individual may freely take part in the cultural life of his community. 3. The promotion and protection of morals and traditional values recognized by the community shall be the duty of the State.'

[19] African Charter on the Rights and Welfare of the Child, 11 July 1990, Art 12, OAU Doc CAB/LEG/24.9/49 (1990), reprinted in (1992) 18 *Commonwealth Law Bulletin* 1112. Art 12 reads in full: '1. States Parties recognize the right of the child to rest and leisure, to engage in play and recreational activities appropriate to the age of the child and to participate freely in cultural life and the arts; 2. States Parties shall respect and promote the right of the child to fully participate in cultural and artistic life and shall encourage the provision of appropriate and equal opportunities for cultural, artistic, recreational and leisure activity.'

[20] Draft Protocol to the African Charter on Human and Peoples' Rights on the Rights of Women in Africa, 13 September 2000, Art 17(1), OAU Doc CAB/LEG/66.6 (2000).

ICESCR, the UN Economic, Social and Cultural Committee only notes that the term 'culture' should be given a wide reading, but refrains from any definition. It holds that even if culture may not seem to be a matter of human rights, it is of fundamental importance to the principle of equality of treatment, freedom of expression, the right to receive and impart information, and the right to the full development of human personality.[21] However, it avoids engaging in any explanation of how the right to cultural participation is related to any of these rights. To the extent that cultural rights have been given any attention at all by this committee, it has focused on the protection of cultural property as intellectual property rights (Article 15(1)(c)).[22] When addressing the challenges posed by globalisation on the advancement of human rights, the contributions of the committee centre on the impact of these challenges on the protection of economic and social rights.[23] Hardly any attention has been given to the impact of globalisation processes on the right to culture.[24]

The lack of attention is also reflected in the work of international human rights committees with the mandate to develop the meaning of the right to cultural participation whether it is in response to individual complaints or in general comments. Although the UN Committee on the Elimination of All Forms of Racial Discrimination has the mandate to receive individual complaints, it has never received any specific allegations about violations of the right in question.[25] Neither has the committee in question expounded on

[21] United Nations, *Fact Sheet No 16 (Rev 1), The Committee on Economic, Social and Cultural Rights*. See also R O'Keefe, 'The "right to take part in cultural life" under Article 15 of the ICESCR' (1998) 47 *International and Comparative Law Quarterly* 904.

[22] The Committee held its Day of General Discussion on 27 November 2000 in co-operation with the World Intellectual Property Organisation on the 'right of everyone to benefit from the protection of the moral and material interests resulting from any scientific, literary or artistic production of which he is the author' (Art 15(1)(c)). The Committee decided, as a follow up to the discussion held, to begin the drafting of a General Comment on Art 15(1)(c). See Note on the twenty fourth session (14 November–1 December 2000). The discussion paper was submitted by Audrey Chapman, 'Approaching Intellectual Property as a Human Right: Obligations Related to Article 15(1)(c)' (Doc E/C 12/2000/12). Other background documents submitted by the Specialised Agencies, United Nations Programmes and individual experts include but are not limited to: '*La Protection des droits culturels par le Comité des droits économiques, sociaux et culturels*' (Doc E/C 12/2000/14); 'Protection of cultural property: an individual and collective right' (Doc E/C12/2000/16); and 'Protecting the rights of Aboriginal and Torres Strait Islander traditional knowledge: Australia' (Doc E/C 12/2000/17).

[23] Committee on Economic, Social and Cultural Rights, 'Statement on Globalization and Economic, Social and Cultural Rights: 11/05/98,' 18th sess, 27 April–15 May 1998, Geneva [available at: <http://www.unhchr.ch/tbs/doc.nsf/0/adc44375895aa10d8025668f003cc06e?Opendocument>]. Last visited on 4 January 2005.

[24] *Ibid*, para 4. The Committee notes that 'an insistence upon higher and higher levels of payment for access to artistic, cultural and heritage-related activities risks undermining the right to participate in cultural life for a significant proportion of any community.'

[25] As of 31 March 2004, the Committee on the Elimination of All Forms of Racial Discrimination [hereinafter CERD] has considered 33 individual complaints none of which specifically concern alleged violations of the right to cultural participation or the meaning of that right. See 'Statistical Survey of Individual Complaints Under the Procedure Governed by Article 14 of the International Convention on the Elimination of All Forms of Racial Discrimination' [available at: <http://www.unhchr.ch/html/menu2/8/stat4.htm>]. Last visited on 4 January 2005.

the meaning of the right to cultural participation in any of its general comments.[26] A somewhat similar situation pertains with respect to the UN Committee on the Elimination of Discrimination against Women. The committee has not assessed the meaning of the right in question in any of its general recommendations or reporting guidelines.[27] The individual complaint procedure is recent and has not dealt with any complaints concerning the right to cultural participation.[28] Neither has the UN Committee on the Rights of the Child set up to monitor the implementation of the rights of children given any substantive content to cultural rights in its general comments or reporting guidelines.[29] In other words, the meaning and importance of this right is left largely unexplored by interpretative human rights institutions at the international level.

THE RIGHT TO ENJOY ONE'S OWN CULTURE

The modest attention paid to the right to culture as a right to cultural participation should be contrasted with the right to enjoy one's own culture. The latter right has been intensively debated from the standpoint of a diversity of different groups, such as peoples, as well as national, ethnic, linguistic, and religious minorities, including migrant workers and indigenous people as well as minority children. What is more, since its affirmation in international human rights law, the right has come to comprise a diversity

[26] As of 12 May 2004, CERD has produced 29 general comments none of which focuses on the right to cultural participation. See 'Compilation of General Comments and General Recommendations adopted by Human Rights Treaty Bodies,' 12 May 2004 (HRI /GEN/1/Rev7), at 198–232.

[27] The Committee on the Elimination of Discrimination against Women [hereinafter CEDAW] has produced 25 general comments none of which deal specifically with the right to cultural participation. See 'Compilation of General Comments and General Recommendations adopted by Human Rights Treaty Bodies,' *ibid*, at 233–290. See also 'Compilation of Guidelines on the Form and Content of Reports to Be Submitted by States Parties to Human Rights Treaties–Addendum,' CEDAW, 5 May 2003 (HRI/GEN/Rev 1/Add 2).

[28] Optional Protocol to the Convention on the Elimination of All Forms of Discrimination against Women, GA Res 54/4, 15 Oct 1999 (A/RES/54/4) (entered into force on 22 December 2000).

[29] The Committee on the Rights of the Child has produced five comments none of which focus on the right to cultural participation. See 'Compilation of General Comments and General Recommendations adopted by Human Rights Treaty Bodies,' 294–351, above n 26. See also 'General Guidelines Regarding the Form and Content of Initial Reports to be Submitted by States Parties under Article 44, paragraph 1(1), of the Convention: 30/10/91' (UN Doc CRC/C/5). The guidelines group together 'education, leisure, and cultural activity' and ask the States Parties to provide in their initial report information about the principal legislative, judicial, administrative and other measures in force in respect of these rights as well as institutional infrastructure for implementing policy in this area, in particular, monitoring strategies and mechanisms, factors and difficulties encountered, and progress achieved in the implementation of the relevant provisions of the convention (para 21). Their periodic reports should include information about activities, programs and campaigns developed in these fields as well as how the right is related to other rights laid down in the convention, including the right to education (see 'General Guidelines for Periodic Reports: 20/11/96', paras 117–118 (UN Doc CRC/C/58)).

of more specific rights, including the right to cultural development, the right to cultural identity and, occasionally, the right to cultural integrity.

The idea of a human right to culture as connoting something like a right of a community to enjoy its own culture was launched for the first time in the context of self-determination rights and minority rights in 1966. In the context of self-determination, the right is essentially understood as a right of peoples to develop their cultures. Thus, according to Article 1(1) of both the International Covenant on Civil and Political Rights (ICCPR)[30] and the ICESCR:

> All peoples have the right of self-determination. By virtue of that right they freely determine their political status and freely pursue their economic, social and cultural development.

Similarly, the African Charter on Human and Peoples' Rights proclaims a peoples' right to cultural development as an aspect of self-determination[31] and so does the Organization for Security and Co-operation in Europe.[32] More generally, however, while the topic of self-determination rights continues to receive immense attention and consideration in academic circles, most recently as a result of the upsurge of nationalist movements and demands for independence, relatively little significance has been given to the meaning of the cultural aspect of that right.

Instead, more attention has been given to the relationship between the right of a people to cultural development and development in general, such as in the Declaration on the Right to Development adopted in 1986.[33] According to this declaration, the right to development entails an entitlement of every human person and all peoples to participate in, contribute to, and enjoy cultural (in addition to economic, social, and political) development in which all human rights and fundamental freedoms can be fully realised (Article 1(1)). In addition, the African Charter on Human and Peoples' Rights recognises a right to the assistance of states parties to the charter to end foreign domination, including cultural domination as a means

[30] International Covenant on Civil and Political Rights, 16 December 1966, Art 1, GA Res 2200 (XXI), UN GAOR, 21st Sess, Supp No 16, at 52, UN Doc A/6316 (1966) [hereinafter ICCPR].

[31] Art 22 reads in full: '1. All peoples shall have the right to their economic, social and cultural development with due regard to their freedom and identity and in the equal enjoyment of the common heritage of mankind; 2. States shall have the duty, individually or collectively, to ensure the exercise of the right to development.'

[32] Helsinki Final Act (Conference for Security and Co-operation in Europe, Summit, 1 August 1975): Questions relating to Security in Europe (Declaration on Principles Guiding the Relation between Participating States). Principle 8 (2) reads in full: 'By virtue of the principle of equal rights and self-determination of peoples, all peoples always have the right, in full freedom, to determine when and as they wish, their internal and external political status, without external interference, and to pursue as they wish their political, economic, social and cultural development.'

[33] Declaration on the Right to Development, GA Res 128, UN GAOR, 41st Sess, Supp No 53, at 186, UN Doc A/41/53 (1986).

of realising the right to cultural development.[34] The preamble of the charter states that:

> The struggle of peoples for their dignity and genuine independence requires not only tolerance from other peoples, but respect and recognition of particular values and traditions.[35]

The World Commission on Culture and Development (UNESCO) has sought to endow the right to cultural development with meaning and significance. According to its findings, culture not only has an instrumental function in development, but is also a desirable end in itself, insofar as it gives meaning to our existence.[36] Nevertheless, given its broad mandate to explore the relationship between culture and development it fails to advance any meaningful definition of the right to cultural development as such.[37]

Far more interest has been accorded to the right to enjoy one's own culture from the standpoint of various minorities, above all, indigenous populations and national minorities, and also, at least to some extent, migrants. It is in this context that right to culture has developed to signify a right to cultural identity and, possibly, a right to cultural integrity. The cultural right of minorities was recognised for the first time in the ICCPR in 1966. According to Article 27 of that covenant:

> In those States in which ethnic, religious or linguistic minorities exist, persons belonging to such minorities shall not be denied the right, in community with the other members of their group, to enjoy their own culture, to profess and practice their own religion, or to use their own language.

Since the adoption of this provision, several instruments have been added to the list, both international and regional, reaffirming and developing the content of the right and what is required by states to secure it. The UN Declaration of the Rights of Persons Belonging to National or Ethnic,

[34] Art 20 reads in full: '1. All peoples shall have the right to existence. They shall have the unquestionable and inalienable right to self-determination. They shall freely determine their political status and shall pursue their economic and social development according to the policy they have freely chosen; 2. Colonized or oppressed peoples shall have the right to free themselves from the bonds of domination by resorting to any means recognized by the international community; 3. All peoples shall have the right to the assistance of the State parties to the present Charter in their liberation struggle against foreign domination, be it political, economic or cultural.'

[35] Para 4 of the Preamble of the African Charter on Human and Peoples' Rights.

[36] UNESCO, *Our Creative Diversity. Report of the World Commission on Culture and Development* (Paris, UNESCO, 1995), 23–24.

[37] But see United Nations Development Programme, *Human Development Report 2004. Cultural Liberty in Today's Diverse World* (New York, United Nations Development Programme, 2004).

Religious or Linguistic Minorities (1992), to begin with, pronounces a right to cultural identity. Pursuant to the declaration:

> States shall protect the existence and the national or ethnic, cultural, religious and linguistic identity of minorities within their respective territories, and shall encourage conditions for the promotion of that identity.[38]

Article 4 of the same declaration stipulates that:

> States shall take measures to create favourable conditions to enable persons belonging to minorities to express their characteristics and to develop their culture, language, religion, traditions and customs, except where specific practices are in violation of national law and contrary to international standards.

The right to enjoy one's own culture is also affirmed in relation to the minority child. According to Article 30 of the Convention on the Rights of the Child:

> In those States in which ethnic, religious or linguistic minorities or persons of indigenous origin exist, a child belonging to such a minority or who is indigenous shall not be denied the right, in community with other members of his or her group, to enjoy his or her own culture, to profess and practice his or her own religion, or to use his or her own language.

However, so far, the UN Committee on the Rights of the Child has not specified the content of this right in its general comments, days of general discussion, or recommendations.

In addition, the right to cultural identity is specifically mentioned as applicable to migrant workers. Thus, the International Convention on the Protection of the Rights of All Migrant Workers and Members of Their Families (1990) stipulates that:

> 1. States Parties shall ensure respect for the cultural identity of migrant workers and members of their families and shall not prevent them from maintaining their cultural links with their State of origin.
> 2. States Parties may take appropriate measures to assist and encourage efforts in this respect.[39]

Notwithstanding the recognition of the right to cultural identity in relation to migrant workers, the most significant development in the field of cultural

[38] Declaration of the Rights of Persons Belonging to National or Ethnic, Religious or Linguistic Minorities, GA Res 47/135 (18 December 1992), Art 1(1).

[39] International Convention on the Protection of the Rights of All Migrant Workers and Members of Their Families, Art 31, GA Res 45/158, GAOR, 45th Sess, UN Doc A/Res/45/158 (1990) (entered into force on 1 July 2003).

rights has taken place in response to claims advanced by indigenous populations. The right of indigenous populations to enjoy their own cultures was made explicit for the first time in the International Labour Organization (ILO) Indigenous and Tribal Peoples Convention (1989) which applies to tribal peoples in independent countries. Pursuant to this convention, states in which indigenous peoples exist have the responsibility to guarantee respect for their cultural integrity, including:

> promoting the full realization of the social, economic and cultural rights of these peoples with respect for their social and cultural identity, their customs and traditions and their institutions.[40]

In addition, states are obliged, in applying the provisions of the convention, to recognise and protect the social, cultural, religious, and spiritual values and practices of these peoples as well as respect the integrity of their values, practices, and institutions (Article 5(a) and (b)). Moreover, in applying national laws and regulations to the peoples concerned, states are obliged to pay due regard to indigenous customs and customary laws (Article 8(1)). The national legal systems are obliged to respect the methods customarily practised by the peoples concerned for dealing with offences committed by their members provided that the methods are compatible with internationally recognised human rights. Finally, indigenous customs in regard to penal matters shall be taken into consideration by the authorities and courts dealing with such cases (Article 9).

The Draft Declaration on the Rights of Indigenous Peoples adopted by the UN Sub-Commission for the Promotion and Protection of Human Rights in 1994 and currently working its way up through the UN system to the UN General Assembly contains elaborate provisions on the meaning of the right to culture from the standpoint of indigenous peoples.[41] As maintained in the draft declaration, indigenous peoples have the right to maintain and strengthen their distinct cultural characteristics as well as their legal systems (Article 4). Furthermore, the indigenous right to culture entails a right to belong to an indigenous community or nation, in accordance with the traditions and customs of the community or nation concerned (Article 9); the right to manifest, practice, develop, and teach their spiritual and religious traditions, customs and ceremonies (Article 13); the right to revitalise, use, develop, and transmit to future generations their histories, languages, oral traditions, philosophies, writing systems and literatures, and to

[40] Convention Concerning Indigenous and Tribal Peoples in Independent Countries, Art 2(b) ILO Conv 169, ILO, 76th Sess, reprinted in (1989) 28 *International Legal Materials* 1382.

[41] Draft Declaration on the Rights of Indigenous Peoples, UN Sub-Commission on Prevention of Discrimination and Protection of Minorities, Res 1994/45, 36th Sess (1994), UN Doc E/CN4/SUB2/1994/2/Add1 (1994).

designate and retain their own names for communities, places, and persons (Article 14); and the right to practise and revitalise their cultural traditions and customs, including:

> [t]he right to protect and develop the past, present and future manifestations of their cultures, such as archaeological and historical sites, artifacts, designs, ceremonies, technologies and visual and performing arts and literature, as well as the right to the restitution of cultural, intellectual, religious and spiritual property taken without their free and informed consent or in violation of their laws, traditions and customs (Article 12).

As indicated by the same draft declaration, indigenous children have a right to separate educational institutions and, in the case of children living outside their community, access to education in their own languages, in a manner appropriate to their cultural methods of teaching and learning (Article 15). Finally, indigenous peoples have the right to establish their own media in their own languages (Article 17) as well as the right to their traditional medicines and health practices (Article 24).

The right to culture in the context of indigenous peoples is usually linked to access to and ownership of lands, territories, waters, and coastal seas. To this end, the draft declaration stipulates that the right to culture comprises:

> [t]he right to own, develop, control and use the lands and territories, including the total environment of the lands, air, waters, coastal seas, sea-ice, flora and fauna and other resources which they have traditionally owned or otherwise occupied or used. This includes the right to the full recognition of their laws, traditions and customs, land-tenure systems and institutions for the development and management of resources, and the right to effective measures by States to prevent any interference with, alienation of or encroachment upon these rights (Article 26).

A similar point was made by the Human Rights Committee in its General Comment on Article 27 in which the committee observes that:

> [c]ulture manifests itself in many forms, including a particular way of life associated with the use of land resources, especially in the case of indigenous peoples. That right may include such traditional activities as fishing or hunting and the right to live in reserves protected by law.[42]

In addition, what it means to enjoy one's culture cannot be determined in the abstract, but must be placed in context. Article 27 not only protects 'traditional means of livelihood of minorities', but also allows 'for adaptation of those means to the modern way of life and ensuing technology'.[43]

[42] 'General Comment No 23: The Rights of Minorities (Art 27): 08/04/94', CCPR/C/21/Rev/Add 5, para 7.

[43] *Mahnika et al v New Zealand* (547/1993), ICCPR, A 156/40 vol II (27 October 2000), para 9.4.

In the European context, significant interest has been given to the right of national minorities to protect their cultural identities and especially their respective languages. According to the Framework Convention for the Protection of National Minorities (1994):[44]

> The Parties undertake to promote the conditions necessary for persons belonging to national minorities to maintain and develop their culture, and to preserve the essential elements of their identity, namely their religion, language, traditions and cultural heritage (Article 5(1)).

Similarly, the Organisation for Security and Cooperation in Europe (OSCE) recognises a right of national minorities to enjoy their own cultures. As indicated by Article 32 of the Document of the Copenhagen Meeting (1990):[45]

> Persons belonging to national minorities have the right freely to express, preserve and develop their ethnic, cultural, linguistic or religious identity and to maintain and develop their culture in all its aspects, free of any attempts at assimilation against their will. In particular, they have the right
>
> 1. to use freely their mother tongue in private as well as in public;
> 2. to establish and maintain their own educational, cultural and religious institutions, organizations or associations, which can seek financial and other contributions as well as public assistance, in conformity with national legislation;
> 3. to profess and practice their religion, including the acquisition, possession and use of religious materials, and to conduct religious educational activities in their mother tongue;
> 4. to establish and maintain unimpeded contacts among themselves within their country as well as contacts across frontiers with citizens of other States with whom they share a common ethnic or national origin, cultural heritage or religious beliefs;
> 5. to disseminate, have access to and exchange information in their mother tongue;
> 6. to establish and maintain organizations or associations within their country and to participate in international non-governmental organizations.
>
> Persons belonging to national minorities can exercise and enjoy their rights individually as well as in community with other members of their group. No disadvantage may arise for a person belonging to a national minority on account of the exercise or non-exercise of any such rights.

[44] Council of Europe Framework Convention for the Protection of National Minorities, 10 November 1994, Europ TS 157.

[45] Document of the Copenhagen Meeting of the Conference on the Human Dimension of the CSCE, 29 June 1990, reprinted in (1990) 29 *International Legal Materials* 1305.

The right of European national minorities to express, develop, and preserve their cultural identities was reaffirmed in the Charter of Paris for a New Europe (1990),[46] and the Charter for European Security (1999)[47] stipulates that there are various concepts of autonomy (as well as other approaches) that constitute ways to preserve and promote the ethnic, cultural, linguistic, and religious identity of national minorities within an existing state.[48]

However, it must be noted that the right of a minority to enjoy its own culture in the form of educational rights is not novel in the European context, but was recognised by the European Court of Human Rights in 1968 as a right protected by the European Convention on the Protection of Human Rights and Fundamental Freedoms. Thus, in the *Belgian Linguistics* case,[49] the court pronounced that the convention entails a right for French-speaking Belgian children to access French-speaking schools in Belgium regardless of their local residence. In more recent years, the court has developed its jurisprudence with respect to freedom of association to comprise a right of a minority to associate to preserve its culture. Accordingly, a state is not permitted to restrict the exercise of that right even when it appears to undermine the traditions and symbols of the majority culture.[50] In the *Gorzelik* case,[51] the court articulated this point further by alluding to the general importance of freedom of association for minority cultures and for a prospering democracy:

> While in the context of Article 11 [freedom of association] the Court has often referred to the essential role played by political parties in ensuring pluralism and democracy, associations formed for other purposes, including those protecting cultural or spiritual heritage, pursuing various socio-economic aims, proclaiming or teaching religion, seeking an ethnic identity or asserting a minority consciousness, are also important to the proper functioning of democracy. For pluralism is also built on the genuine recognition of, and respect for, diversity and the dynamics of cultural traditions, ethnic and cultural identities, religious beliefs, artistic, literary and socio-economic ideas

[46] Charter of Paris for a New Europe, Conference on Security and Co-operation in Europe (21 November 1990), reprinted in (1991) 30 *International Legal Materials* 190. The section on 'Human Rights, Democracy and the Rule of Law' pronounces that: 'We affirm that the ethnic, cultural, linguistic, and religious identity of national minorities will be protected and that persons belonging to national minorities have the right freely to express, preserve and develop that identity without any discrimination and in full equality before the law.' The section on 'The Human Dimension' reads: 'We reaffirm our deep conviction that friendly relations among our peoples, as well as peace, justice, stability and democracy, require that the ethnic, cultural, linguistic and religious identity of national minorities be protected and conditions for the promotion of that identity be created.' See also 'Report of the CSCE Meeting of Experts on National Minorities' (19 Jul 1991), reprinted in (1991) 30 *International Legal Materials* 1692, section 3(4).

[47] Charter for European Security, Organization for Security and Co-operation in Europe (19 November 1999) reprinted in (2000) 39 *International Legal Materials* 255.

[48] *Ibid*, para 19.

[49] *Relating to Certain Aspects of the Laws on the Use of Languages in Education in Belgium* Series A no 6 (1968).

[50] *Sidiropolous and Others v Greece* no 26695/95 ECHR 1998–IV.

[51] *Gorzelik and Others v Poland*, no 44158/98, judgment of 17 February 2004.

> and concepts. The harmonious interaction of persons and groups with varied identities is essential for achieving social cohesion. It is only natural that, where a civil society is functioning in a healthy manner, the participation of citizens in the democratic process is to a large extent achieved through belonging to associations in which they may integrate with each other and pursue collectively common objectives.[52]

The court continued by noting that:

> Freedom of association is particularly important for persons belonging to minorities, including national and ethnic minorities, and, as laid down in the Preamble to the Council of Europe's Framework Convention, 'a pluralist and genuinely democratic society should not only respect the ethnic, cultural, linguistic and religious identity of each person belonging to a national minority, but also create appropriate conditions enabling them to express, preserve and develop this identity.' Indeed, forming an association in order to express and promote its identity may be instrumental in helping a minority to preserve and uphold its rights.[53]

At the same time, the European Court of Human Rights has refused to endorse the claim advanced by two Muslim female students that it is a critical aspect of their religious freedom to be able to wear their headscarves in higher education in Turkey. One case was struck out of the list when the applicant informed the court that she wished to withdraw her petition without any explanation.[54] In the other case, the court ruled in favour of Turkey's ban based on a consideration of the rights and freedoms of others, the prevalence of extremist political movements, and the virtues of the principle of secularism.[55]

The regional human rights law of the Americas does not entail an explicit right of minorities to enjoy their own cultures. However, a draft declaration on the rights of indigenous peoples is underway.[56] That declaration, if adopted, will recognise a right to cultural integrity for indigenous peoples (Article VII). For the time being, the cultural enjoyment of minorities is protected by other rights guaranteed in the American Declaration of Human Rights (1948). To begin with, the declaration stipulates that individuals have the right to associate with others to promote, exercise, and protect legitimate interests of a cultural nature (Article XXII). More critically, the Inter-American Court of Human Rights has pronounced that the right to

[52] *Ibid*, para 92.

[53] *Ibid*, para 93. It must be noted that, in this case, the Court did not find any violation of Art 11 of the Convention.

[54] *Zeynep Tekin v Turkey*, no 41556/98, judgment of 29 June 2004.

[55] *Leyla Sahin v Turkey*, no 44774/98, judgment of 29 June 2004, para 110.

[56] Proposed American Declaration on the Rights of Indigenous Populations, Permanent Council of the Organisation of American States, 6 December 2000, OEA/SerK/XVI GT/DADIN/doc 1/99 rev 2.

property in the American Convention on Human Rights (1969) protects the close tie between indigenous peoples and their lands. This tie is a necessary precondition for their cultural survival. In the words of the court:

> Among indigenous peoples there is a communitarian tradition regarding a communal form of collective property of the land, in the sense that ownership of the land is not centered on an individual but rather on the group and its community. Indigenous groups, by the fact of their very existence, have the right to live freely in their own territory; the close ties of indigenous people with the land must be recognized and understood as the fundamental basis of their cultures, their spiritual life, their integrity, and their economic survival. For indigenous communities, relations to the land are not merely a matter of possession and production but a material and spiritual element which they must fully enjoy, even to preserve their cultural legacy and transmit it to future generations.[57]

To sum up, the idea of a right to culture as a right to enjoy one's own culture, in particular, in the form of a right to cultural identity, is gaining momentum in international human rights law, both in the form of the adoption of new instruments as well as in jurisprudence, in particular, as a right designed to protect certain minority cultures, notably indigenous peoples. In the absence of any critical account of the way in which the right to cultural identity is related to other human rights, such as the right to cultural participation, the dominant understanding of what the right to culture consists of in more concrete terms and to whom it applies is likely to remain unchallenged.

CULTURE AS OBSTACLE OR BARRIER

To the extent that culture has become an issue in contemporary international human rights debates about law and policy, it is usually thought of as warranting the pronouncement of an enabling or empowering right for certain communities (peoples and minorities). Only occasionally is culture presented in a less favourable light; emphasis is then placed on the obstacles or barriers it may pose to the equal enjoyment of international human rights. This is especially true in the context of women's rights. According to Article 5(a) of the Convention on the Elimination of Discrimination against Women (1979),[58] States Parties shall take all appropriate measures:

> To modify the social and cultural patterns of conduct of men and women, with a view to achieving the elimination of prejudices and customary and all other

[57] *Mayagna (Sumo) Awas Tingni Community v Nicaragua*, judgment of 31 August 2001, IACHR Series C no 66 (2000), para 149.

[58] Convention on the Elimination of All Forms of Discrimination against Women, 18 December 1979, GA Res 34/180, UN GAOR, 34th Sess, Supp No 46, at 193, UN Doc A/34/46 (1980) (entered into force on 3 September 1981).

> practices which are based on the idea of the inferiority or the superiority of either of the sexes or on stereotyped roles for men and women.

Also the Beijing Declaration and Platform of Action (1995)[59] emphasises the idea of culture as a possible barrier and obstacle to the equal enjoyment of all human rights (para 32).[60] All the same, this notion of culture remains undeveloped. It is only touched upon by the UN Committee on the Elimination of Discrimination against Women in some of its general comments. It is expected that it will develop this notion further in response to individual communications. So far, only three communications have been registered.[61]

However, with respect to other vulnerable groups, say, children, immigrants or ethnic, religious or linguistic minorities, the idea of culture as a potential obstacle or barrier to the enjoyment of human rights is left unexplored at the level of international law.

CULTURE AS HARMFUL PRACTICE

Finally, some attention has been given to the fact that culture may harbour harmful practices. For example, Article 4 of the Declaration on the Elimination of Violence against Women (1993)[62] stipulates that:

> States should condemn violence against women and should not invoke any custom, tradition or religious consideration to avoid their obligations with respect to its elimination.

In a similar vein, the Inter-American Convention on the Prevention, Punishment and Eradication of Violence against Women (1994)[63] holds that the right of every woman to be free from violence includes, among others:

> The right of women to be valued and educated free of stereotyped patterns of behavior and social and cultural practices based on concepts of inferiority or subordination (Article 6(b)).

[59] Beijing Declaration and Platform of Action. Report of the Fourth World Conference on Women, Beijing, 15 Sept 1995, UN Doc A/CONF 177/20 (1995).

[60] Para 32 of the Beijing Declaration reads: '[We are determined to:] Intensify efforts to ensure equal enjoyment of all human rights and fundamental freedoms for all women and girls who face multiple barriers to their empowerment and advancement because of such factors as their race, age, language, ethnicity, culture, religion, or disability, or because they are indigenous people.'

[61] 'Overview of the current working methods of the Committee on the Elimination of Discrimination against Women', 20 January 2004, CEDAW/C/2004/I/4/Add 1/Rev 1.

[62] Declaration on the Elimination of Violence against Women, GA Res 48/104, UN GAOR, 48th Sess, Supp No 49, at 217, UN Doc A/48/49 (1993).

[63] Inter-American Convention on the Prevention, Punishment and Eradication of Violence against Women ('Convention of Belem Do Para'), GA 24th Sess, 9 June 1994, reprinted in 33 *International Legal Materials* 1534.

In addition, the Draft Protocol to the African Charter on the Rights of Women in Africa (2000)[64] lists a number of practices (female circumcision, polygamy, etc) considered to be harmful to women. The Protocol stipulates that states are obliged to modify the social and cultural patterns of conduct, including public education, with a view to achieving the elimination of harmful cultural and traditional practices (Article 2(a)).[65] States should also condemn and eliminate all harmful practices (including those actions intended to ameliorate or preserve harmful practices such as the medicalisation and para-medicalisation of female genital mutilation and scarification) in order to effect a total elimination of such practices (Article 6(b)) as well as outlaw polygamy (Article 7(c)).

The African Charter on the Rights and Welfare of the Child similarly acknowledges that culture is not merely something that African children have a right to enjoy, but may entail harmful practices that must be prohibited. According to Article 21 of the charter, there are harmful cultural practices known to seriously affect the welfare, dignity, normal growth, and development of children, in particular, discriminatory practices on grounds of sex, and child marriages.[66]

Notwithstanding the partial recognition of culture as a source of harm and violence, however, it is mostly confined to women and children in Africa; the universal significance of this claim and its relationship to the right to enjoy one's own culture is neglected.

In summary, the idea of a right to culture as a right of certain minorities, in particular, national minorities and indigenous peoples, to develop and preserve their cultural identities is gaining momentum at the expense of other cultural rights, notably the right to cultural participation. In addition, other notions of culture and their impact on human rights, namely the notion of culture as an obstacle or barrier to the enjoyment of international human rights (as well as harbouring practices of violence in contravention with those rights) have been largely secondary. The modest attention paid to cultural rights by the various international human rights institutions

[64] Draft Protocol to the African Charter on Human and Peoples' Rights on the Rights of Women in Africa [final version], Organisation of African Unity, 13 September 2000, Doc CAB/LEG/66.6.

[65] Art 2(2) of the Draft Protocol reads: 'States Parties shall modify the social and cultural patterns of conduct of men and women through specific actions, such as: (a) public education, with a view to achieving the elimination of harmful cultural and traditional practices and all other practices which are based on the idea of the inferiority or the superiority of either of the sexes, or on stereotyped roles for men and women [...].'

[66] Art 21 of the African Charter on the Rights and Welfare of the Child reads: 'States Parties to the present Charter shall take all appropriate measures to eliminate harmful social and cultural practices affecting the welfare, dignity, normal growth and development of the child and in particular: (a) those customs and practices discriminatory to the child on the grounds of sex or other status; 2. Child marriage and the betrothal of girls and boys shall be prohibited and effective action, including legislation, shall be taken to specify the minimum age of marriage to be 18 years and make registration of all marriages in an official registry compulsory.'

mandated to expound the content and significance of those rights reinforces a deep-rooted sentiment about the irrelevance or superfluity of cultural rights. As this chapter conveys, the sole exception to this rule is the advancement of the right to culture as a right of certain minorities to enjoy their own cultures.

3

A Critique of the Current Human Rights Approach to Culture

MUCH RESEARCH IN the field of human rights is influenced by the key issues of the day. So is this study. Unlike most human rights research, however, it is not framed by hard law, or soft, for that matter. It is my contention that our task as human rights scholars is not confined to the interpretation of existing international legal provisions nor to the assessment of the efficacy of current international institutions assigned to monitor the implementation of human rights on the ground; it is also to reflect upon, and critically examine, a human rights approach from the outside, as it were, to clarify its shortcomings, and to draw attention to new tasks that still lie ahead of us.

Since the present study may be a less conventional piece of work in the field, it is necessary to first explain some of my criticisms of the current human rights approach to questions about rights and justice and how these misgivings have come to influence my choice of method. The more detailed criticisms of the current approach necessitate a comment at some length, but it is fundamental to gain a clear understanding of the background to the particular focus of my work. Of special concern are the attitudes that I believe have become distinct for a human rights approach: avoidance, idealism, simplicity and, more recently, particularism. These attitudes may have been acceptable at the time of adopting the Universal Declaration of Human Rights in 1948 and conducive for the concept of human rights to reach the degree of maturity it has today. Perhaps this development made it possible to regard problems of culture faced by individuals as a matter of critical importance within a human rights framework, as this study does, instead of as a challenge to the same. However, it is far from certain whether these are the attitudes that human rights researchers *should* have, and continue to insist upon, in the face of disagreement, complexity, scarcity of goods in demand, and other less than ideal conditions that public and civic actors assigned and committed to secure respect for human rights are forced to grapple with in their work, often on a daily basis. These attitudes made sense in the context of the need to reach a level of abstraction and generality that could possibly elicit agreement across cultures. It is doubtful whether the same attitudes are helpful in answering the new issues that arise as a result of multitude of efforts by various actors to ensure respect for human rights.

AVOIDANCE

What is meant by avoidance? Avoiding controversial propositions about deep values is often said to be a useful strategy for reaching broad agreement on the importance of a point of common concern. Since disagreement may be futile, not the least when religious and moral consciences are engaged, the precept of avoidance may be not only perceived as the more reasonable position, but also deemed necessary in order to prevent conflicts and violence from breaking out.[1] However, if avoidance is a necessary concession in a sensitive political climate so as to maintain fragile channels of communication, it is doubtful if it is supposed to apply to human rights scholars in their academic work as well.[2] As Ronald Dworkin states in his criticism of the political liberal idea of avoidance first and foremost advanced by John Rawls,[3] scholars in the field of rights and justice can hardly be expected to adjust their proposals and answers in the light of what may be accepted by the relevant addressees. In fact, it would be 'foolish to expect … [a philosophical theory] to provide answers that everyone in the relevant community would accept'.[4]

Dworkin's remark ought to have resonance in the human rights field, especially in the light of the fact that human rights are supposed to offer a *critical* standard for the evaluation of law and policy of various powerful institutions and actors. The same rights are also expected to provide a basis for developing more *forward-looking* propositions, models, and persuasive arguments about what a given human right (or cluster of such rights) requires on the ground, so to speak, here and now. Both the more critical as well as forward-looking tasks appear to necessitate a more careful consideration of what deeper value or principle those engaged in human rights rhetoric ultimately seek to communicate and protect. The account of culture and human rights advanced in this study assumes that the deeper purpose of human rights is to secure a minimum provision of respect for individual freedom. However, this commitment does not compel us to make a choice between a concern for liberty and a concern for well-being. As Amartya Sen suggests, the individual interests in liberty (agency) and well-being (which

[1] J Rawls, *Political Liberalism* (New York, Columbia University Press, 1995), especially the paperback introduction.

[2] See eg S Holmes, *Passions and Constraint: On the Theory of Liberal Democracy* (Chicago, University of Chicago Press, 1995), at 10.

[3] J Rawls, *Political Liberalism* (New York, Columbia University Press, 1995).

[4] R Dworkin, *Sovereign Virtue: The Theory and Practice of Equality* (Cambridge Mass, Harvard University Press, 2000), at 322.

seem to lie at the root of human rights) might best be understood as two aspects of freedom.[5] Nor does this commitment deny the importance of positive collective action; on the contrary, such a commitment seems to go hand-in-hand with the need to set up and maintain schemes of social co-operation resolving re-distributive issues.[6] It is in the light of these considerations, it is held, that freedom must replace avoidance.

Thus, while it seems correct, as Charles Taylor notes, that the concept of human rights (or the legal culture in which such rights are embedded) 'could travel better if separated from some of its underlying justifications,'[7] as Michael Ignatieff also notes, a persistent avoidance of a substantive set of justifications that could lend additional support and credence to what is supposed to be *self-evident* to all has become the cause of a spiritual crisis.[8] The need for a more robust account of what is supposed to be the deeper concern behind human rights must be understood in the light of a growing sentiment of relativism of values in some philosophical circles reinforcing a positivist outlook on matters of human rights and exaggerated beliefs in legalism. Nonetheless, once the claim about moral objectivity (ie the existence of a set of independent moral norms) had been brought into question—and few claims are so controversial as this one is today—the proposition about the true value upon which the concept of human rights might ultimately rest lost support.[9] However, if this mood prevents academics from more constructive thinking, the relativist sentiment has hardly had an impact on more practical work in the field. Never before have so many international and national institutions as well as non-governmental actors been engaged in human rights work as now. One notable example is the serious effort made by the United States and the member states of the European Union to implement the human right to periodical elections outside their own borders. If these governments have second thoughts about continuing their human rights programmes, it is not likely to depend on a loss of conviction about the universal validity of the values they currently promote. Instead, it is more likely to depend on doubts about the efficacy or eventual

[5] A Sen, 'Well-being, Agency, and Freedom' (1985) 82 *The Journal of Philosophy* 185.

[6] S Holmes and C Sunstein, *The Cost of Rights: Why Liberty Depends on Taxes* (New York, Norton & Company, 1999).

[7] C Taylor, 'Conditions of an Unforced Consensus on Human Rights' in JR Bauer and DA Bell (eds), *The East Asian Challenge for Human Rights* (New York, Cambridge University Press, 1999), at 126.

[8] M Ignatieff, 'Whose Universal Values? The Crisis in Human Rights': A discussion paper prepared for *Stichting Praemium Erasmianum* on the occasion of the award of the Erasmus Prize to Mary Robinson (Amsterdam, November 1999), 44 ff.

[9] R Rorty, 'Human Rights, Rationality, and Sentimentality' in S Shute and S Hurley (eds), *On Human Rights: The Oxford Amnesty Lectures 1993* (New York, Harper Collins Publishers, 1993). See also Brian Barry's criticism of the Amnesty Lectures on Human Rights for their relativistic flavour: B Barry, *Culture and Equality* (Oxford, Polity Press, 2001), at 5.

success of their specific programmes.[10] In a similar way, the delay in crafting a human rights policy for the EU can hardly be said to depend on a growing sense of sentimentality or relativism, but is better understood as the result of lengthy discussions about a possible lack of competence in the human rights field.[11] The sentimentality of some philosophers offers no persuasive reason for these actors to change their course of action, and rightly so.

Thus, a more promising approach to the new set of issues ensuing from efforts to implement human rights is a more robust and engaging stance even if people are likely to disagree as a result. Scholars in the field of human rights must play an active role—not merely as critics—but also in offering models, lines of reasoning, and conceptual frameworks, that seem more conducive than others, given a commitment to human rights.

IDEALISM

The claim that a human rights approach should be forward-looking is not meant as a pleading for reinforcing attitudes of idealism sometimes associated with human rights advocacy. On the contrary, part of what it means to be forward-looking is to consider, and come to terms with, the less than ideal conditions that often pertain to this world, within established parameters of legal and social inquiry. This claim is not supposed to disconcert anybody about the universal validity of human rights; instead, it is intended to direct attention to the need for a complementary set of tools once faced with the question as to what a commitment to ensuring respect requires in more precise terms and whether the answers we give are likely to differ across time and place. If human rights-orientated research is supposed to provide normative guidance to problems that occur under conditions of scarcity of goods, intolerance, disagreements, and institutional arrangements already in place, a shift of focus onto theories about authority, stability, legitimacy, and social justice seems both urgent and necessary.

One illustration of idealism in human rights public forums is the spirit in which the 'third generation rights', including the right to culture in its current formulation, have been introduced. Similarly to other rights of the 'third wave' (rights to a healthy environment, to development and peace, as well as to be different),[12] the right to culture was articulated in aspirational

[10] See eg T Carothers, *Aiding Democracy Abroad: The Learning Curve* (Washington DC, Carnegie Endowment for International Peace, 1999). Carothers' argument about the need for cultural sensitivity in transnational assistance presupposes that relevant sponsors already agree about the universal validity of human rights (at 334).

[11] Charter of Fundamental Rights of the European Union, 2000 OJC/364/01.

[12] P Alston, 'A Third Generation of Solidarity Rights: Progressive Development or Obfuscation of International Human Rights Law?' (1982) 29 *Netherlands International Law Review* 307. For a recent discussion of these rights, in particular, their collective dimension, see also P Alston (ed), *Peoples' Rights* (New York, Oxford University Press, 2002).

terms from its very inception. This shift in the spirit of human rights discussions may be a sign of optimism, but it is also the result of the felt need to place new issues onto the international public human rights agenda. Such efforts must be accompanied by persuasive reasons so as to convince others about the importance of the matter. Given the need to find the desired inclusion of a point attractive in the eyes of others, it is not unusual to try to stress what is likely to be gained therefrom. The paradox is that such efforts make these new rights look like aspirations when they, in fact, refer to basic preconditions crucial for any individual to be able to exercise her rights and freedoms in adequate ways.

My contention is that the inclusion of 'third generation rights' expresses a broader change in the spirit of international human rights deliberations. It entails a move away from the idea of human rights as the foundation for a morality of duty (minimum provision) on to an idea of human rights as the foundation for a morality of aspiration (an ideal).[13] However, concerns about the importance of a healthy environment, development, peace, difference, and so on, need not be interpreted as aspirational only, but also as pointing towards minimum conditions necessary for the ability to fully enjoy and exercise agency and freedom. As we shall see, the deeper concerns behind the right to culture do not necessarily differ in this respect. Thus, apart from making things seem possible when they might not be, a flavour of idealism may also—quite paradoxically—make rights look less basic than they, in fact, are.

SIMPLICITY

Who is supposed to ensure respect for human rights? Until the second and third waves of human rights claims, the assumption that human rights issues were a matter for the courts, and thus outside the bounds of political life and beyond rules of negotiation and compromise, was not in question. Indeed, once put to work, human rights are supposed to frame and limit the range of issues subject for negotiation and compromise. As Jeremy Waldron notes:

> In the first instance, the idea of rights is a claim about political justifications, in particular that there are limits on what can be justified. In social and political life, individuals and groups inevitably suffer disappointments, frustrations, losses, setbacks, defeats, and even harms of various sorts. No one can get everything he wants. Rights imply limits on the harm and losses any individual or group may reasonably be expected to put up with; they indicate that certain losses and harms are simply not to be imposed on any individual or group for any reason.[14]

[13] See L Fuller, *The Morality of Law* (New Haven, Yale University Press, 1969), at 5–9.
[14] J Waldron, 'Rights and Majorities: Rousseau Revisited' in J Waldron, *Liberal Rights: Collected Papers* (1981–1991) (New York, Cambridge University Press, 1993), at 400.

This understanding of the function of rights is reflected in current institutional divisions. Thus, for example, the specification of what rights in the realm of civic freedoms require is usually reserved to constitutional courts or regional ones such as the European Court of Human Rights. To submit such issues to politics would be to place individual interests in liberty and well-being in the hands of the mighty, those whose power warrants the need for constitutional protection of freedom in the first place. For the purposes of this analysis, the reasonableness of these institutional arrangements is not contested. It is the way most states known to have good human rights records, at least comparatively speaking, are arranged.

Even so, an exclusive focus on rights as side-constraints on the political process makes the requirements of respect look simple to fulfil. However, it is far from certain what the 'constraint' at hand would consist of, substantively speaking. Neither is it clear whether all human rights issues are more suitably dealt with in the courtroom instead of the legislature, especially when they go beyond ensuring a minimum protection of civic freedoms and aspire to cover more ground. Imagine, for instance, if a group of people attached to a particular culture aspires to set up or maintain their own court system or the like in the midst of a plural society. In fact, a more nuanced account of various institutions assigned to ensure protection for human rights suggests that it is a mistake to assume that once talk of human rights enters legislative assemblies it is a sign that they have lost their high moral status and are now subject to the same rules of negotiation and compromise as any other political matter.[15]

Thus, a more nuanced account of who is expected to ensure respect is called for before it can be concluded that talk of rights in political life is a sign that something has gone wrong.[16] By no means all human rights are most suitably safeguarded by law-applying institutions insofar as they might require collective action, legislative revisions, and adjustments so as to be properly enforced. Since the actual implementation of human rights generates political questions about fair distributive schemes as well as the need for legislative action, such an effort often becomes relevant for politics in an obvious and welcoming sense. A somewhat different consideration has to do with the fact that various rights-uses may come into conflict and must be specified and adjusted. In addition, since most rights are costly and priorities must be made, the actual protection of any given right raises a range of issues that may be more suitably dealt with by the legislative authority than by the judicial branch.

[15] J Waldron, *Law and Disagreement* (Oxford, Clarendon Press, 1999), especially ch 10: 'Between Rights and Bills of Rights', 211.

[16] For a criticism of judicial review, see M Tushnet, *Taking the Constitution Away from the Courts* (Princeton, Princeton University Press, 1999); JH Ely, *Democracy and Distrust: A Theory of Judicial Review* (Cambridge, Harvard University Press, 1980); and J Waldron, 'A Right-based Critique of Constitutional Rights' (1993) 13 *Oxford Journal of Legal Studies* 18.

Given this background, it seems reasonable to conclude that few rights are in principle without political relevance. Even basic rights to housing or clean water need to be discussed in a political context since they raise various issues of common concern including limits to ownership or industry regulations, priority in budget allocations, and so on. In addition, the right to a healthy environment may direct attention to current foreign policy and the need for transnational discussion insofar as pollution may be caused by industries located in other states. And more general still, even if everybody is committed to ensure respect for human rights, it will in all likelihood continue to be a matter of dispute and disagreement what such a commitment requires on the part of official institutions and ordinary individuals in order to secure them. Thus, to insist on simplicity is not necessarily the most conducive way to achieve respect for human rights in practice. A more theoretically informed analysis must not be oblivious of this fact.

PARTICULARISM

It is unfortunate that the new claims associated with culture and advanced as a matter of human right do not seem to consider the requirements of universalisability imposed on any human rights claim. A human rights claim must be possible to state in universal terms as a claim to a good that can reasonably be said to be wanted or desired by all regardless of location or opinion. A human right is a right that applies to all individuals and not merely a few. Thus, to call something a human right is to say something about its scope of application.[17] If a right applies to a few, it is still a right, of course, but it is not a *human* right. This distinction is of particular importance when evaluating international debates about cultural rights. Such debates are often pitched in terms of particular rights of minorities as though the very introduction of the term culture is a way of talking about particular or special rights.[18]

This is not to say that particular or special rights may ultimately be derived from a universal principle of deep and pervasive concern. Once faced with the task of implementing a given human right, it may well be the case that the fairest way to do so is not necessarily to give everyone the same right, but pay attention to differences in terms of actual aims and commitments. From having been regarded as a language in which we express universal and broad concerns, the language of rights may re-occur in political discussions as a way of specifying what a given human right requires in

[17] J Waldron, 'Nonsense Upon Stilts? A Reply' in J Waldron, *Nonsense Upon Stilts: Bentham, Burke and Marx on the Rights of Man* (New York, Meutheu, 1987), at 163.

[18] See eg J Donnelly, 'Human Rights, Individual Rights and Collective Rights' in J Berting *et al* (eds), *Human Rights in a Pluralist World: Individuals and Collectivities* (Westport, Meckler Corporation, 1990), at 55.

more concrete terms.[19] The trouble with this approach begins if the deeper justification for particular rights is unclear, ambiguous or deeply contested. It makes special treatment of particular cases look arbitrary and, at worst, unfair, not least from the standpoint of those who do not stand to benefit from them.

One case in point is the right to culture, at least in its current formulation. Is the ultimate purpose of that right to protect the conditions for a sense of belonging or community, identity-formation, or liberty (a context of choice)? If the inclusion of a right to culture is supposed to direct attention to some aspect of the human condition that has not been given sufficient attention, it must be possible to state this claim in a way that is intelligible and agreeable to all. At present, however, the right to culture has been designated to suit a set of particular hopes or aspirations associated with one range of cultures, namely, indigenous cultures and their members' particular interests in hunting, fishing, living a life on a reserve, and so on. For example, in its comment to Article 27 of the International Covenant on Civil and Political Rights made in 1994, the UN Human Rights Committee states that:

> With regard to the exercise of the cultural rights protected under article 27, the Committee observes that culture manifests itself in many forms, including a particular way of life associated with the use of land resources, specially in the case of indigenous peoples. That right may include such traditional activities as fishing or hunting and the right to live in reserves protected by law.[20]

This understanding of the right to culture has evidently been influenced by the urgency of responding to the fate of individuals attached to indigenous cultures. The urgency must be understood in the light of the fact that the difference between their cultures compared with the culture dominating their respective governments is usually more radical than others. More importantly, their cultural difference has not merely been ignored, but regarded as intolerable by most governments claiming authority over conduct on the lands where the members of indigenous cultures live. Their circumstance is also defined in terms of poverty. Finally, until recently, no effort had been made by governments to redress the historical injustice done to their ancestors. In particular, no attempt had been made to make financial reparation. In this sense, indigenous individuals are victims of injustice thrice-over. No doubt, the special consideration of indigenous people is warranted; however,

[19] J Waldron, 'A Right-based Critique of Constitutional Rights', above n 16.

[20] 'General Comment No 23 (50) on Article 27/ Minority Rights', Human Rights Committee, 50th Sess, 1314th meeting, 6 April 1994, Doc CCPR/C/21/Rev 1/Add 5.

it does not help us to clarify the more general basis for being concerned with culture in the first place.[21]

Why not instead simply concentrate on those who do complain and object to the injustices done to them? One unfortunate consequence of an exclusive focus on actual claims advanced by particular groups is that it makes us oblivious to the fact that there may be others similarly situated, but whose hardships are currently ignored. Furthermore, if the claims of a group have been brought into public light it might also—not always but sometimes—indicate that they have already become a relatively powerful group. Assistance by civic and political actors (notably, NGOs and foreign governments) may be crucial to get one's particular claims and concerns considered by one's government. However, since NGOs may depend on public funds they might select victims of injustice with whom it is easier to empathise and whose situation evokes guilt in others. A government may take advantage of a partial dependence on public funds by NGOs. Given this background, it is far from certain whether all similarly situated receive the same assistance with respect to claims-making by voluntary actors.

The trouble confronting human rights scholars and others attempting to develop more principled accounts of what respect for human rights requires in more concrete terms must face a problem debated between choice theorists and benefit theorists of rights.[22] While the former endorse a case-by-case approach, the latter compel us to think about the importance of enforcing a given right in more general terms. The choice theorists assume that a right-holder chooses whether or not to enforce the right he has against others. Benefit theorists, in contrast, argue that a choice-oriented approach may lead to grossly unfair results. Above all, a choice theory seems to imply that those whose rights are not recognised have *chosen* not to demand that their rights be enforced. However, we know that there are several factors at work that may inhibit the individual from seeking to enforce his rights, not only his relative power compared with others, but also his more general attitude towards complaints.[23] Thus, for example, Don Herzog explains that silent acceptance (acquiescence) is evidently not a reliable indicator of fairness.[24] And, as Hannah Arendt contends, there are effective ways of silencing an individual who suffers from injustice. One method is to deprive him of his status as citizen since it is this status that secures an individual's political rights (rights to vote, stand for elections, and

[21] For a comprehensive analysis of the range of arguments employed by indigenous peoples and their advocates, see B Kingsbury, 'Reconciling Five Competing Conceptual Structures of Indigenous Peoples' Claims in International and Comparative Law', in P Alston (ed), *Peoples' Rights*, above n 12.

[22] See eg J Waldron, *Theories of Rights* (New York, Oxford University Press, 1984), at 9 ff.

[23] R Hughes, *Culture of Complaint: The Fraying of America* (New York, Oxford University Press, 1993).

[24] D Herzog, *Happy Slaves: A Critique of Consent Theory* (Chicago, University of Chicago Press, 1980).

hold public office) and the right to remain in the country.[25] In other words, a particularist outlook risks being insensitive to the actual problems faced by individuals who are supposed to ensure that their own rights are respected.

As indicated earlier on in this section, particularism in the sense of searching for suitable solutions to different cases is not necessarily incompatible with a commitment to human rights. However, we must explain why different solutions may be called for to respond to a more general human concern and why some solutions are better in one kind of case than in others. In other words, it becomes immensely important to sort out what it takes to be entitled to a set of particular rights. This is a serious problem confronted by human rights scholars in the field of minority rights. The endless debates about the correct criterion for being entitled to minority protection under Article 27 of the Covenant on Civil and Political Rights indicate that the specification of this kind of criterion is by no means an uncomplicated or insignificant task.[26] Indeed, it is by no means a coincidence that the criterion for minority status is unspecified in the International Covenant on Civil and Political Rights (Article 27) and the Council of Europe Framework Convention for the Protection of National Minorities. Thus, another reason for thinking about the relation between culture and human rights in more general terms has to do with the need to clarify the deeper concerns behind the introduction of culture. It may assist in explaining what is at stake insofar as culture is concerned prior to a search for possible institutional solutions with due regard for the circumstances pertaining in a given society.

A COMMENT ON THE RIGHT TO CULTURE

Recognition of the complexity and difficulty that inheres in the notion of culture is warranted in the light of the persistent supposition that the idea of community and, above all, the nation represent the archetype of culture. Concomitant to this understanding is the idea that culture is something that one can have a right *to* in the same way as one has a right to housing, clean water, or nutrition. For example, in a recent UNESCO report, the right to culture is presented as a right to a way of life. As it holds, 'cultural freedom ... is a collective freedom. It refers to the right of a group or people to follow a way of its choice.'[27] In a similar vein, the drafters of the European

[25] H Arendt, *Origins of Totalitarianism* (New York, Harcourt Brace Jovanovich, 1951).

[26] But see F Capotorti, *Study on the Rights of Persons Belonging to Ethnic, Religious and Linguistic Minorities* (UN Publications, 1979). Capotorti defines the notion of minority in a human rights context as: 'a group numerically inferior to the rest of the population of a State, in a non-dominant position, whose members—being nationals of the State—possess ethnic, religious or linguistic characteristics differing from those of the rest of the population and show, if only implicitly, a sense of solidarity, directed towards preserving their culture, traditions or language.'

[27] World Commission on Culture and Development, *Our Creative Diversity*. Report submitted to UNESCO and the United Nations in November 1995 (Paris, UNESCO, 1998).

Framework Convention for the Protection of National Minorities assert that the purpose of the right to culture is to protect aspirations shared by the members of a national minority 'to develop their culture, and to preserve the essential elements of their identity, namely their religion, language, traditions and cultural heritage'.[28] The understandings of culture in the sense relevant to the aim of securing respect for human rights do not succeed in exhibiting the—sometimes vast—differences between the cultures of the individual and the minority to which he belongs as well as the culture dominating his government.[29] These troubling facts have led to a fundamental and radical disagreement among academics as well as professionals not only as to what actions a right to culture may legitimise, but also about the ultimate purpose for which we want and need that right.

The idea of a right to culture in its current formulation finds support among contemporary philosophers who regret the persistent lack of attention to culture when thinking about rights and justice. According to Will Kymlicka, the struggle for recognition of culture has been successful insofar as it has led to 'a growing awareness of the importance of interests usually ignored by liberal theorists of justice, eg interests in recognition, identity, language, and cultural membership.'[30] Several philosophers argue that a right to culture really captures a set of new interests and concerns which are not well understood within the Rule of Law or the distributive paradigm. In Charles Taylor's view, such a right is supposed to protect the necessary conditions for identity-formation, ie the integrity or survival of the nation. The rise of nationalist movements is a sign of the failure to ensure respect for—and recognition of—the existence of a plurality of nations constituting vital sources of identification. Taylor defends the idea that each of us depends on our national membership to enable us to develop a sense of identity. This is something people need and want apart from things like primary goods (rights, opportunities, income and wealth) or the like.[31]

Also more liberal interpretations of culture tend to be inspired by the nation. If pressed on the question of the nature of the social environment believed to be conducive for rights-use, liberal philosophers tend to look to the nation with its shared language and institutional arrangements.[32] It is in this spirit that Kymlicka develops his argument about the (liberal) nation as

[28] Council of Europe Framework Convention for the Protection of National Minorities, Art 5.

[29] See eg A Shachar, 'The Puzzle of Interlocking Power Hierarchies: Sharing the Pieces of Jurisdictional Authority' (2000) 35 *Harvard Civil Rights-Civil Liberties Law Review* 385.

[30] W Kymlicka and W Norman, 'Introduction' in W Kymlicka and W Norman (eds), *Citizenship in Diverse Societies* (New York, Oxford University Press, 2000), at 5.

[31] See C Taylor, 'The Politics of Recognition' in A Gutman, *Multiculturalism: Examining the Politics of Recognition* (Princeton, Princeton University Press, 1994).

[32] A Margalit and J Raz, 'National Self-determination' (1990) 87 *The Journal of Philosophy* 439; W Kymlicka, *Multicultural Citizenship* (New York, Oxford University Press, 1995); and Y Tamir, *Liberal Nationalism* (Princeton, Princeton University Press, 1993).

a 'context of choice' or a 'cultural structure'[33] which is of fundamental importance for making intelligent judgements about the things we want to be and do in life. The national culture is the background condition crucial for the enjoyment of agency and freedom. As Kymlicka writes:

> Our language and history are the media through which we come to an awareness of the options available to us, and their significance; and this is a precondition of making intelligent judgments about how to lead our lives. We make judgments by examining the cultural structure ... What follows from this? Liberals should be concerned with the fate of cultural structures, not because they have some moral status of their own, but because it's only through having a rich and secure cultural structure that people can become aware, in a vivid way, of the options available to them, and intelligently examine their value.[34]

The present study does not contest the importance of a person's relation to the language (or languages) he or she acquires for the full enjoyment of agency and freedom. The acquisition of a rich language and cultural knowledge enables us to express ourselves, communicate with others, and deliberate about what to do. Thus, I agree with Kymlicka that the reason for caring about culture has to do with its impact on individual freedom. My concern is what is left out of sight by such a thin conception of culture, namely more important aspects which are allegedly vehicles not only for feelings of commonality and community, but also for opposition, alienation, ignorance, etc.

By no means all cultures can usefully be characterised in terms of their distinct languages. Although their characteristics at any given time can (and do) change across time, whether deliberately (as in the case of legislative innovation), or unintentionally (as in the case of traditions subject to drift), it is odd to think that culture is *only* about language. If we want to explain what troubles feminists and other cultural critics and what is troubling about definitions of culture such as those presupposing that 'islands, communities, ethnic groups, nations, civilisations, and so on, have common cultures, ie shared manners of doing things, distinct, characteristic, one apiece' now subject to belated apologies by some anthropologists, the solution is not necessarily to rob the notion of culture of virtually all its content.[35]

This is one reservation to the idea of culture as simply referring to the language of a nation. A second reservation has to do with the idea of

[33] See eg R Dworkin, *A Matter of Principle* (Cambridge Mass, Harvard University Press, 1985), at 230–233; and W Kymlicka, *Liberalism, Community and Culture* (Oxford, Oxford University Press, 1989), at 165.

[34] W Kymlicka, *Liberalism, Community and Culture*, above n 33, at 165.

[35] For a critical reflection on these movements in academic studies, see C Geertz, *After the Fact: Two Countries, Four Decades, One Anthropologist* (Cambridge Mass, Harvard University Press, 1995), 42.

associating culture with the land issue. Land is obviously an important asset for cultures. Its value can be measured in terms of the space it provides, but it is often measured in terms of its natural resources. A piece of land may also have symbolic value from the standpoint of a given culture. Even so, this analysis does not regard culture as a basis for making legitimate claims on land. I intend to explain, in brief terms, the background to this modest position. The right to culture in its current formulation seems to include a right of a group of people not merely to access, but also to own and control, a piece of land with which their culture has historical ties. Once such a right is stated in universal terms, however, it is far from clear whether the right to land can remain as an integral part of a right to culture. First of all, it seems to suggest that there is a natural territorial home for each culture. It thereby fails to recognise fierce competition about sovereignty over one and the same piece of land. For this reason, it seems to hold out a promise impossible to achieve in practice. These conflicts are difficult enough; a study of culture for the purposes of human rights cannot hope to resolve them.

Secondly, not all cultures aspire to isolation or separation; many want to move about in the world and mingle with others. Such cultures—often religious or cosmopolitan ones—will in all likelihood contest the claim to absolute local control over land, and thus, of borders. The particular interests of the latter kind of culture seem more consistent with the claims about ownership associated with human rights and a commitment to ensure respect, namely, the idea that ultimately the surface of the earth and its natural resources is owned in common. Classical scholars such as John Locke and Immanuel Kant who contributed immensely to the modern formulation of human rights also complemented their accounts of rights with theories about ownership. They shared the assumption about common ownership of the surface of the earth. The preoccupation with land in human rights debates can be explained by the fact that the establishment of a multicultural state is often caused by forced invasion, conquest,[36] 'discovery',[37] colonisation of inhabited land by foreign powers, and other forms of expansion. It is an experience shared by most European national minorities and indigenous peoples. Still, a right to land may be better

[36] For a recognition of the wrongs done by conquest, see eg John Locke who wrote at length about the injustice of acquisitions and transfer of land without consent. See Chapter XVI with the title 'Of Conquest' in J Locke, *Two Treaties of Government* P Laslett (ed) (Cambridge, Cambridge University Press, 1988), at 384 ff.

[37] See eg J Crawford, *The Creation of States in International Law* (New York, Oxford University Press, 1979), at 176–184. Crawford explains how the European powers made use of the concept of the *res nullius* which was legal in form but often political in application since it involved the occupation of areas in Asia and Africa which were often in fact the seat of organised communities.

understood as a historical right and not a universal right.[38] Ethnic revivals are often fuelled with resentments about historic injustices inherited from the past. Such historic injustices are often a source of dissatisfaction (well-founded or not) with the current government. It is not necessarily the result of disrespect for a pure right to culture.

To this should be added that the concept of human rights is intelligible only in the light of cosmopolitan presuppositions about the morally relevant community.[39] Such presuppositions shape the way in which we approach questions about respect, such as what *kind* of respect we owe one another (which is more consistent with 'recognition respect' as opposed to 'status respect'),[40] as well as to *whom* we owe such respect (eg whether exclusion of some from the circle of respect is ever justified on the basis of, say, their cultural membership).[41]

A cosmopolitan background is the only one capable of accounting for the possibility of multiculturalism inside the same social and political organisation. It provides a basis for the supposition that people are able to interact with one another in spite of cultural differences and develop common vocabularies and currencies in order to facilitate such interaction. It does not deny the fact that cultures differ from place to place, change and evolve over time, and affect people in some way. Neither does this background commit us to a vision of co-operative endeavours among people from different cultures as effortless or necessarily wanted and celebrated by everybody. A cosmopolitan view appears to be the only viable background to a study of the relation between culture and human rights in the light of ongoing processes of multiculturalisation of local legal frameworks for social interaction and the accompanying recognition of the fact that it is *possible* for people from many different parts, or all parts, to live together.

What is distinct about a cosmopolitan approach is not that it advocates the need for exclusive reliance on global institutions or something like a

[38] See generally J Waldron, 'Superseding Historic Injustices' (1992) 103 *Ethics* 4; and A Føllesdal, 'Indigenous Minorities and the Shadow of Injustice Past' (Oslo, ARENA Working Papers 98/7). See also I Brownlie, *Principles of Public International Law* 4th edn (New York, Oxford University Press, 1990), at 131 ff. Brownlie states that, while international law prohibits transfers by the use of force, in practice such transfers are made legal over time by rules of prescription and, possibly, acquiescence (silent acceptance). Further, it is sometimes legalised by bilateral or multilateral peace treaties.

[39] See generally T Pogge, 'Cosmopolitanism and Sovereignty' (1992) 103 *Ethics* 48; J Waldron, 'Minority Cultures and the Cosmopolitan Alternative' (1992) 25 *University of Michigan Journal of Law Reform* 751; and J Waldron, 'What is Cosmopolitan?' (2000) 8 *The Journal of Political Philosophy* 227.

[40] See generally SL Darwell, 'Two Kinds of Respect' (1977) 88 *Ethics* 36, at 38–39. 'Appraisal' respect depends on the excellence of particular characteristics. Some characteristics are more deserving than others are (merit and desert). 'Recognition' respect, in contrast, depends on features every individual in principle shares with every other such as that all are persons deliberating about what to do.

[41] M Nussbaum with Respondents, *For Love of Country: Debating the Limits of Patriotism* J Cohen (ed) (Boston MA, Beacon Press, 1996).

world government. Rather, the primary concern is to examine what is required to ensure effective and adequate respect for all individuals regardless of location leaving it an open question what sort of *institutional* arrangement would be more effective for realising such a commitment. This approach seems indeterminate as to whether such a commitment is best achieved through a patchwork of local legal systems, or, alternatively, overlapping legal regimes, instead of a single global legal system and government.[42] The acknowledgement of viable local institutional arrangements does not necessarily come into conflict with a cosmopolitan background assumption about the relevant moral community. Thus, it does not tie us to a local understanding of what is a fair distribution of income and wealth and who stands to benefit from such distribution.[43] It only indicates that the legal and moral communities do not necessarily coincide with one another.

Obviously influenced by international events, however, international legal scholarship and recent philosophical contributions have been largely preoccupied with issues about self-determination, de-centralisation, or national government. In an important sense, these institutional solutions have been paramount to the development of current understandings of what people want or aspire to once talk of culture is in the air. However, the specific institutional solutions to issues that arise as a result of cultural difference depends, in part, on the number of individuals involved, and whether they are scattered across the territory or appear as a united body in one part of the country. Until now, not much attention has been paid specifically to concerns about justice and right that occur when separation as an institutional response is not available, is not practically possible, or is undesirable, or when groups of people for other reasons must find a way of living together and establish, maintain, and administrate a set of laws in spite of their various backgrounds and attachments. At present, the main bulk of institutions in many places creating or conferring responsibilities, entitlements, rights, and duties, including legislative assemblies, courts, welfare institutions, health care services, social agencies, and educational institutions (to the extent that they exist at all) are usually expected to house a diversity of cultures.

Still, we may ask if this kind of multiculturalism is to be considered as a lasting social fact in the same way as the nation? In other words, does it call for serious consideration and, possibly, accommodation in mainstream theory? Unless public institutions successfully manage to suppress difference in terms of moral, ethical, or religious views about what ultimately makes life

[42] But see J Waldron, 'Special Ties and Natural Duties' (1993) 22 *Philosophy and Public Affairs* 3.

[43] T Pogge, 'The Global Resources Dividend' in DA Crocker and T Linden (eds), *Ethics of Consumption: The Good Life, Justice and Global Stewardship* (Lanham, MD, Rowman & Littlefield, 1998); T Pogge, 'Human Flourishing and Universal Justice' (1999) 16 *Social Philosophy* 33; and C Beitz, *Political Theory of International Relations* (Princeton, Princeton University Press, 1999), at 136–143.

worthwhile, such difference is expected to remain. As John Rawls states, 'for political purposes, a plurality of reasonable yet incompatible comprehensive doctrines is the normal result of the exercise of human reason within the framework of the free institutions of a constitutional democratic regime.'[44] However, the claim about multiculturalism as a permanent fact also depends on exogenous factors: even if every local government in principle has sovereignty over its territory and so may decide whether or not to accept large-scale immigration, its authority is nevertheless circumscribed by duties of justice such as the duty of rescue and hospitality.[45] In addition, to the extent that a government depends on foreign investment, labour forces, outside assistance, etc, its people may have to accept multiculturalism even when they believe it is not in their interest to do so. Nor does the reality that cultures are proximate to one another and are—willingly or reluctantly—seeking to come to terms with one another necessarily result in convergence. As Robert Axelrod predicts, human interaction does not necessarily lead to convergence or assimilation of cultural differences. Some cultures assimilate or converge while others do not.[46] It is a mistake, then, to assume that multiculturalism is a phenomenon which is soon to fade or else is avoidable.

This background lends credence to the argument about the fundamental importance of placing the claim about culture as a quality possessed by the individual firmly in normative theorising about the centrality of culture to the aim of ensuring effective and adequate protection of international human rights. It also conveys the need for caution and recognition of difficulty in attempts to make generalisations about the context of rights-use. Any given context is bound to differ not only between places, but also across time. People are also likely to vary in their ideological convictions as to what the ideal society ought to be like. A human rights approach to culture confined to the nation—whether liberal or communitarian in spirit—is inapt to tackle claims of culture depending on differences between the culture of the individual and the cultural framework in use by the public institutions in his or her place of residence. A more comprehensive approach is needed to redress this neglect.

[44] J Rawls, *Political Liberalism*, above n 1, *xviii*.

[45] I Kant, 'To Perpetual Peace. A Philosophical Sketch (1795)' in *Perpetual Peace and Other Essays*, T Humphrey (trans). (Indianapolis, Hackett Publishing Company, 1983), sec 358. According to Kant: '*Hospitality* (hospitableness) means the right of an alien not to be treated as an enemy upon his arrival in another's country. If it can be done without destroying him, he can be turned away; but as long as he behaves peaceably he cannot be treated as an enemy. He may request the *right* to be a *permanent visitor* (which would require a special, charitable agreement to make him a fellow inhabitant for a certain period) but the *right to visit*, to associate, belongs to all men by virtue of their common ownership of the earth's surface; for since the earth is a globe, they cannot scatter themselves infinitely, but must, finally, tolerate living in close proximity, because originally no one had a greater right to any region of the earth than anyone else.'

[46] R Axelrod, 'The Dissemination of Culture. A Model with Local Convergence and Global Polarization' (1997) 41 *Journal of Conflict Resolution* 203.

4

The Cultural Dimension of the Individual: A Fresh Start

RE-CONCEPTUALISING CULTURE

THE HUMAN RIGHTS approach to culture developed and defended in this book builds on the claim that culture is first and foremost a quality possessed by the individual that directly influences his or her ability to enjoy the rights and freedoms as recognised in international human rights law in effective and meaningful ways. The cultural dimension of the individual consists of three elements:

1. skills (cultural equipment);
2. cultural norms (*adiaphora*); and
3. ideology (comprehensive doctrine).

In brief, the notion of 'cultural equipment' consists of skills, know-how, tools, and so on.[1] The category of *adiaphora*, in contrast, refers to cultural norms and rules regulating human activities that are viewed as ultimately indifferent from the standpoint of the cosmopolitan law.[2] Such activities include, but are not limited to, ways of dress, diet, marriage, divorce, caring for the elderly and sick, disposing of the dead, and much else. The third aspect of culture, finally, captures political convictions about right and justice having their source in religious, ethical and philosophical comprehensive doctrines.[3]

The critical relevance of each of the facets of culture—skills, norms, and ideology—to advance respect for human rights will be explained in the four subsequent chapters. Suffice it to note for now that all have fundamental implications for human action. In general terms, if a person's skills enable/disable action, norms and ideological outlook shape and, to some extent, define the purpose and manner of action. The claim about the critical role and significance of culture in human action is familiar to social

[1] The term 'cultural equipment' has been borrowed from A Swidler, 'Culture in Action: Symbols and Strategies' (1986) 51 *American Sociological Review* 273.

[2] See generally I Kant, *Lectures on Ethics*, P Heath and JB Schneewind (eds), P Heath (trans) (Cambridge, Cambridge University Press, 1997), at 262–263.

[3] The notion of 'comprehensive doctrine' is defined and developed by J Rawls, *Political Liberalism* (New York, Columbia University Press, 1995), at 13 and 175.

theorists and anthropologists. It is known as the 'subjective-behavioural' approach. This approach, Robert Wuthnow explains, understands culture, not merely as an inner state (feelings and experience), but also as a vehicle for commitments, utterances, and actions.[4] As the anthropologist Sherry Ortner affirms, to focus on culture is to focus on human action, not only on the sources of such action (needs, interests, fears, etc), but also factors inhibiting, constraining, or rendering action impossible.[5]

The skills, norms, and ideological outlook which together constitute the cultural dimension of the individual are generally understood as the product of membership in society. From this standpoint, the cultural dimension is primarily acquired and learned. This understanding of the source of culture finds support in Edward Tylor's view on culture presented in his book *Primitive Culture* published in 1871. According to him:

> Culture or civilization, taken in its wide ethnographic sense, is that complex whole which includes knowledge, belief, art, morals, law, custom, and any other capabilities and habits acquired by man as a member of society.[6]

The affirmation of culture as skills, norms, and views that we learn and acquire is not meant to indicate that all people relate in the same way to their culture. It is a mistake to speak of the culture of a people as though all who are affiliated to that culture are reasonably similar with respect to some psychological attribute, characteristic, or behaviour. As a research team in the field of psychology and education notes, culture at the societal level describes average tendencies; at the same time, it cannot capture all behaviours of all people in that culture.[7] There are important individual differences in cultural receptivity. Such differences can be observed in the degree to which people adopt and engage in the attitudes, values, beliefs, and behaviours characterising their culture. As the team describes this phenomenon, if a person is in accord with shared values and behaviours then that culture resides in him. However, if the same person does not share those values or behaviours, then he does not share that culture. Still, it can be said that culture exists on multiple levels across individuals within groups as well as across groups within larger groups (ie within an organisation). A second reservation to Tylor's definition is its stress on men and women as recipients

[4] R Wuthnow, *Meaning and Moral Order: Explorations in Cultural Analysis* (Berkeley, University of California Press, 1987), at 337–338.

[5] SB Ortner, 'Theory in Anthropology since the Sixties' in NB Dirks, G Eley and SB Ortner (eds) *Culture/Power/History: A Reader in Contemporary Social Theory* (Princeton NJ, Princeton University Press, 1994), at 394–396.

[6] E Tylor, *Primitive Culture* (New York, Harper & Row Publishers, 1958) [originally published 1871], at 1.

[7] C Ratzlaff, D Matsumoto, N Kouznetsova, J Raroque, and R Ray, 'Individual Psychological Culture and Subjective Well-being', in E Diener and EM Suh (eds), *Culture and Subjective Well-Being* (Cambridge Mass, MIT Press, 2000), at 39.

of culture. Obviously, people are not only recipients but also creators of culture even if the extent to which human creativity is encouraged varies from culture to culture.

In addition to being acquired and learned, culture is also generally understood as fabricated and not 'natural'.[8] However, while constructed, and, thus, in principle changeable and adjustable at any particular point in time, it is nevertheless possible to say something more substantive about the content of the cultural dimension of any given individual.

The claim that culture should first and foremost be understood as a quality possessed by the individual does not deny that organisations (public and private, social, political, and legal) also have cultural dimensions. However, it takes seriously the reality that the cultural dimensions of the individual and any given organisation are not necessarily identical with one another. While culture as a quality of the individual may be of normative significance in a way that the culture of any given social or political organisation is not, the latter nevertheless plays a role in this analysis. Whether people are able to make effective use of their rights in a meaningful way depends, at least in part, upon the character of their social environment as well as the culture in use by the public institutions in their place of residence, work, and life.

The notions of 'public culture' and 'social culture' capture two main types of culture that the individual is related to besides her own culture. According to Rawls, 'social culture' (also called the 'background culture' of civil society) refers to the 'culture of daily life, of its many associations, churches, universities, learned and scientific societies, and clubs and teams.' 'Public political culture', in contrast, comprises

> the political institutions of a constitutional regime and the public traditions of their interpretation (including those of the judiciary), as well as historic texts and documents that are common knowledge.[9]

In the present study, the term 'public institutions' is not confined to legal and political institutions, but covers public health care, prisons, public schools, unemployment agencies, etc. Problems created by cultural differences are especially frequent in the context of these institutions. What is relevant for us is that the individual's culture may correlate with the social and public cultures, but the different cultures may also diverge in the sense that the individual does not possess the skills, observe the cultural norms, or affirm the ideological outlook currently dominating public and social institutions in his or her society. A rather complicated picture of the relation between culture and human rights begins to emerge, but this is precisely my point.

[8] See, for example, I Kant, *Lectures on Ethics*, above n 2, at 262–263.
[9] J Rawls, *Political Liberalism*, above n 3, at 13–14.

One obvious illustration of the cultural differences in focus and deemed pertinent to human rights protection is that between newcomers (immigrants, refugees, etc) and the public and social institutions of their host country. That said, the conceptual framework advanced in this study purports to be applicable to any case where cultural differences in terms of skills, norms, and ideological outlook are present. Such differences have many sources. Society may fragment into so many pieces and factions creating a distance, opposition, or alienation that was not always there for reasons not all of which are well understood. A cultural difference between individuals or between individuals and their public institutions can come about as a result of human mobility or the annexation of inhabited land by a foreign government. It is also the product of free democratic institutions. For the purposes of this analysis, however, it is simply assumed that multiculturalism is a fact of social life in many places—rendering the problem of cultural variation a significant one in principle.

The acknowledgement of cultural variations between rights-holders and their public institutions is a useful starting point for understanding and/or explaining social and political behaviours in a multicultural context. Above all, these variations may prompt non-compliance with generally applicable laws in force. Let me allude to some cases of non-compliance with laws explained in reference to a person's cultural background or attachment in conflict with (or unrelated to) the cultural framework in use by public institutions making, enforcing, and interpreting the laws in force. It is my conviction that the relative frequency of instances involving legal non-compliance explained in terms of differing cultural background or attachment compared to the dominant culture is a sign of inability to conform to the laws that claim authority over conduct if the cultural differences are too great. The cases that are listed below direct attention to the impact of culture on human activities that, in Western societies at least, are regulated as a matter of law:

1. Two members of the Native American Church living in Oregon in the United States are fired from a drug rehabilitation organisation for misconduct having ingested *peyote*, a hallucinogenic drug, at a ceremony in their church. The law in their place of residence makes it a felony to knowingly and intentionally possess a drug. Due to the alleged misconduct, the two men are denied unemployment benefits. Once before the court, however, they defend their act on the basis that their drug-use has sacramental significance and, therefore, differs from drug-use in its conventional meaning.[10]
2. Three French Muslim girls arrive at school wearing headscarves in contravention of French local school regulations prohibiting provocative

[10] *Employment Division v Smith*, 494 US 872 (1990).

dress. They explain to the relevant school authorities that it is part of their culture to dress in this way.[11]

3. A British Sikh refuses to comply with a regulation requiring him to wear a crash helmet when riding a motorbike. The Sikh explains that the regulation is in conflict with his culture-specific dress-code.[12]
4. The members of the Amish community in the United States explain that their convictions as to how life ought to be led prevent them from complying with Wisconsin's mandatory education laws requiring them to send their children to school until the age of 16. The Amish stress co-operative farming and homemaking skills in conflict with values of intellectualism and competitiveness promoted in the public schools.[13]
5. A Buddhist in an Austrian prison resists compliance with prison rules because the rules de facto require him to violate his religious prescriptions to grow a beard.[14] A similar case is that of a Sikh prisoner in Britain who resists compliance with prison rules due to his religious prescriptions requiring him not to clean his cell and to wear a turban.[15]
6. A 21-year-old Iranian man in Britain undertakes a Muslim marriage ceremony with a girl aged 14½ years without permission from her father. They live together for four months until the man is arrested, tried, convicted, and sentenced to nine months' imprisonment for under-age sex, which is prohibited by the British Sexual Offences Act of 1956. The man explains that marrying minors, even without parents' consent (from 12 years old), is permitted by Islamic law.[16]
7. An Indian man refuses to give his ex-wife the allowance he owes her according to Indian law. He explains that he gives what the Shari'at law specifies he owes her.[17]
8. Kargar, an Afghan refugee who has been living in Maine in the United States for four years is reported for gross sexual assault for having kissed his son's penis on two occasions.[18] Maine's gross sexual assault

[11] See *Avis No* 346893 *du* 27 Novembre 1989. *Assemblée générale plénière* (1990). *L'actualité juridique—Droit administratif* (AJDA) 39 (1990). For a translation of the judgment of *Conseil d'Etat*, in K Boyle and J Sheen (eds), *Freedom of Religion and Belief: A World Report* (London, Routledge, 1997), at 298–300.

[12] Appl 7992/77, *X v the United Kingdom*, European Commission on Human Rights, D&R 14 (1979) 234.

[13] *Wisconsin v Yoder*, 406 US 205 (1972).

[14] Appl 1753/63, *X v Austria*, European Commission on Human Rights, *Yearbook* VIII (1965) 174.

[15] Appl 8231/78, *X v the United Kingdom*, European Commission on Human Rights, D&R 28 (1982) 5.

[16] Appl 11579/85, *Khan v the United Kingdom*, European Commission on Human Rights D&R 48 (1986) 253. For a comment on the case, see R Gleave, 'Elements of Religious Discrimination in Europe: The Position of Muslim Minorities,' in SV Konstadinidis (ed), *A People's Europe: Turning a Concept Into Content* (Aldershot, Dartmouth, 1999), 100 ff.

[17] See V Das, 'Cultural Rights and the Definition of Community,' in O Mendelsohn and U Baxi (eds), *The Rights of Subordinated Peoples* (Bombay, Oxford University Press, 1994).

[18] *State v Kargar*, 679 A 2d 81 (Me 1996).

statute prohibits any contact between an adult's mouth and a child's penis, and thus, does not require intent or sexual gratification.[19] Kargar submits cultural evidence by arguing that his conduct is consistent with the Law of Afghanistan which prohibits sexual abuse and punishes such acts with death penalty. More significantly, his act is considered neither wrong nor sexual under Islamic law. In fact, according to that law, his act is not only considered innocent, but also appropriate.[20]

9. An Arab man living in Sweden kills his daughter for having adopted a liberal life-style. He refers to the unacceptability in Arab culture of her choice to live unmarried with a man. He explains that the killing was necessary to restore family honour.[21]
10. A Laotian-American woman is abducted from her place of work at Fresno State University and forced to have sexual intercourse against her will. Her Hmong immigrant assailant explains that, among his tribe, such behaviour is not only accepted, but expected: it is the customary way to choose a bride.[22]
11. A Japanese-American woman drowns her two young children in Santa Monica and then attempts to kill herself because her husband had been unfaithful to her. She explains that, though it is an act of honour prohibited by law, it continues to be a custom in some Japanese regions.[23]
12. A Mexican woman living in the United States is prosecuted for a serious drug offence.[24] She pleads guilty to participating in a conspiracy with her boyfriend and a friend of his to distribute methamphetamine,

[19] Kargar received an 18-month suspended prison sentence, and was placed on probation for three years with the condition that he learn English. Kargar's convictions also exposed him to deportation under federal law. Pursuant to current US deportation statutes, an alien is deportable if he is convicted of two 'crimes involving moral turpitude, not arising out of a single scheme of criminal misconduct' even if no prison sentence is imposed. See Appellant's Brief at 15–16, Kargar (No 7719, CUM–95–300).

[20] A professor at the University of Arizona and the Director of the Afghan Mujahideen Information Bureau verified this evidence. A caseworker from the Maine Department of Human Services (DHS), who had investigated the incident after the arrest, also testified. Kargar himself explained that, consistent with his Islamic culture, by kissing Rahmadan's penis—a body part that is 'not the holiest or cleanest'—he was showing how much he truly loved his son. The submitted evidence was also supported by an Ahman, or priest, in the Maine Muslim community who stated that the conduct for which Kargar had been convicted was deemed innocent, non-sexual, and appropriate in Islamic Afghan culture.

[21] Åsa Eldén, '"The Killing Seemed to Be Necessary": Arab Cultural Affiliation as an Extenuating Circumstance in a Swedish Verdict' (1998) 6 *NORA: Nordic Journal of Women's Studies* 89.

[22] *People v Moua*. Record of Court Proceedings, No 315972–0 (Super Ct Fresno County, 7 Feb, 1985).

[23] *People v Kimura*. Record of Court Proceedings, No A–091133 (Super Ct LA County, 21 Nov, 1985).

[24] *United States of America, Plaintiff-Appellant v Maira Bernice Guzman, Defendant Appellee,* No 99–2169 (3 Jan, 2001) (236 F3d 830; 2001 US App).

> but asks for a '25-level downward departure' because Mexican cultural norms dictate submission to her boyfriend's will.[25] She had gone with him in defiance of her family's wishes and it would have been humiliating for her to break with him and return to her family, especially since, despite their being unmarried, she was pregnant with his child.

How should courts and other public institutions approach and respond to these cases? Should all appeals to culture in a public institutional context be treated in a like manner as a matter of principle? Alternatively, are some appeals to be singled out for special attention while others to be left aside? At present, uncertainty pertains as to the role of culture in human action and its possible significance in reasoning about justice and right in a multicultural environment. As a result, human rights courts, such as the European Court of Human Rights, and constitutional courts, such as the US Federal Supreme Court, tend to avoid engaging in the deeper reasons for lawbreaking when culture is involved.

EQUALITY BEFORE THE LAW

One question that continues to preoccupy human rights scholars, and rightly so, is what rights, if any, we have by virtue of our humanity. It is in this context that the doctrine of cultural relativism is intensively debated, and also whether there is a right to culture that ought to be integrated into the general list of rights in international law. This is the approach to culture and rights dominating the current international human rights debate. However, I believe there are important reasons to shed light on another set of questions arising in the field of human rights implementation. We should ask what international human rights law is ultimately for, and what duties and obligations are generated by the deeper concerns which that law is predicated upon. It is my contention that culture takes on a particular urgency once states and other public entities, including international organisations, seek to secure protection for human rights in more concrete terms. A formalistic approach is not sufficient to secure such protection.

The response usually deemed unsatisfactory by anybody concerned with societal inequality is a formal Rule of Law response. From that perspective, a minimum provision of respect for persons is granted if everyone is treated alike before the law (equality before the law). Whatever rights there might be, the least to be expected is that they be the same for all. The trouble with this idea is that it fails to consider whether people are able to make effective

[25] The sentencing judge accepted the complaint and sentenced her to time served (three days), six months of home detention, plus an additional two and a half years of supervised release instead of 57 to 71 months in prison.

use of their rights and whether they are able to do so in a way that is meaningful and important to them. Still, it is well known that a range of obstacles may get in the way and seriously impede the ability to enjoy agency and freedom including poverty, chronic ill-health, etc. The Rule of Law principle of equality before the law guarantees consistency, but is entirely ignorant as to whether everybody is able to, in fact, benefit from his or her rights.

Nor does a formal Rule of Law approach take account of the claim about the need to formulate laws and policies to suit the kinds of things people wish to be and do. No matter how well-designed it seems to be from the outside, a legal system fails to consider something of fundamental importance if it does not consider and, if need be, accommodate, what people, in fact, try to be and do in their lives. Thus, while a state may distribute a set of rights equally in the sense of granting everyone the same set, it may not succeed in ensuring that that set is adequate in the eyes of the right-holder. In a different light, then, a human rights approach to culture must be attentive to, and integrate, real concerns put forward by social justice theorists. That said, however, it must be recognised that, so far, no theorist of social justice has considered culture as creating obstacles or barriers to the enjoyment of rights and freedoms in the sense discussed in this book. Even so, social justice theorists do articulate the basis for considering unwarranted obstacles or barriers as raising legitimate demands on the state and do succeed in specifying concerns that are of special importance in the area of human rights protection.

In summary, it is a mistake to suppose that the principle of equality before the law is sufficient to protect human rights. That approach does not offer a basis for paying attention to the impact of cultural difference on the enjoyment of human rights and instead treats everybody alike. It rests on a crude version of what a commitment to respect for persons means and requires and, as this study indicates, amounts to an unjustifiable neglect of the socio-cultural conditions imposed upon people in multicultural societies. Above all, it fails to recognise the fundamental ways in which a person's cultural difference from the cultural framework dominating the public institutions in his place of residence impedes his ability to benefit from his rights and risks rendering the rights he formally has on hand worthless in the light of his actual aims and aspirations.

As shall be demonstrated in the four succeeding chapters, the circumstances related to cultural differences in terms of skills, norms, and ideological outlook generate duties and responsibilities on states and other relevant public entities. These duties go beyond merely ensuring the conditions for such enjoyment through legislative action to require states and public authorities to pay attention to particular cases where such conditions are absent and to respond to failures to comply with law in a way consistent with the aim of ensuring a minimum provision of respect for individual freedom. The realisation of this aim may justify deviations from the principle of equality before the law.

5

Problems of Cultural Equipment

FOR PEOPLE TO be able to exercise their rights, they must know about their rights, how to relate their rights to those of others, and how to exercise their rights in a way that does not subject them, involuntarily, to sanction. However, the effective exercise of rights presupposes access to the cultural framework that defines the social and cultural existence of the scheme of rights in force. This is the upshot of the argument about the importance of possessing suitable cultural equipment in order to enjoy the full range of rights and freedoms. The lack of such equipment, it is suggested, generates new and unprecedented questions in the field of justice.

CULTURAL EQUIPMENT

Are people's cultural differences similar to a difference in terms of skills or capabilities (personal resources), or are they more akin to differences in tastes, preferences, convictions, character, and other aspects of personality?[1] It may appear as an abuse of the term 'culture' to reduce it to aspects of people's resources or aspects of personality, as I shall suggest. Such an approach indicates that culture is a quality of the individual rather than the group, and thus leads us away from what many regard as the real issues at stake in multicultural politics, namely, the need to consider and accommodate communal aspirations for cultural survival into a human rights framework. Nevertheless, although an individualistic outlook does not exclude the possibility of considering communal aspirations as well,[2] it insists that

[1] See generally R Dworkin, *Sovereign Virtue: The Theory and Practice of Equality* (Cambridge Mass, Harvard University Press, 2000), at 322–323. I employ the distinction made by Ronald Dworkin concerning different aspects of persons and their relevance/irrelevance for social justice (distributional equality). First of all, aspects of personality consist of ambition (tastes, preferences, and convictions as well as overall plan of life) and character (energy, industry, doggedness, etc). Secondly, personal resources refer to physical and mental health and ability, general fitness and capacities, including wealth-talent. These resources differ from impersonal ones which refer to resources that can be reassigned from one person to another, including wealth and property.

[2] J Waldron, 'Can Communal Goods be Human Rights?' in J Waldron, *Liberal Rights: Collected Papers (1981–1991)* (New York, Cambridge University Press, 1993).

the individual is the ultimate source of moral claims.[3] It assumes that the more fundamental concern is with the fate of individuals, one-by-one, rather than the community, and that these two concerns may come apart. Thus, while the argument advanced in this chapter does not rule out the possibility of paying attention to community-oriented concerns as well, it suggests that the basic concern must be to secure effective protection of individual interests in liberty and well-being. Cultural difference is thought to be directly relevant insofar as it affects these endeavours.[4]

It is suggested that we must look to the individual's cultural resources—language and other skills (cultivated through education and training), informal know-how, familiarity with local habits, styles, and customs—to find out whether a person is sufficiently equipped in cultural terms to enjoy and exercise fully his or her agency and freedom. Culture, Ann Swidler affirms, shapes action, not by providing ultimate ends, but by providing a repertoire or tool-kit of habits, skills and styles from which people construct strategies of action. It consists of

> symbolic vehicles of meaning, including beliefs, ritual practices, art forms, and ceremonies, as well as informal cultural practices such as language, gossip, stories, and rituals of daily life.[5]

Thus, culture is more like a style or a set of skills and habits rather than a set of preferences or needs.[6] This aspect of culture is of decisive significance for the individual's ability to move about in his place of residence, and to take advantage of various opportunities. The well-equipped have an advantage compared with those lacking such equipment.

The Possibility of Adjustment

Some aspects of a person's culture are acquired while others are learned. There are important differences between learning and acquisition. According to James Paul Gee, acquisition is

> a process of [understanding] something by exposure to models, a process of trial and error, and practice within social groups, without formal teaching. It happens in natural settings that are meaningful and functional in the sense that

[3] See generally J Rawls, *Theory of Justice* (Cambridge Mass, Belknap Press of Harvard University Press, 1999), at 233–234. The centrality of individualistic assumptions to liberal theory is affirmed by John Rawls who holds that only persons (as opposed to communities) are to be viewed as ultimate units of moral concern.

[4] See A Sen, 'Well-being, Agency, and Freedom' (1985) *The Journal of Philosophy* 169 at 185 ff. Sen holds that well-being and agency (liberty) are two aspects of individual freedom.

[5] A Swidler, 'Culture in Action: Symbols and Strategies' (1986) *American Sociological Review* 273 at 273.

[6] *Ibid*, at 275.

> acquirers know that they need to acquire the things they are exposed to in order to function and that they in fact want to so function.[7]

Learning, in contrast, is

> a process that involves conscious knowledge gained through teaching (though not necessarily from someone officially designated as a teacher) or through certain life experiences that trigger conscious reflection. This teaching or reflection involves explanation and analysis, that is, breaking down the thing to be learned into its analytical parts. It inherently involves attaining, along with the matter being taught, some degree of meta-knowledge about the matter.[8]

Gee notes that most of what we know and understand is derived from a mixture of acquisition and learning, and that some cultures emphasise one mode over the other. While acquisition facilitates performance, learning tends toward discursive knowledge—the ability to talk about, analyse, and explain things.[9]

It is certainly possible to move about in the world despite cultural differences, and also to find temporary solutions to communication problems. A more permanent settlement in a new environment, however, requires a new tool-kit for a person not to be disabled. Habits, skills, styles, and know-how cover aspects of culture that can be acquired or learnt by new arrivals. A relative lack of suitable cultural resources is not thought to be a permanent disability. None of these things are impossible to learn, but it takes time. Benedict Anderson defends the possibility of learning most eloquently when contesting the idea of language as an instrument of exclusion. As he observes, anyone can learn any language, 'limited only by the fatality of Babel: no one lives long enough to learn *all* languages'.[10] Like other types of differences, cultural difference is a matter of degree. It obviously takes less time for a Swede to learn Danish or Norwegian than, say, Chinese or Russian. This is not to say that it is impossible for a Swede to learn these, for her more difficult, languages as well, but that she needs more time. People's ability to learn culture-specific skills also depends on biological factors, such as age, health, and also talent and motivation.

So far, it has been assumed that the individual usually has the cultural equipment suitable for her location. Her resources are not necessarily limited to this, though, and may extend to familiarity or knowledge of a variety of languages, habits, styles, and skills useful for many different places. Acquaintance with the habits, styles, and customs in places other than one's

[7] JP Gee, *The Social Mind: Language, Ideology and Social Practice* (New York, Bergin and Garvey, 1992), at 113–114.
[8] *Ibid.*
[9] *Ibid.*
[10] B Anderson, *Imagined Communities: Reflections on the Origins and Spread of Nationalism* (London, Verso, 1991), at 133–134.

own is sometimes explained by territorial closeness, but not necessarily so. The assumed link between territorial closeness and familiarity with certain skills and habits is undermined by the prevalence of factors such as education, media, the web, travels, romantic love, literature, and other methods of acquiring cosmopolitan cultural equipment. As a result, most people leading their lives in the industrialised world today may be more familiar with the language, habits, styles, and customs of whoever happens to dominate the cultural industry rather than with the particular patterns of those leading their lives nearby. This background lends credence to the assertion that the individual may be generally well-equipped to move about in the world, or may otherwise choose a destination for which she already has the suitable culture-specific tools on hand. Even so, it does not seem reasonable to assume that most new arrivals are well-equipped in this way considering the common motives for embarking on their travels (motives that I shall shortly discuss in more detail in connection with the choice–circumstance distinction).

The claim about the possibility of adjustment might appear overburdened by a documented reluctance towards acquiring a suitable tool-kit, even if it seems to be the most rational thing to do once one has settled in a new social environment. If new arrivals stick to their culture in spite of the obstacles imposed as a result, does it indicate that their culture might be of ultimate worth for them, or is it a sign that people are simply unable to change their particular ways once socialised into a certain culture? Is non-acquisition a form of conscientious objection indicating that an individual's culture—whatever its particular shape and content—commands absolute allegiance and loyalty wherever the individual happens to be? Is it because people in principle can be said to prefer their own culture before any other, regardless of the conditions imposed on them as a result?

There are various models available to explain the phenomenon of cultural resistance. One approach accounts for this behaviour in the image of *homo economicus* who generally adapts to changing circumstances and is always on the lookout for improvements. If he does not acquire a new tool-kit it must depend on the fact that he would not gain anything thereby. This is how Swidler explains the relative lack of upward mobility from the lower strata in society (assuming, as she does, that the different strata within one and the same society have different cultures). As she puts it: 'One can hardly pursue success in a world where the accepted skills, styles and informal know-how, are unfamiliar. One does better to look for a line of action for which one already has the cultural equipment.'[11] On this model, it only seems rational not to acquire a new tool-kit in the case of uncertainty about the period of settlement perhaps boosted by a hope of early safe return. To gain a new tool-kit is not an effortless activity and it seems rational to embark on

[11] A Swidler, 'Culture in Action: Symbols and Strategies', above n 5, at 275.

this task only if the period of stay is expected to be more permanent. Furthermore, non-adjustment may also be the result of having more urgent undertakings to attend to such as that of securing daily food sustenance, water supply, security, shelter, etc. If the lack of the bare essentials for survival persists over time an individual might become indifferent towards the acquisition of a new tool-kit even if that was part of his initial plan. This appears to be a perfectly rational reaction if no real option to learn is within reach.[12]

Though there are inevitably high costs involved in changing tool-kits, reluctance towards adjustment nevertheless seems to be a more complicated phenomenon than Swidler wants to admit. For example, her account fails to appreciate the possible significance of social norms and the fact that people are also social beings. The reference to social norms as a variable for explaining behaviour may at first appear to involve a rejection of a rational choice model in favour of an entirely different approach. The latter depicts humans as mindlessly complying with social norms acquired in early years and as insensitive to changing circumstances and availability of new information (*homo sociologicus*). Even so, the impact of social norms has come to receive remarkable attention from rational choice scholars seeking to explain human behaviour on the basis of individualistic assumptions. According to Jon Elster, social norms can be understood as emotional and behavioural propensities of individuals. In their simplest form, social norms are unconditional and postulate 'do *x* or don't do *x*'. However, more complex norms have a conditional form: 'if you do *y*, then do *x*' or 'if others do *y*, then do *x*'. An even more complex norm says 'if it would be good if all did *x*, then do *x*.'[13] The fact that the propensities are shared with others and maintained through interactions with others does not undermine the claim that they are propensities of individuals.[14] Indeed, a consideration of culture as entailing social norms is consistent with 'methodological individualism' which explains social institutions and social change as the result of the action and interaction of individuals.[15] Instead of regarding rational choice and social norms as opposites of one another, Elster suggests that social norms ought to be integrated as a variable within the framework of rational choice.[16] Thus, the importance of considering the impact of social norms does not necessarily come into conflict with principles of rationality. As Steven Lukes affirms, 'there is no basic contrast between rationality and social norms'. In other words, there is no opposition between rational and

[12] J Elster, *Sour Grapes: Studies in the Subversion of Rationality* (New York, Cambridge University Press, 1983).

[13] J Elster, *Nuts and Bolts for the Social Sciences* (New York, Cambridge University Press, 1989), at 113.

[14] J Elster, 'Rationality and Social Norms' (1991) 32 *Archive Européene Sociologique* 109, at 113–114.

[15] J Elster, *Nuts and Bolts for the Social Sciences*, above n 13, at 13 and J Elster, 'Rationality and Social Norms' above n 14, at 109.

[16] J Elster, *Nuts and Bolts for the Social Sciences*, above n 13, at 113.

norm-guided action. Lukes continues by noting that if the task is to explain why people follow norms and why they follow one set of norms rather than another, the most promising strategy will be one that will make as much norm-following as possible come out as rational. The task of explaining human behaviour surely involves finding out what reasons may lead people to follow the norms they do, ie why they dress or eat in a certain way, pursue vengeance or honour, etc.[17]

How does the recognition of the possible significance of social norms come to bear on our analysis? The introduction of social norms may deepen our understanding of a variety of issues underlying cases of cultural resistance. For example, imagine the insiders of culture *A* must flee from the place they have inhabited for years because of a sudden famine, natural disaster, or civil war. Most of them arrive at the borders of a neighbouring country whose inhabitants share a culture, *B*, that differs remarkably from culture *A*. Suppose, then, that the *A*s are stranded in the new place and must seek to establish a common life together with the *B*s. It turns out that most of the *A*s do not acquire the skills, styles, and know-how suitable to their new place even if it appears to be to their advantage to do so. Many obstacles may get in the way and impede acquisition of a new tool-kit. Say the new arrivals share a norm of revenge towards the *B*s who not so long ago sought to invade the territory of the *A*s. All of a sudden they find themselves dependent on those they had come to regard as their enemy. This fact obviously does not inhibit their ability to learn *about* the culture of the *B*s. On the contrary, the *A*s are expected to be attentive to the habits and styles of the *B*s—not to *identify* with them—but to prepare for attack or defence. This situation is not exceptional. People fleeing from their country often end up at the borders of a neighbouring country, and it is not unusual that neighbouring countries have a long history of both friendly and hostile relations.

Against this background, it is possible to conclude that several variables are at play in the case of acquiring or, as the case may be, not acquiring suitable cultural equipment none of which necessarily indicate that people do not care for such equipment or would reject it were they given the opportunity to acquire it. Documented cases of non-adjustment do not constitute evidence that people naturally attach great value to their tool-kit nor that adjustment is impossible once socialised into one culture. This type of explanation is deeply problematic to sustain as an overall account of the sources of cultural resistance. Such an account would require a careful assessment of the actual choice situation, the circumstances imposed, as well as a consideration of social norms.

[17] S Lukes, 'Rationality of Social Norms' (1991) 32 *Archive Européene Sociologique* 142, at 147.

Potential Limits to this Claim

Until now, no attention has been given to the question of the degree of permanence of the background assumptions against which the notion of cultural equipment makes sense. Above all, situations might arise in which the idea that it is possible to discern suitable cultural equipment for a given place is rendered obsolete. For one thing, the particular content of the tool-kit of a people is not stable over time, but revised to accommodate changing circumstances and improved in the light of new information about more effective or rightful ways of organising strategies of action. In other words, what is generally considered as a suitable tool-kit for a certain place is not fixed once and for all. Thus, to substantiate it and say 'this is our culture' (this is how we harvest, build roads, trade, organise our common affairs, punish criminals, etc) and 'that is theirs' is to take a 'snapshot' of two cultures that may prevent them from evolving, changing, adapting, and mingling with each other and other cultures.[18] This is not an unusual reaction once people have become aware of what is special and distinct about their culture as opposed to others. Another problem with this approach is that it seems to indicate that adjustment is a responsibility for new arrivals and not a mutual cause.

One possible objection to the notion of cultural equipment and its attendant claim about the disadvantage of lacking suitable equipment is that a multicultural society is better understood as one in which skills, habits, styles, etc are simply diverse and that it must be more reasonable to suppose that new arrivals and native-born will select among, combine in various ways, or reject a range of various tool-kits. That is to say, it may not be possible to identify any given cultural equipment at any given time that could be said to be advantageous for everybody regardless of what they wish to be and do. Adrian Favell seems to indicate that these are the effects of the construction and consolidation of the European Union. Its member states can no longer be understood as self-contained bordered units within which new arrivals do better by adjusting their skills, styles, and habits to their new location. According to Favell, 'culturally, Europe as a whole appears to be fragmenting into a collection of smaller regional units and transnational cultural ties, as well as moving towards a more Europeanised common culture.'[19] Against this background, he envisions the coming of a state of affairs where the requirement imposed by national governments that new arrivals must integrate into the dominant national culture is rendered obsolete.[20]

Though we may speculate how things will be some time in the future, such speculation fails to provide a reasonable basis for taking stock of the

[18] J Waldron, 'Minority Cultures and the Cosmopolitan Alternative' (1992) 25 *University of Michigan Journal of Law Reform* 751, at 787–788.

[19] A Favell, 'The Europeanisation of Immigration Politics' (1998) 2 *European Integration. Online Papers*, at 2 [available at: <http://eiop.or.at/eiop/texte/1998-010a.htm>]. Last visited on 23 October 1999.

[20] *Ibid*, at 3.

obstacles or disadvantages faced by new arrivals here and now. Moreover, even if the image of Europe as comprising a set of diverse national cultures each with their own distinct style appears to fade, this development by no means renders our initial claim irrelevant.[21] What ultimately matters is not whether a particular tool-kit is designed for a region, neighbourhood, or to fit the idea of a common European culture, but only that it is possible to identify a tool-kit more suitable than others for the context in which people lead their lives.

The North American case of the aspirations of the Amish provides an example of a somewhat different complication. The Amish believe that the question about a person's skills, habits, or styles is based on a prior conception of rightful conduct, independent of actual conditions pertaining to a person's environment. The Amish emphasise co-operative farming and house-making skills and not the intellectualism and competitiveness promoted in public schools (from their standpoint informed by a radically different conception of the good). Therefore, the Amish appealed to the US Supreme Court that their children should be exempted from the compulsory public school requirement past the eighth grade. Their children's cultural equipment ought to be selected on the basis of a prior idea about its intended use: in their view, Bible study. All-purpose cultural equipment must be withheld insofar as it appears to encourage—that is, provide the tools for—a life-style in conflict with their convictions about how life is to be led.[22] These ideals, the Amish representatives conclude, must shape the educational policy relating to their children.

The Amish case directs attention to the possibility of conscientious efforts to control the selection of culture guided by a conviction about knowledge of the right and good. The Amish parents are not alone in their critical attitude towards teaching (their) children the skills and tools associated with values of competitiveness and intellectualism. Their protests remind us about the difficulty which inheres in the question as to what kind of cultural equipment a child is supposed to acquire and learn. Regardless of whether we—as citizens—affirm that children should acquire the tool-kit crucial for them to be citizens of the world,[23] or whether we agree with the

[21] But see J Raz and A Margalit, 'National Self-determination' (1990) 87 *The Journal of Philosophy* 439, at 443–444. Raz and Margalit oppose the claim about the fading character of national cultures. Their argument about self-determination presupposes that there are groups with 'a common character and a common culture that encompass many, varied, and important aspects of life, a culture that defines or marks a variety of forms or styles of life, types of activities, occupations, pursuits, and relationships. With national groups we expect to find national cuisines, distinctive architectural styles, a common language, distinctive literary and artistic traditions, national music, customs, dress, ceremonies, and holidays, etc.' Raz and Margalit continue by noting that the serious candidates for national self-determination 'have pervasive cultures and their identity is determined at least in part by their culture.'

[22] *Wisconsin v Yoder*, 406 US 205 (1972).

[23] M Nussbaum with Respondents, *For Love of Country: Debating the Limits to Patriotism* J Cohen (ed) (Boston MA, Beacon Press, 1996).

Amish about the sufficiency of basic reading and writing skills, we are likely to disagree with others about that. The Amish contend that it must be up to each (parent) to decide. Others argue that cultural equipment is obviously a matter of common concern for society as a whole. The concept of cultural equipment houses a diversity of substantive answers to the question of suitable cultural equipment within some range. It nevertheless regards the Amish objection as a critical case insofar as their objection seems to contravene the principle of familiarity—and of cultural impurity—in favour of withdrawal and separation, a principle that is fundamental to the claim about cultural equipment. Their objection indicates that shared cultural equipment necessary to discuss these matters is not the same as agreeing about ends, ie what any equipment is ultimately for.

LACK OF SUITABLE EQUIPMENT: CHOICE OR CIRCUMSTANCE?

One issue that arises from any attempt to ascertain whether difference in terms of cultural equipment is morally relevant is whether the content of an individual's equipment is supposed to be understood as the result of choice, thus, as something that the individual is capable of taking responsibility for and adjusting in the light of social change or simply by a change of residence. The choice–circumstance distinction is usually seen as decisive for liberal social justice theorists in determining whether a condition imposed upon a class of individuals qualifies as a circumstance requiring positive collective action. Hence, it is of great importance to examine how this distinction bears upon this analysis.

Whether human mobility across borders is a matter of choice or circumstance has come to be played out in the debate between cosmopolitans and nationalists. This debate entertains the idea that a cosmopolitan understanding of cultures as overlapping and criss-crossing one another rather than as separate islands each with their own distinct social organisation indicates that human travels and movements across borders cannot capture the possible disadvantages of new arrivals and that only a more communitarian understanding of culture can explain their circumstance. It is my contention that this assumption is a mistake. The cosmopolitan contribution to multicultural debates is a conception of culture that articulates why it is *at all* possible for humans to move across the surface of the earth and adjust to new places. Cultural differences are matters of degree. A cosmopolitan understanding of culture does not deny the possibility of making a distinction between individuals who like to move about in the world and think of their travels and settlements in remote places as adventurous and self-fulfilling, and groups of individuals and families whose travels are driven by necessity and who are motivated by a search for a safer place and basic goods for survival and sustenance. It is the part of the *aim* of the former to mingle and mix with different others in various places. They might have prepared themselves for this sort of life-style—always on the lookout for cultural resources suitable to pursue their aim. To learn about cultures in distant places and to move around in the world is part of a cosmopolitan's conception of the good life. This is not necessarily the case for refugees whose cultural equipment may be vastly deficient for their new environment.[24]

How should we understand the fate of new arrivals? Will Kymlicka whose account of the basis for minority rights relies on a more nationalist conception of culture believes that it is possible to make a general claim about an individual's relationship to his place of birth and upbringing. He criticises the cosmopolitan image of culture in that it grossly overestimates the extent to which people do, in fact, move across borders and downplays the costs involved for those who do. Of course, Kymlicka's reference to empirical data indicating a relative lack of human mobility in support of his contention about the individual's attachment to his culture of birth and upbringing ignores the prevalence of other factors—perhaps more significant ones than cultural difference—that must be considered as relevant variables in explaining this outcome.[25] A person who wishes to look for alternative places of settlement is confronted with a range of obstacles—most notably migration controls, but also a lack of means—that not only hampers, but *de facto* blocks the possibility of realising a plan involving settlement somewhere else. Kymlicka argues that individuals who do settle in a new social environment pay a high cost in terms of having lost a familiar place: their own cultural context. This cost must be eliminated. However, unlike this study which insists that it is possible to adjust to and be familiar with various places (and that there is nothing inherently regrettable in

[24] For a most comprehensive account of the various definitions of the term 'refugees', see GS Goodwin-Gill, *The Refugee in International Law,* 2nd edn (New York, Oxford University Press, 1996). Goodwin-Gill explains that: 'In ordinary language, it [the term 'refugee'] has a broader, looser meaning, signifying someone in flight, who seeks to escape conditions or personal circumstances found to be intolerable. The destination is not relevant; the flight is to freedom, to safety. Likewise, the reasons for flight may be many; flight from oppression, from a threat to life or liberty, flight from prosecution; flight from deprivation, from grinding poverty; flight from war or civil strife; flight from natural disasters, earthquake, flood, drought, famine. Implicit in the ordinary meaning of the word 'refugee' lies an assumption that the person concerned is worth of being, and ought to be, assisted, and, if necessary, protected from the causes and consequences of flight' (at 3). The legal definition is much more restrictive and excludes 'economic refugees' and makes a distinction between victims of natural disasters and victims of conditions or disasters with a human origin (at 3–4). Thus, according to Art 1(a) of the 1951 Convention Relating to the Status of Refugees, 'the term "refugee" shall apply to any person who: ... (2) As a result of events occurring before 1 January 1951 and owing to a well-founded fear of being persecuted for reasons of race, religion, nationality, membership of a particular social group or political opinion, is outside the country of his nationality and is unable or, owing to such fear, is unwilling to avail himself of the protection of that country; or who, not having a nationality and being outside the country of his former habitual residence as a result of such events, is unable or, owing to such fear, is unwilling to return to it.' In this book, the term 'refugee' is used in its broader sense.

[25] W Kymlicka, *Multicultural Citizenship* (New York, Oxford University Press, 1995), at 85–86.

moving about), Kymlicka orients his argument in a different direction more similar to that developed by Rawls in his more recent writings. Instead of fully exploring the possibility of facilitating adjustment to a different environment, both look to the question of the fate of migrants as not having relevance for social justice in the way indicated in the present study.[26]

Their more general idea is that the circumstance of new arrivals created by migration is a matter of partial (or non-) compliance with the principles of justice in many parts of the world, thus, a matter of *non-ideal* theory.[27] If the many existing local institutional arrangements were just, so it is held, migration would not exist or at least not be as significant as it is today. This reflection is sound considering that human movement across borders is often driven by necessity and amounts to flights from threat to life, persecution, war, poverty, and other unbearable conditions. In several cases characterised in terms of lack of suitable cultural equipment, it is wrongful conduct by government and other powerful agents that has driven people away from the context with which they are familiar. Their point is that even if migration were never to disappear entirely—even in a more well-ordered world[28]—there would no longer be any reason for paying special attention to people's cultural differences and, consequently, no reason for seeking to rectify the obstacles and disadvantages to which such differences amount. Then, migration would be limited to persons who *want* to move about in the world and think of their travels as enriching.[29] Of course, we may speculate about the extent to which people (if the opportunity were available) could be said to want to move about in the world and be free to look for alternative places of settlement, or whether people are inclined to remain in the context familiar to them. In other words, we may speculate as to whether an ever growing human mobility is explained in terms of necessity or whether it is boosted by curiosity and labour incentives in the more global market created by extensive transnational commerce, investment,

[26] J Rawls, *The Law of Peoples* (Cambridge Mass, Harvard University Press, 1999).

[27] For a distinction between ideal and non-ideal theory, see J Rawls, *Theory of Justice*, above n 3, at 216. According to Rawls, *ideal theory* assumes strict compliance and focuses on the principles that characterise a well-ordered society under favourable circumstances. It develops a conception of a perfectly just basic structure and the corresponding duties and obligations of persons under fixed constraints. *Non-ideal theory*, in contrast, is articulated after an ideal conception of justice has been chosen; only then do the parties behind the 'veil of ignorance' ask which principles to adopt under less favourable conditions. One part of non-ideal theory consists of the principles for governing adjustments to natural limitations and historical contingencies, and the other of principles for meeting injustice.

[28] But see J Rawls, *The Law of Peoples*, above n 26, at 9. According to Rawls, migration motivated by religious and ethnic persecution, political oppression, starvation and famine, population pressure, and the inequality and subjection of women would be eliminated as a serious problem in a realistic utopia.

[29] See generally J Waldron, 'Minority Cultures and the Cosmopolitan Alternative', above n 18, at 762.

business, and trade,[30] but this does not suggest anything in the way of how to respond to the questions of justice that arise here and now.

Kymlicka has a response to the fate of new arrivals in terms of their cultural difference, though. He holds that the individual entitlement to full enjoyment of culture depends on the actual distance from it. If we are far away from our culture—in geographical terms—we have no legitimate claim to cultural engagement. In this sense, the possibility of cultural engagement in a multicultural society is not the same for everyone. This is Kymlicka's response to the claims by new arrivals to enjoy their culture. However, his approach ignores the question of cultural equipment and focuses exclusively on culture as a background condition—a context of choice—for the pursuit of various aims. It seems to presuppose that cultures are not something that people carry with them when they move about in the world, but are materialised in various local social organisations tied to a certain place. This understanding of culture naturally indicates that if an individual leaves his place of birth and upbringing he forfeits his right to enjoy his culture to the full; it is a choice he makes and he must bear the consequences of that choice.[31] All the same, it is not reasonable to assume that all new arrivals have chosen to lay down their claim to full enjoyment of culture as Kymlicka also points out. On the contrary, it may have been their cultural engagements that were perceived as intolerable and eventually led them to embark on their journey. They did not choose to relinquish their right; in fact, they refused to do so.

Nevertheless, insofar as human movement is driven by necessity, Kymlicka continues, it is an injustice done by the government in the country of origin and it is this government that is ultimately responsible for the circumstance of refugees in socio-cultural terms. Their cultural difference is not a direct concern for the native-born in the host country. Of course, for Kymlicka, full enjoyment of culture requires the establishment of a set of social and political institutions in the form of self-government. Even so, if a group of newcomers resists any attempt to adjust their culture, and instead aspires towards separation and ultimately self-government, it would look like (and, in fact, amount to) an attempt to acquire land and other natural resources rather than genuine cultural engagement. To the extent that their action amounts to a joint effort to establish the *conditions* perceived as crucial for cultural engagement, it is necessary to examine the legitimacy of such a move in the light of what constitutes a fair distribution of land. Still, none of these considerations help us to respond to the question whether cultural differences largely introduced by human mobility involve new questions of justice.

[30] See eg I Kant, 'To Perpetual Peace. A Philosophical Sketch (1795)' in *Perpetual Peace and Other Essays*, Ted Humphrey (trans) (Indianapolis, Hackett Publishing Company, 1983), sec 364. According to Kant, commerce brings people into peaceful relations with one another.

[31] See especially W Kymlicka, *Multicultural Citizenship*, above n 25, at 96.

My argument is that it is a mistake to treat migration as a matter for partial compliance or non-ideal theory. It makes it seem as though the possible injustice done to newcomers is not done here by us, but elsewhere and by others.[32] It lends credence to the belief that the trouble faced by refugees must be resolved by foreign policy and by serious attempts to ensure respect for human rights and fair schemes of co-operation everywhere. No doubt, this is a basic concern. Nevertheless, even if the phenomenon of multiculturalism is often the upshot of other injustices, once we are brought into relation with one another—no matter how—we have a duty to come to terms with one another and to set up or maintain fair schemes of social co-operation.[33] The more general claim about the need to receive new arrivals is based on the idea of natural duties, ie duties that hold between persons irrespective of their institutional relationship. One such duty is the duty of mutual aid, ie to help one another when a person is in need or in jeopardy provided that one can do so without excessive risk or loss to oneself.[34] Guy Goodwin-Gill holds that implicit in the term 'refugee' is the assumption that the individual in question is worthy of being—and ought to be—assisted and, if necessary, protected from the causes of his refuge.[35] Furthermore, if new arrivals intend to remain on a certain territory where a group of individuals has set up and already participates in an ongoing scheme of social co-operation supposed to fairly distribute the benefits and burdens associated with such a co-operative scheme, it is necessary to shift the focus onto principles regulating the accommodation of arrivals into such schemes, and to the question whether they are owed compensation or some form of assistance as a result of their circumstance. To the extent that their arrival is the result of circumstance so is their incomplete cultural equipment.

[32] But see T Pogge, 'The Global Resources Dividend' in DA Crocker and T Linden (eds), *Ethics of Consumption: The Good Life, Justice and Global Stewardship* (Lanham, MD, Rowman & Littlefield, 1998), at 505. According to Pogge, poverty or 'radical inequality' is an injustice for which citizens in affluent democracies are actually responsible. Thus, in his view, citizens of the affluent democracies are causally entwined in the misery of the poor and we cannot release ourselves from involvement as long as their misery continues.

[33] See I Kant, *Metaphysics of Morals*, Mary Gregor (trans) (Cambridge, Cambridge University Press, 1991), at 158–159; and J Waldron, 'Redressing Historic Injustice' (2002) 52 *University of Toronto Law Journal* 135. According to Waldron, the 'proximity principle' can usefully be applied to problems related to multiculturalism and identity politics.

[34] J Rawls, *Theory of Justice*, above n 3, at 98–99. Rawls defines 'natural duties' as duties that apply to everybody without any consideration of voluntary acts. Natural duties have no necessary connection with institutions or social practices, 'hold between persons irrespective of their institutional relationships; they obtain between all as equal moral persons. In this sense the natural duties are owed not only to definite individuals, say to those co-operating together in a particular social arrangement, but to persons generally.'

[35] GS Goodwin-Gill, *The Refugee in International Law*, above n 24, at 3.

CULTURAL EQUIPMENT AND INDIVIDUAL FREEDOM

The reality of vast differences in terms of suitable cultural equipment tells us something about the difference—sometimes enormous—in the *worth* of basic liberties among the inhabitants of a place. A formal assignment of rights and freedoms is not a sufficient measure to secure effective freedoms. For example, a parliamentary enactment of, say, a Bill of Rights does not consider that people differ—sometimes vastly—in their ability to utilise the rights and freedoms listed in that Bill. Conditions upon the individual due to want of means, malnutrition, chronic disease, mental or physical disability seriously inhibit individual ability and can eventually destroy all the faculties crucial to fully enjoy and exercise agency and freedom.[36] Rawls affirms that 'poverty, ignorance and lack of means' amount to serious obstacles to the capacity to take advantage of rights and freedoms. On his account, these kinds of obstacles affect the *worth* of rights and freedoms from the standpoint of the individual. The worth of freedom for any given individual is measured in terms of his or her capacity to advance ends.[37] In the worst case, then, an individual whose circumstance prevents him from making use of his rights may regard them as worth next to nothing. The recognition of difference in terms of the worth of rights formally assigned to everyone tells us something about the importance of carefully examining the conditions crucial for effective freedom. One such condition, it is contended here, is suitable cultural equipment.

This condition seems to be of direct relevance for social justice. Though social justice theorists agree that poverty is an especially distressful and urgent obstacle, their limited focus does not seem to exclude the possibility of paying attention to other kinds of obstacles as well. Amartya Sen, for example, advances an account of justice that considers a broad variety of social and biological factors documented to have a serious impact on freedom.[38] According to Sen, such factors warrant consideration as well. More generally, theories of justice must be shaped by what we ultimately care about, namely, to secure respect for freedom. This concern necessitates a direct focus on the ability to convert primary goods (including basic liberties) into effective freedoms. An exclusive focus on income and wealth ignores a broad range of factors known to obstruct individual ability to move around, to lead a healthy life, to participate in the life of the community, and

[36] J Waldron, 'Rights' in R Goodin and P Pettit (eds), *A Companion to Contemporary Political Philosophy* (Oxford, Blackwell, 1993), at 578–579.

[37] J Rawls, *Theory of Justice*, above n 3, 179 ff. See also J Rawls, *Political Liberalism* (New York, Columbia University Press, 1995), 324 ff.

[38] A Sen, 'Justice: Means versus Freedom' (1990) 19 *Philosophy and Public Affairs* 111, at 116. Sen explains that we must distinguish capability—representing freedom actually enjoyed—from both (1) primary goods (and other resources), and (2) actually chosen lives. Sen concludes that neither primary goods nor resources, more broadly defined, can represent the capability a person actually enjoys.

to take advantage of employment and educational opportunities.[39] Of particular concern is the way in which inadequate cultural equipment inhibits—and sometimes renders practically impossible—access to law and public institutions as well as impeding the ability to participate in the economic and political life in one's place of residence. Finally, the same condition also has a serious impact on the distributive process. Without suitable cultural equipment on hand the individual might not be able to secure a fair share of income and wealth in that process.

Access to Law and Public Institutions

First of all, suitable cultural equipment is crucial to be able to access the law that claims authority and jurisdiction in one's place of residence. Since the law is usually communicated in a mode suited to the native-born, it is by no means evident that new arrivals and others who differ in cultural terms are able to appreciate what rights they have as a matter of law, nor what is required by them in terms of conduct. For example, the individual may have certain rights as an employee or as an unemployed person. He or she may have rights to healthcare in case of illness, or the right to housing in case of homelessness. However, without any knowledge of these rights the individual will naturally not make use of them. Apart from having access to the rights-aspect of law, it is also essential for freedom to be familiar with its duty-aspect. Unless the individual is acquainted with the legal duties imposed on conduct she risks punishment for conduct she did not know was unlawful. As Rawls notes, ignorance has a serious impact on individual freedom since the individual does not know how to behave in order to avoid legal punishment.[40]

In a situation of diverse cultural equipment, access requires that the law be communicated in a language or through the use of signs readily perceived by all its addressees. It also requires familiarity with the scheme of interpretation in use by courts and administrative agencies. Unless a law has been communicated with due regard for the culture(s) of the addressees, it fails to meet the requirement of accessibility. As modest as this claim appears to be it nevertheless places noteworthy burdens on the public institutions of a culturally diverse population. In a more culturally homogeneous setting, it is not unusual that practices of communication are regarded as 'natural' and 'parochial' (non-political). As society is becoming increasingly multicultural, however, the language and signs employed by public institutions to advertise laws can become fraught with political significance. Having said that, it is a mistake to assume that once the inhabitants of a place care for their practices that facilitate communication, something has gone wrong. To the extent that

[39] A Sen, 'Justice: Means versus Freedom', above n 38, at 116.
[40] J Rawls, *Theory of Justice*, above n 3, at 212.

shared practices of communication are lacking some official position on how to respond to a culturally diverse situation is warranted.

My argument about the centrality of cultural equipment is universal although it singles out newcomers as a critical case. However, the circumstance of deficient cultural equipment is not limited to newcomers, but is experienced by any individual whose legal system rapidly changes in form and content. Above all, it is experienced in times of radical political change brought about by revolution, or in periods of radical re-settlement of the question of authority, say, in case of transition from dictatorship to democracy.[41] Consideration of cultural equipment must be part of any theory of justice that accommodates disagreement about justice and right. As argued in the seventh chapter of this book, ideological disagreement is expected in a multicultural society. Changes in ideology are known to affect the range and kind of rights and duties we have as individuals. Quite regardless of whether it is a more conservative government replacing a more socialist one, or the other way around, the least to be expected is that the individual is able to know about his or her legal rights and duties.

There are several strategies available to respond—at least in part—to a condition of inaccessibility due to incomplete cultural equipment. Private initiatives to secure familiarity must be considered. Cultural associations are often established so as to create a context to meet and mingle with like-minded others. It is often a natural part of the activities of such associations to inform newcomers with similar cultural make-up about the law in force and how it applies to their conduct. These are spontaneous initiatives often launched by cultures with a considerable membership in a given location. As such, they cannot be relied upon as the definitive solution to the problem of inaccessible laws. Thus, public initiatives are called for. Such initiatives may cover translation and language education. For example, it is a well-established practice among the law-making bodies of the European Union to advertise their laws with due regard for different public cultures of the member states.[42] The circumstance of newcomers is often neglected. One area where their circumstance has been accorded central importance is in their first encounters with European public authorities. Consideration of difference in cultural equipment is made at the time of arrival and application for entry of asylum-seekers and workers. According to a recent EU legal draft, national public authorities are obliged to provide interpreters and translators so as to establish effective channels of communication con-

[41] I thank Jeremy Waldron for alerting me to the relevance of cultural equipment in a 'closed' society and for discussing with me in what sense it may be so.

[42] PM Hearn and DF Button (eds), *Language Industries Atlas* (Amsterdam, IOS Press for CEC, Brussels and Luxembourg, 1994). There are over 40 indigenous languages and major language variants spoken by the 380 million people of the EU, mostly of Romanesque or Germanic origin, together with a smaller number of languages of Celtic, Finno-Ugric or Basque stock. Even so, the law is only translated into the official languages, not all indigenous languages. Trevor Hartley claims that multilingualism is one of the causes of the uncertainty

sidering the obvious multicultural setting at the borders to 'safe havens'. According to the draft Council Directive, new arrivals have the right to be informed about the laws on exit and entry in an accessible mode.[43] Even so, the public institutions of the EU and its member states must continue to grapple with the question of individual access to law in a multicultural environment so as to ensure efficacy of a given legal system, and, as suggested in this study, for the sake of securing a minimum provision of respect.

Sustainable solutions to overcome the reality of communicative interruptions between public institutions and parts of their population is by no means self-evident.[44] The trouble may not be fully overcome by way of translation. This depends, in part, on the absence of terms in various languages that mean exactly the same thing. For translation to be effective, the translator must be capable of diminishing the gap not only between various languages, but also between different cultures. The translator must have advanced linguistic competence coupled with good translation skills, possess cultural awareness and an education sensitive to the requirements of

problem in Community law. Every item of Community legislation is promulgated in each of the working languages of the Community. At present, there are 11 of these—Danish, Dutch, English, Finnish, French, German, Greek, Italian, Portuguese, Spanish and Swedish. The text of a given provision is not always the same in each of these languages. It is not possible to apply the English text in England, the French in France and the Danish in Denmark, etc. The European Court has rejected this because it would lead to the fragmentation of the Community legal system (see *Stauder v City of Ulm*, Case 29/69, [1969] ECR 419 (para 3 of the judgment); see also *Moksel v BALM*, Case 55/87, [1988] ECR 3845 (para 15 of the judgment)). Instead, the Court has said that all language-versions are equal, even if in practice, the Court seems to give more weight to the French version. The problem of different language-versions normally does not become apparent until the case comes before the European Court. For a discussion of interpretative problems having their source in multilingualism, see TC Hartley, *Constitutional Problems of the European Union* (Oxford, Hart Publishing, 1999), at 68–71.

[43] A recent example is a proposal by the EU Commission for a Council Directive on Minimum Standards on Procedures in Member States for Granting and Withdrawing Refugee Status (Brussels, 20.9.2000) (COM (2000) 578 final, 2000/0238 CNS). Art 7 of the draft sets out procedural guarantees for every asylum applicant. Thus, para (a) reads: 'Member States must inform each applicant, prior to examination of his asylum application, of the procedure to be followed, and of his rights and obligations during the procedure, in a language which he understands. This could be done for example by giving the applicant a standard document about the procedure in a language he can read and to give him time to read it or by explaining the procedure to him in a film in a language he understands. It could also be done orally by the authorities or by organisations assigned this task.' In addition, para (b) stipulates that: 'According to this point, applicants must be given the services of an interpreter, whenever necessary, for submitting their case to the competent authorities. These services must be paid for out of public funds if the interpreter is demanded by a competent authority.' See also Art 9 (1) (a) of the Amended Proposal for a Council Directive on Minimum Standards on Procedures in Member States for Granting and Withdrawing Refugee Status (Brussels, 03.07.2002) (COM (2002) 326 final/2).

[44] J-P Malhaic, 'The Formulation of Translation Strategies for Cultural References' in C Hoffmann (ed), *Language, Culture and Communication in Contemporary Europe* (Philadelphia, Multilingual Matters, 1996), at 132. There are different translation strategies: one is 'exoticism' (ie plunge the addressees into the source culture); another is 'cultural borrowing' (a systematic attempt to convert the source culture setting into the culture of the addresses) (at 134).

equivalence so as to avoid misunderstandings and misinterpretations.[45] At the same time, it should be noted that translation and interpretation are costly undertakings.[46] The alternative is to accept a period of adjustment and acquisition of cultural equipment. During this period, no obvious answer to the question of responsibility for compliance with particular laws having their source in lack of access may be available.[47]

Finally, the cultural equipment in use by various public institutions is likely to change as the result of multiculturalism. In many cases, public institutions must engage in, and as the case may be, accommodate, the variation that exists with respect to the different cultural equipment on hand. It is important that institutions of childcare, education and healthcare services are not too distant from the various cultures of families, communities, and neighbourhoods since such distance may hamper the prospects of providing the goods in demand. For example, a recent study of classroom diversity in the United States indicates that, while the population of children is rapidly becoming more ethnically and culturally diverse, the population of white middle-class female teachers remains stable. The mismatch between children's home cultures and the cultures of schools plays havoc with student achievement. Disproportionately high numbers of minority, immigrant, isolated, and poor children perform consistently less well academically than white, middle-class students. This phenomenon is explained in terms of what two anthropologists define as different 'funds of knowledge' among children. Children from different homes, communities, and economic backgrounds acquire different 'funds of knowledge' and these differences are not considered in school.[48] The cultural difference consists of various social and linguistic practices and the historically accumulated bodies of knowledge that are essential to the students' homes and communities. Although the children are immersed in rich and stimulating language environments, the difference between the worlds they know at home and the world of school is experienced as vast. The difference between the culture at home and the culture in school leads to misunderstandings and confusion and makes the school an uncomfortable place for those whose cultures do not correspond neatly with

[45] J Laver and J Roukens, 'The Global Information Society and Europe's Linguistic and Cultural Heritage', in C Hoffmann (ed), *Language, Culture and Communication in Contemporary Europe*, *ibid*.

[46] *Ibid*. Laver and Roukens inform us that, in 1988, it was estimated that in the EU alone some 100 million pages of text are translated each year by a work-force of 100,000 and at a cost of 10 billion ECU. There is a steady increase in the volume of text translated. Given the need for transmitting large quantities of information and the wish to preserve linguistic diversity, access by all citizens of the EU to user-friendly and effective translation tools for all European languages will be indispensable (at 14–15). The European Commission is the most prominent user of multilingual language technology. It translates a million pages a year through the work of 1,500 professional translators (at 23–24).

[47] See generally chapter eight of this book.

[48] C Vélez-Ibáñez and J Greenberg, 'Formation and Transformation of Funds of Knowledge Among US Mexican Housholds' (1993) 23 *Anthropology and Education Quarterly* 313.

the culture of the school. This cultural difference obviously has an impact on the ability to perform well in school.[49]

As a study on the health and adjustment of immigrant children and families indicates, for many immigrants arriving in the United States today, access to healthcare is likely to be complicated by cultural perceptions of health and healthcare that differ from Western concepts and by communication problems caused by language barriers.[50] Culture shapes perceptions, explanations, and experiences of illness, help-seeking patterns, and responses to treatment. The fears of immigrant parents that healthcare providers will fail to understand or will even disparage their beliefs about their children's health and healthcare, whether founded or not, may discourage healthcare use.[51] As a matter of fact, there is a strong consensus among healthcare professionals that the delivery of high-quality healthcare and mental health services to immigrant children and their families must be done in ways that are *culturally competent* and *culturally sensitive*; above all, it must take into account language barriers.[52]

These are but a few examples of the kinds of difficulties that arise in a public institutional context due to cultural difference. They raise issues about the difficulties encountered as a result of cultural difference between the individual and her public institutions. Such difference has an obvious impact on the ability of children to enjoy the goods of education and healthcare and of people more generally to enjoy the goods that have been formally assigned to all.

[49] See A Rosebery, E Mcintyre and N González, 'Connecting Students' Cultures to Instruction' in E McIntyre, A Rosebery and N González (eds), *Classroom Diversity: Connecting Curriculum to Students' Lives* (Portsmouth, NH, Heinemann, 2001), at 2–3. See generally PG Ramsey, 'Caring for Children in a Diverse World' in B Spodek and ON Saracho (eds), *Issues in Child Care. Yearbook in Early Childhood Education*, vol 3 (New York, Teachers College Press, 1992) 88–106, at 92–94; and P Ramsey, *Teaching and Learning in a Diverse World: Multicultural Education for Young Children* (New York, Teachers College, Columbia University, 1987).

[50] DJ Hernandez and E Charney (eds), *From Generation to Generation: The Health and Well-being of Children in Immigrant Families.* Report by the Committee on the Health and Adjustment of Immigrant Children and Families, Board on Children, Youth and Families, National Research Council, Institute of Medicine (Washington, National Academy Press, 1998), at 150.

[51] See eg P Mrazek and RJ Haggerty (eds), *Reducing Risks for Mental Disorders: Frontiers for Preventive Intervention Research.* Report by the Committee on Prevention of Mental Disorders, Division of Biobehavioral Sciences and Mental Disorders, Institute of Medicine (Washington DC, National Academy Press, 1994). But see CNH Jenkins, L Tao, SJ McPhee, S Stewart and T Ha Ngoc, 'Health Care Access and Preventive Care among Vietnamese Immigrants: Do Traditional Beliefs and Practices Pose Barriers?' (1996) 43 *Social Science and Medicine* 1049. According to this study, the differing beliefs of Vietnamese immigrants did not constitute a barrier to accessing Western medicine.

[52] P Mrazek and RJ Haggerty (eds), *Reducing Risks for Mental Disorders: Frontiers for Preventive Intervention Research, ibid* at 151.

Participation in Political Life

Cultural difference in the sense relevant here influences the individual's ability to play a role in political life, that is, to exercise political rights. Apart from the withholding of recognition of political rights, one reason why newcomers are not likely to engage in political discussions in their new place of residence, work, and life is that, unlike the native-born, recent arrivals often lack the cultural equipment crucial to be full participants in such discussions. Even when political rights have been secured, a deficiency in culture-specific know-how and skills often remains as an obstacle creating a cultural barrier between those whose cultures differ from the native-born and those engaged in discussions in the public forum. It might also explain why newcomers and others similarly situated, culturally speaking, have recourse to non-argumentative strategies such as symbolic acts and gestures (protests and demonstrations) or real acts (civil disobedience) in an attempt to address the agents of the public forum about their particular claims and concerns. Since the background to the politics of exclusion is complicated, it will be discussed separately and in greater detail in the seventh chapter of this book.

There is a tendency to refrain from public efforts to design measures to facilitate discussion with those whose cultures differ and to secure conditions for universal political involvement. One trouble is that political engagement often requires skills and know-how that go far beyond the basic cultural equipment in focus. It is evidently not an issue of language skills alone. Members of political parties as well as members of parliament and government offices are expected to be well informed about a vast range of issues—not least about what are considered to be the more pertinent concerns in their community—as well as the historical background to on-going legislative discussions. As stated earlier in this chapter, none of these things are impossible to learn, but it takes time. Against this background, the acquisition of cultural equipment sufficient for engagement in common political institutional tasks seems an aspiration. Even so, to the extent that a right to take part in political affairs is not solely founded on an idea about the need for self-expression, but is supposed to represent one of the more vital channels of communication on matters of common concern, the centrality of cultural equipment can hardly be ignored—even from a basic democratic standpoint.

The EU with its culturally diverse parliamentary assembly has sought to resolve the problems posed by vast differences in cultural equipment among its citizens and their political representatives in an innovative manner. The participants in common deliberations in the European Parliament may select the language with which they are more familiar (as long as it is considered an officially recognised language) when advancing proposals about law and policy or forwarding objections and counter-arguments. The European

Parliament provides services for simultaneous translation when the parliamentarians assemble. Critics believe that this is an unreasonably costly solution and that some alternative must be forthcoming especially in the light of the EU enlargement, which inevitably involves accommodating more languages into the EU institutional structure and organisation. However, since the details of common cultural equipment remain unspecified, the current solution seems to be the only one available, at least for now. One dilemma that is likely to impede a resettlement of this issue is that far from all inhabitants are sufficiently familiar with any specific language. Another problem refers to the politicisation of the question of what language all EU citizens are expected to learn and use in their public discussions with one another.

Participation in Economic Life

Actual engagement in economic activities and the ability to take advantage of employment opportunities usually require suitable cultural equipment. There are nevertheless difficulties involved in seeking to generalise the extent to which culture-specific skills and know-how acquired in and for a certain place are useful in the marketplace elsewhere. The impact of deficient suitable equipment is less obvious in a place whose government controls and manipulates immigration flows so as to ensure that people already possess the culture-specific skills and tools upon arrival to meet the general demands by the labour market. In addition, even if an individual's skills and know-how are unfamiliar to consumers in his new place of residence, it might be possible to introduce such skills and know-how, thereby creating new needs for foods, services, and so on, among the more permanent population. In this sense, an individual's original skills may prove to be an asset in a foreign marketplace.

In addition, formal networks established by cultural fellows often assist newcomers to find employment. Indeed, upon arrival the newcomer might be absorbed by an ever-growing cultural community of like fellows and continue to speak his native language in everyday life as well as engage in trade and services established in and for the insiders of his community. The importance of cultural fellows has been documented by the Spanish experience of receiving a group of refugees from South East Asia. The Spanish government provided the newcomers with housing, clothing, and food as well as language instruction and information about Spanish customs and traditions during their first months of stay. The refugees were then located to different regions of Spain where they had been offered jobs. After two months, however, most of them had returned to Madrid, complaining about hard work and lack of friendship. Just a few weeks later most of them had left without notice to France. One Spanish social worker involved in the reception explains that the Spanish and French governments have adopted the same reception policies and that their motive for departure was the

Laotian and Vietnamese settlements in France.[53] Among social workers, it is a well-known fact that immigrant settlements are often better equipped to assist newcomers find a job, and can also provide them with natural forums for friendship and community.[54]

Thus, public efforts cannot replace informal networks. Even so, public authorities will still have a role to play in newcomers' endeavours to acquire a new tool-kit. Sometimes an interest in acquiring suitable equipment comes into conflict with other concerns. The paradox is that in times of a flourishing labour market new arrivals are often offered a job immediately upon arrival, a job that does not require any culture-specific skills and may be appreciated by the newcomer who usually wishes to be self-sufficient. As a result, the acquisition process is usually delayed. Their lack of suitable equipment may only be brought to the attention of social agencies when they lose that job or for other reasons become dependent on public assistance. Under less favourable labour market conditions, by contrast, newcomers are more likely to complete the courses provided by the government.[55]

The cultural disadvantage in economic life must be understood in light of the fact that the labour market has become vastly regulated and organised with categories, prototypes, as well as standardised educational and training requirements. This reality is even more striking when the orders and hierarchies are well established and fixed, the rules of success clear, and the cultural capital (the currency of a prestigious form of know-how) widely recognised.[56] The importance of having suitable cultural equipment is felt by most of us. Even national elites may be badly equipped to take advantage of new repertoires of practices and avenues being developed (such as EU institutions) since this requires a different cultural capital.[57] All the same, the argument advanced in this chapter does not consider concerns for lack of *excellence*, but is motivated by the need to ensure the minimum socio-cultural conditions to be able to exercise rights and freedoms. One such condition is the possession of the culture-specific skills and know-how suitable for one's place of residence.

CULTURAL DIFFERENCE AND ITS RELEVANCE TO SOCIAL JUSTICE

In spite of the direct relevance of cultural difference for ensuring effective protection of rights and freedoms, the concerns raised by theorists of multi-

[53] MJ Santa Cruz Robles, 'Refugees from South-East Asia in Spain: The Challenge of Hope' in D Joly and R Cohen (eds), *Reluctant Hosts: Europe and Its Refugees* (Aldershot, Avebury, 1989).

[54] Personal interview with Swedish social secretaries in Stockholm region on 20 April 2001.

[55] *Ibid.*

[56] See P Bourdieu, *Distinction: A Social Critique of the Judgement of Taste* (Cambridge, Mass, Harvard University Press, 1998); and P Bourdieu, *The State Nobility: Elite Schools in the Field of Power* (Stanford, Stanford University Press, 1996).

[57] A Favell, 'The Europeanisation of Immigration Politics', above n 19, at 8.

culturalism have failed to engage liberal theorists of social justice, and perhaps even reinforced the tendency to avoid these and similarly controversial issues.[58] From the standpoint of a political liberal account of social justice, the trouble is that some subjects of law would be treated differently from others on what appear to be contestable grounds. To treat every individual in the same way is thought to secure an equal right to equal basic liberties.[59] The purpose of this section is to examine the basis for the principle of equal treatment. Of primary interest is whether there are any considerations that stand in the way of accommodating a concern for variation in terms of cultural equipment into the framework of a more general account of social justice. It is suggested that the principle of equal treatment may not be an obstacle to differential treatment.

Formally speaking, the principle of equal treatment does not rule out differential treatment insofar as reasons can be given for the deviation. Several scholars contend that equal treatment is best considered as a starting point, ie as a 'default' position when thinking about the way people ought to be treated by agents of the public forum. In a legal context, the principle is considered as a fundamental precept of the Rule of Law. Equality before the law refers to the equal subjection of all inhabitants to the law that claims authority over their conduct by virtue of their territorial location. It stipulates that courts and other law-applying institutions are to apply the law impartially and interpret it consistently. Similar cases are to be treated similarly and different cases differently. However, though the principle of equality before the law is fundamental to the legal order, it still leaves open the question of what, if anything, makes a case different from others and what, if anything, should be done about that. The accompanying rules of impartiality and consistency in application require that if one case is treated differently before the law then all other similar cases must be treated alike. The reasons for treating people differently must be stated in statutes or precedents.[60]

[58] See generally J Rawls, *Political Liberalism*, above n 37; and S Macedo, *Liberal Virtues: Citizenship, Virtue and Community in Liberal Constitutionalism* (Oxford, Clarendon Press, 1990).

[59] J Rawls, *Theory of Justice*, above n 3, at 53; and J Rawls, *Political Liberalism*, above n 37 at 291. In *Theory of Justice*, Rawls states that the basic liberties are political liberty (the right to vote and hold public office) and freedom of speech and assembly; liberty of conscience and freedom of thought; freedom of the person, which includes freedom from psychological oppression and physical assault and dismemberment (integrity of the person); the right to hold personal property and freedom from arbitrary arrest and seizure as defined by the concept of the rule of law. These liberties are to be equal by the first principle. In *Political Liberalism*, Rawls gives a similar list: the 'equal basic liberties' include freedom of thought and liberty of conscience, the political liberties and freedom of association, as well as the freedoms specified by the liberty and integrity of the person; and the rights and liberties covered by the rules of law.

[60] See generally J Rawls, *Theory of Justice*, above n 3, at 51, 206, 442. Rawls explains that the 'conception of formal justice, the regular and impartial administration of public rules, becomes the rule of law when applied to the legal system' (at 206).

According to Isaiah Berlin, the principle of equal treatment is a demand for rationality and non-arbitrariness.[61] What it requires, Gerald Gaus explains, is that 'any discriminatory act—any action that provides differential advantages or burdens—stands in need of justification; any unjustified discriminatory act calls for redress'.[62] The primary aim of this principle may be to secure the legitimate exercise of authority. As Joseph Raz maintains, for authorities to be legitimate they must act for reasons and their legitimacy depends on a degree of success in doing so.[63] Stated in this general way, the principle of equal treatment seems to leave open the possibility of accommodating vast differences in terms of culture. If it is possible to explain why an individual's culture may be a ground for differential treatment then the requirements of reason imposed by equal treatment are respected. The question, then, is whether liberal accounts of social justice provide substantive reasons for taking account of the cultural difference in focus.

Liberal Approaches to Interpersonal Difference

It is possible to discern at least three different liberal accounts of justice for the purpose of establishing the permissibility or necessity of differential treatment for the sake of achieving justice or fairness. The accounts in focus are defined as the primary goods approach, equality of resources, and the basic capability approach, and have been developed by John Rawls, Ronald Dworkin, and Amartya Sen respectively. Though none of these approaches discusses the possible relevance of *cultural* difference (as opposed to other types of difference) among the beneficiaries, their respective accounts assist in ascertaining the basis for regarding an interpersonal variation as directly relevant to thinking about justice.

The primary goods approach recognises the existence of interpersonal differences in terms of moral, intellectual, and physical capacities and skills. However, it then assumes that all individuals have the essential minimum degree of skills and capacities that enable them to be fully co-operating members of society over a complete life.[64] The primary goods approach, therefore, fails to provide reasons for supposing that people may not actually be sufficiently equipped in the way assumed in the outset. Rawls explains that there are practical reasons for this neglect. The primary goods approach is limited to basic questions. It does not purport to answer *all* questions (involving difference) that may appear before the agents of the public forum. The assumption about sufficient similarity across individuals

[61] I Berlin, 'Equality as an Ideal' in FA Olafson (ed), *Justice and Social Policy* (Englewood Cliffs NJ, Prentice Hall, 1961), 128–150. But see R Norman, *Free and Equal: A Philosophical Examination of Political Values* (Oxford, Oxford University Press, 1987), at 57–58.

[62] G Gaus, *Social Philosophy* (New York, ME Sharpe Inc, 1999), at 119.

[63] J Raz, *Ethics in the Public Domain: Essays in the Morality of Law and Politics* (New York, Oxford University Press, 1994), at 220.

[64] J Rawls, *Political Liberalism*, above n 37, at 183.

is not supposed to rule out, once and for all, claims about the need for considering conditions such as lack of health or physical or mental disabilities.[65] Thus, for example, Rawls states that his approach is consistent with a consideration of unequal welfare or unequal capabilities.[66] Still, while not excluding the possible significance of variations in terms of skills and other personal resources, the primary goods approach does not single out conditions that warrant special attention.[67]

Amartya Sen advances an important alternative to the political liberal approach. In his basic capability approach, he subordinates the issue of equal treatment to what he affirms must be our primary concern, namely, to secure respect for individual freedom. As Sen puts it, if it is individual freedom we ultimately care about 'then that is what we do and possession of goods is instrumentally and contingently valuable only to the extent it helps in the achievement of things we do value viz. capabilities.'[68] Such a concern requires a direct focus on individual ability to convert primary goods or resources into effective freedoms. A broad variety of social and biological differences are known to obstruct individual capacity to make use of means assigned to everybody alike.[69] Hence, Sen argues that an account of fairness, ie an account of what is required by the agents of the public forum in order

[65] J Rawls, *Theory of Justice*, above n 3, at 83–84, and J Rawls, *Political Liberalism*, above n 37, at 185. In *Theory of Justice*, Rawls informs us that 'various refinements will certainly be necessary in practice (...) I shall assume that everyone has physical needs and psychological capacities within the normal range, so that the questions of health care and mental capacity do not arise.' Such questions are considered 'hard cases'. In *Political Liberalism*, Rawls holds that primary goods adequately respond to all kinds of differences except in case of illness or accident that places people below the line.

[66] J Rawls, *Theory of Justice*, above n 3, at 266–267, 446–447; and J Rawls, *Political Liberalism*, above n 37, at 185–186. In *Theory of Justice*, Rawls explains that the 'second priority rule' (the priority of justice over efficiency and welfare) stipulates that: 'The second principle of justice is lexically prior to the principle of efficiency and that of maximizing the sum of advantages; and fair opportunity is prior to the difference principle. There are two cases: (a) an inequality of opportunity must enhance the opportunities of those with the lesser opportunity; (b) an excessive rate of saving must on balance mitigate the burden of those bearing this hardship' (at 266–267). However, welfare as the criterion for justice is rejected. Rawls holds that a policy that tries to make the same proportionate contribution to each person's life to realise the best life he is capable of would require a measure of estimating the relative goodness of plans of life, and a way of measuring what counts as an equal proportionate contribution to persons with different conceptions of the good. The consequences would be that the greater abilities of some may give them a stronger claim on social resources irrespective of compensating disadvantages to others (at 446–447).

[67] See J Rawls, *The Law of Peoples*, above n 26, at 13. The extent to which the primary goods approach permits direct concern with difference is nevertheless unclear. In more recent writings, Rawls appears to move away from his previous statement in favour of a more comprehensive theory of interpersonal difference. He notes that the simplifying assumptions about citizens' capabilities are necessary since 'the idea of effective basic capabilities without those or similar assumptions calls for more information than political society can conceivably acquire and sensibly apply.'

[68] A Sen, 'Rights and Capabilities' in A Sen, *Resources, Values and Development* (Oxford, Basil Blackwell, 1984), at 317.

[69] A Sen, 'Justice: Means versus Freedom', above n 38, at 116.

to ensure respect on the ground, must pay attention both to the individual's actual ends as well as his or her powers to convert primary goods or resources into the achievement of ends.[70] The basic capability approach does not rule out the relevance of an interpersonal variation in advance. Such variation may be relevant insofar as it involves obstacles inhibiting some from making effective use of their freedoms.

Though equality of resources advanced by Ronald Dworkin is limited to resources, it, too, indicates the possible significance of interpersonal variation. On his view, to be treated equally is not necessarily the same as being treated as equals by the government. Sometimes the claim about the right to be treated as equals requires equal treatment, but not always so.[71] According to Dworkin, whether a person is entitled to equal resources depends on the source of the present inequality. It makes a difference if a person lacks resources because of his lack of health, strength, and talent (personal resources) or if it depends on his personality (ambitions, tastes, characters, convictions). Thus, what is decisive for the way a government is to distribute resources is whether a person has gambled away almost all he had, say, or whether his lack of resources is the result of mental or physical disabilities.[72]

While Dworkin, Rawls, and Sen disagree about the centrality of human differences, in terms of skills, capabilities, and other similar properties, to the field of justice, all seem to agree about the possible importance of this kind of variation for law and policy-making by actual legislatures. In other words, whether there are grounds for differential treatment for reasons related to cultural difference is an open question. If this exploration fails to inform us about the substantive reasons for differential treatment in the distribution of rights, responsibilities, and burdens in a multicultural society, it nevertheless indicates that an exclusive focus on equal treatment fails to provide a conclusive response. The central question is not whether a given concern would involve differential treatment; instead, we should ask, in the spirit of the basic capability approach, whether all people are able to make effective use of their freedoms in spite of their cultural difference. We may also ask, in the spirit of Dworkin's conception of equality, whether all can be said to be treated as equals in a multicultural environment in ignorance of the nature of the circumstance defined in cultural terms.

One issue considered neither by Dworkin nor Sen is that of stability which is central to Rawls' account. Does a concern with stability rule out any claim that implies differential treatment? Rawls argues that the fact of reasonable pluralism (ie the fact of diverse yet reasonable comprehensive doctrines) imposes practical as well as political limits to our field of moral and social inquiry. According to Rawls, a focus on the political realm

[70] *Ibid* at 120.

[71] R Dworkin, *A Matter of Principle* (Cambridge Mass, Harvard University Press, 1985), at 190.

[72] R Dworkin, *Sovereign Virtue*, above n 1, at 286.

appropriately limits our understanding about the range and kinds of goods it is reasonable to claim and how the various claims are to be defended and balanced against one another.[73] The claims considered must be limited to *political* ideas of the good. It means that ideas of the good must be shared or shareable by all individual citizens regarded as free and equal.[74] This limitation is necessary given the fact of a plurality of 'comprehensive doctrines'.[75] At the same time, this limitation is not supposed to be unfortunate since each person is assumed to want and desire roughly the same bundle of primary goods in order to be free and equal.[76] The primary goods are rights, income and wealth, opportunities, and other all-purpose means.[77]

An equal distribution of goods is supported by a concern with stability. An unequal distribution of, say, income and wealth on the basis of difference in terms of actual expenses is likely to destabilise institutional settlements. Such distributions are likely to be met with ferocious objections by those who lose out, cause instability and, in the worst case, can lead to civil strife.[78] Imagine, for example, that government *A* decides to distribute resources to different religious communities residing in the territory on the basis of their differing expenses. The budget of community *X* vastly exceeds the budget of communities *Y* and *Z* due to its significant pilgrimage expenses. Not only is it necessary to consider that the members of community *Y* and *Z* will pay attention to what *X* receives compared to them, but also the fact that community *X* receives more than their members will inevitably be perceived as a kind of promotion, if not outright discrimination. The way *Y* and *Z* are likely to respond to the perceived injustice depends on various factors. They may simply raise their budget request for the following year. However, they may also react more strongly if they have the power to do so, and if the inequality is significant.

[73] J Rawls, *Political Liberalism*, above n 37, at 179.

[74] *Ibid* at 176.

[75] *Ibid*, at 175. Rawls explains that: 'A doctrine is fully comprehensive when it covers all recognized values and virtues within one rather precisely articulated scheme of thought; whereas a doctrine is only partially comprehensive when it comprises certain (but not all) nonpolitical values and virtues and is rather loosely articulated.'

[76] *Ibid*, at 180.

[77] J Rawls, *Theory of Justice*, above n 3, at 54; and, J Rawls, *Political Liberalism*, above n 37, at 180. In *Political Liberalism*, the list is not considered as closed but can be extended. Rawls holds that 'provided due precautions are taken, we can, if need be, expand the list to include other goods, for example, leisure time, and even certain mental states such as freedom from physical pain' (J Rawls, *Political Liberalism*, at 181–182). It must be noted that the list of primary goods remains essentially the same in *Theory of Justice* and in *Political Liberalism*. One main difference between these two accounts is the assumption about who can reasonably be said to want these kinds of goods. *Theory* affirms that these are goods desired by every rational man. In *Political Liberalism*, however, these are thought of as goods desired by citizens regarded as free and equal in a liberal society. However, whether this limitation amounts to any differentiation between citizens from birth and citizens at the age of reason is unclear considering the assumption that society is closed.

[78] J Rawls, *Political Liberalism*, above n 37, at 330.

This seems to be Rawls' understanding of the relationship between unequal distributions and instability. In practice, however, the issue is often more subtle. For example, imagine that *X* is an immigrant religion. Its budget exceeds those of *Y* and *Z* since it wishes to build a house of worship that is currently lacking. *X*, therefore, receives more than *Y* and *Z* whose members already have access to houses of worship that were built centuries ago. The purpose of the unequal distribution is to ensure equal access to religion and not simply meet the differing expenses. In the absence of religious quarrels, such unequal distribution may be regarded as fair from the standpoint of *Y* and *Z*.

The link between unequal treatment and instability is certainly not rendered less significant for the agents of the public forum purporting to do justice in a multicultural environment. The differential treatment of various cultures in a distributive scheme is likely to be perceived in a similar way. In addition, since cultures tend to have ties to religious, ethical, or philosophical doctrines whose norms, ideas, values, or principles aspire to have universal applicability, it is expected that cultures seek to promote teachings of their doctrines elsewhere. The awareness of these aspects of cultures is likely to induce the members of less powerful cultures to fear domination, oppression, and control by those with more resources at their disposal. However, the claim that all subjects need to be treated equally for merely prudential reasons fails to be convincing. For example, prudential concerns are more relevant in the distribution of goods that are wanted by all (eg money) than in relation to goods not necessarily wanted by all (eg exemptions from dress regulations in the workplace). What seems more critical to stability when distributing goods that are not necessarily wanted by all is the acceptability of the *reasons* for differential treatment instead of an equal *versus* unequal treatment as such.

Apart from the argument based on stability, a second possible objection against differential treatment is that people are assumed to take responsibility for their aims and aspirations; it is part of what free and equal citizens can reasonably expect of one another.[79] The objection proceeds on the assumption that each individual is endowed with the moral power for a conception of the good. The moral power includes the ability to revise, change, and adjust one's aims in the light of social and legal changes. Taking responsibility for tastes and preferences, whether or not they have arisen from actual choices, is a special case of that responsibility. Similarly, people are assumed to be capable of adjusting their aims and aspirations in the light of what they can reasonably demand from one another in terms of goods (rights, opportunities, income, and wealth).[80]

[79] *Ibid*, at 189–190. John Rawls states that: 'each is expected by others to adapt their conception of the good to their expected fair share of primary goods. The only restriction on plans of life is their being compatible with the public principles of justice, and claims may be advanced only for certain kinds of things (primary goods) and in ways specified by those principles.'

[80] *Ibid*, at 34, 185.

The idea that people can be said to choose their preferences and tastes has sometimes come under attack by sociologists who state that most people do not deliberately or conscientiously select their tastes, preferences, and convictions. Instead, they are acquired or shaped by television, magazines, commercial industries, and other powerful cultural agents documented to have a certain grip on the mind of people. Even so, while tastes and preferences may often be acquired unintentionally, this reality does not challenge the fundamental claim about a human capacity for a conception of the good.[81] As this study suggests, however, the claim about the need to shift the focus onto the cultural dimension of the individual may not raise the issue about the nature of preferences and tastes, but instead alert us to the vast discrepancies in terms of actual distributions of suitable cultural equipment.

Effects on the Distributive Process

Apart from seriously affecting the human capacity for making use of rights and freedoms, the cultural disadvantage defined in terms of deficient cultural equipment influences the ability to secure a fair share of income or resources in the distributive process. This contention is supported by empirical evidence about disproportionately low wages among newcomers compared to native-born workers in Britain. The inequality in question is explained by newcomers' lack of sufficient language skills.[82] As a result, in the absence of any consideration of cultural difference, the distributive process is likely to be unfair. However, social justice theories may be able to accommodate such discrepancies once they have been brought to their attention. Although, for example, neither Rawls nor Dworkin pays direct attention to the impact of cultural difference on the distributive process, their accounts seem to leave ample space to take this impact into account. While the circumstance of lacking suitable cultural equipment obviously does not count as an excuse for not seeking to secure one's own material provision, the cultural disadvantage should not be underestimated.

Dworkin formulates an account of distributional equality apt to consider the significance of cultural variety. In particular, his account considers the particular history of every individual in determining what he or she should have in terms of material resources.[83] As he contends, some conditions are

[81] *Ibid*, at 185. Incapacitating preferences and tastes that make someone unable to co-operate normally are treated as a special case. It is considered as a medical or psychiatric situation that needs to be treated separately.

[82] This claim finds empirical support in research in economics. See eg C Dustmann and F Fabbri, 'Language Proficiency and Labour Market Performance of Immigrants in the UK', Centre for Economic Policy Research. Discussion Paper Series, DP 2487 (June 2000).

[83] See generally R Dworkin, *Sovereign Virtue*, above n 1, at 65–119. According to Dworkin's account, all resources are regarded as available for distribution (including those privately owned). The account is limited by what resources and raw materials are available and how much there is of each (at 65). The initial division is guided by the envy test: 'the true measure of the social resources devoted to the life of one person is fixed by asking how important, in fact, that resource is for others. It insists that the cost, measured in that way, figures in each

present right from birth while others develop later and happen to us rather suddenly and unexpectedly (say, a chronic disease or a natural disaster). Deficient cultural equipment is a condition which is never present from birth, but occurs later in life. Still, it tends to be the result of necessity rather than sheer lack of curiosity. Dworkin limits his account to the lack of skills originating in lack of talent. However, if what is decisive is that lack of skills depends on circumstance (of which lack of talent is but one example) and not choice, lack of suitable cultural equipment clearly also fits the bill.

The circumstance of newcomers is determined by looking to the motives for leaving a familiar context in the first place. If the individual had no choice but to leave despite his lack of a tool-kit suitable for his destination, he cannot reasonably be held responsible for his lack of such a tool-kit. As indicated in the previous paragraph, the critical question from the standpoint of equality of resources is whether the individual's settlement is *voluntary* or not. However, there are evidently practical difficulties when seeking to apply the choice–circumstance distinction to newcomers seeking entry and residence.[84] Firstly, there may be no clear or obvious line to draw between choice and circumstance. In debates about the meaning of the term 'refugee', the 'economic refugee' is often regarded as a critical case. Furthermore, even if there are officially established criteria for refugee status, there are enormous complications involved in the gathering of evidence to verify a particular statement. Indeed, it is not unusual that the decisions about entry are made on a case-by-case basis.[85] Finally, it is also difficult to determine whether a lack of suitable cultural skills is still a circumstance after years of residence.

Dworkin holds that an individual who lacks skills cannot expect to receive the same amount of benefits as an individual with a serious disability. Still, he or she can reasonably expect some benefit. The equality of resources approach states that inequality in the distribution of resources explained by lack of skills constitutes unfairness, and must be rectified by periodical re-distributions.[86] Although handicaps and lack of skills have similar effects on the distribution of resources, unlike handicaps, an individual's level of skills is (at least roughly) known before he insures. In other words, a lack of skills is not a matter of future contingency, but of personal history.[87]

person's sense of what is rightly his, and in each person's judgment of what life he should lead, given that command of justice' (at 70).

[84] *Ibid*, at 324. Dworkin admits that there are practical difficulties involved in the choice–circumstance distinction such as in the case of a failure to find employment at a decent wage.

[85] See eg GS Goodwin-Gill, *The Refugee in International Law*, above n 24, at 350 ff. The determination of refugee status demonstrates the difficulties with case-by-case determination of whether the fear is well-founded, whether what is feared is persecution, and whether the persecution feared is attributable to any of the reasons specified in the 1951 Refugee Convention.

[86] R Dworkin, *Sovereign Virtue*, above n 1, at 90–92. Dworkin explains that unfair differences are those traceable to genetic luck, to talents that make some people prosperous but are denied to others.

[87] *Ibid*, at 93.

Even so, Dworkin continues his argument by adding that people would insure also against a lack of skills even if it would be at a much lower premium than, say, a handicap insurance would be.[88] This line of reasoning indicates that the circumstance of lacking suitable equipment for the labour market may be a reason for distributing benefits as well even if incomplete equipment is voluntary.

The primary goods approach developed by Rawls does not pay direct attention to any differences among individuals whatsoever. Its basic claim is that every individual party to a scheme of social co-operation must secure a fair share of income and wealth in the distributive process. Such a share is regarded as necessary in order to make adequate use of basic liberties assigned to everyone alike.[89] Poverty and lack of means are unacceptable conditions about which something must be done. According to the primary goods approach, if the distributive process is controlled by the difference principle, fairness in the distributive process is secured. The difference principle stipulates that the worst-off in society must not become worse off as a result of an unequal distribution of income and wealth. Thus, primary goods are to be distributed equally unless an unequal distribution makes the least advantaged better off. The distribution of income and wealth or authority need not be equal, but it must be to everyone's benefit.[90] If newcomers belong to the worst-off group, their fate defined in economic terms seems accounted for by the primary goods approach.

However, in *A Theory of Justice*, Rawls directly considers the importance of an appropriate scheme of background institutions to secure fairness in the distributive process. One such institution is education. Rawls acknowledges that the distributive process cannot be fair unless this background institution is in place. Thus, he stresses the importance of allocating resources for education in order to enhance the long-term prospects of those who suffer social misfortune.[91] The value of education should not be understood merely in terms of economic efficiency and social welfare, but

[88] *Ibid*, at 108. Dworkin develops a theory of redistribution for differential talents while also mentioning the alternative possibility to devote special resources to the training of those whose talents, as things fall out, place them lower on the income scale. He explains that this proposition is part of the larger question of an egalitarian theory of education, but does not develop this idea any further.

[89] According to 'Justice as Fairness', what ultimately matters is that no one is below the line. It focuses on the worst-off in society and thereby remains insensitive towards variations in distribution among individuals above the worst-off economic class. This limited approach to secure the minimum conditions has been criticised, for example, by Dworkin, *ibid*, at 113.

[90] J Rawls, *Theory of Justice*, above n 3 at 53.

[91] *Ibid*, at 83. Rawls singles out three main kinds of contingencies of the least advantaged. The group includes persons whose family and class origins are more disadvantaged than others, whose natural endowments (as realised) permit them to fare less well, and whose fortune and luck in the course of life turn out to be less happy, all within the normal range and with the relevant measures based on social primary goods.

> equally if not more important is the role of education in enabling a person to enjoy the culture of his society and to take part in its affairs, and in this way to provide for each individual a secure sense of his own worth.[92]

Therefore, a concern with equal opportunities includes taking due account of access to 'cultural knowledge and skills'[93] and to 'education and culture'.[94]

The background institution of education is often lacking in a multicultural society. In this sense, the approach supports the contention about the importance of paying attention to cultural difference in a serious effort to ensure fairness in the distributive process. It is of fundamental importance to provide educational opportunities in order to establish the conditions necessary for distributions to be fair.[95] Such an educational policy is expected to reduce the disadvantage faced by newcomers compared with native-born citizens from birth in securing a fair share of income and wealth. Some might find this proposal objectionable on the basis that this sort of educational policy fails to acknowledge the importance of a *multicultural* education purporting to cover diverse cultural knowledge and skills. However, multicultural education is an aspiration. The kind of education I have in mind is more basic and seeks to secure the bare essentials of the cultural equipment necessary to ensure a minimum provision of respect for individuals regardless of location.

Hence, even an approach to social justice that is confined to the fair distribution of resources (that is, income and wealth) may be compelled to consider—directly or indirectly—the serious impact that difference in terms of suitable cultural equipment is likely to have on that distribution. As suggested in this chapter, however, the difference in terms of equipment is more significant than that and raises independent and unprecedented issues in the field of justice apart from and beyond its impact on the distributive process.

CONCLUSION

The aim of this chapter has been to explain one basic sense in which culture is of critical importance in securing effective protection of human rights in a multicultural environment. To this end, the chapter has advanced the claim about the fundamental importance of possessing cultural equipment suitable for one's place of residence, work, and living. The term cultural

[92] *Ibid,* at 87.

[93] *Ibid,* at 63, 92.

[94] *Ibid,* at 243; and J Rawls, *Political Liberalism,* above n 37, at 181. According to Rawls, this opportunity is not a separate primary good. But see T Pogge, *Realizing Rawls* (Ithaca, Cornell University Press, 1989), at 167.

[95] Of course, this is not the only measure involved in settlement policies. See generally D Joly, *Haven or Hell: Asylum Policies and Refugees in Europe* (New York, St Martin's Press, 1996), at *xii.* Joly asserts that settlement policies (are supposed to) cover housing, health, reception centres, education, and employment.

equipment refers to skills, know-how, styles as well as familiarity with habits and customs. It consists of aspects of culture which are learned and acquired as a result of socialisation (acquisition) and education (learning).

The obstacles and barriers created by the circumstance characterised in terms of deficient cultural equipment are of particular importance in the field of human rights implementation inasmuch as they inhibit the individual enjoyment of freedom. The circumstance seriously influences the individual's capacity to access laws and public institutions, to play a role in political life, to take advantage of opportunities made available in the marketplace, and to secure a fair share of income and wealth.

From a social justice perspective, the circumstance warrants special attention and concern; inasmuch as deficient equipment tends to be unwarranted and often created by factors other than choice, and, as indicated by the basic capability approach, must be a central concern by virtue of the serious impact it has on individual freedom, the circumstance characterised in terms of deficient cultural equipment calls for public collective action. Still, we might ask how to address and respond to the fact of diverse cultural equipment from the standpoint of human rights. A human rights approach is not confined to a focus on public action in the field of implementation. Additionally, and as noted in the second chapter, a human rights approach should refrain from idealistic and simplistic solutions that hide the stark realities that public and civic actors in the field of human rights must consider and accommodate, often on a daily basis.

Surely, while the reality of diverse cultural equipment and its impact on the efficacy of rights is readily understood, it is less certain what should be done about it, how it should be done, and what priorities should be made under conditions of scarcity. To simply reiterate the truism 'ought implies can' seems unsatisfactory. Even so, it is still of critical importance to spell out what states can do. States have a range of options at their disposal. Some states are capable of offering language education to newcomers and do so. These policies are urged by virtue of a commitment to secure respect for human rights in a multicultural society. But what about closing territorial borders or being selective in terms of who may come? Are these the kinds of policies that also would be supported by the human rights approach to culture advanced in this study?

Obviously, problems of cultural equipment are less important than rescuing lives and alleviating poverty. Besides, alleviating burdens imposed on the individual as a result of deficient equipment is not confined to public collective action; it also raises questions of civic responsibility. The acquisition of suitable cultural equipment by newcomers and others similarly situated in cultural terms enables people to communicate with one another and resolve matters of common concern. Acquiring such equipment is an expression of civic responsibility. However, a human rights approach also entails a pleading for compassion and understanding for problems or difficulties that in principle can be understood and felt by anybody. From this standpoint, the recognition of the problems created by deficient cultural equipment is supposed to caution the more fortunate who often blame newcomers for their inability to assume civic responsibility. As pointed out in the beginning of this chapter, acquiring suitable cultural equipment is difficult and takes time. While it is in principle an expression of civic responsibility to try to do so and a social justice concern that states facilitate this process, the difficulties involved must be kept in mind in the formulation of the obligations of states in this regard.

6

Adiaphora and Adequacy

WHAT ARE CULTURAL norms? How are they acquired? Why do they matter? Why does the observance of such norms matter from the standpoint of human rights

The previous chapter advanced a claim about the need to consider suitable cultural equipment as a condition for the effective exercise of rights and freedoms. The purpose of considering cultural equipment as one aspect of culture of critical importance in a human rights framework depends on its instrumental value for enjoying human rights in a multicultural environment. However, the argument from cultural equipment alone is not sufficient for understanding the relationship between culture and rights; in addition, it is pivotal to consider the role of cultural norms and rules in human action and their possible worth for people. This chapter, then, introduces the notion of *adiaphora* to capture the nature of human affairs that are usually governed by cultural norms and their supposed moral irrelevance, above all, in classical liberal philosophy. These affairs include activities such as ways of dress, diet, prayer, child-rearing, marriage, and divorce. Notwithstanding the oft-made assumption about the moral indifference of these activities, however, the particular cultural norms governing these kinds of activities tend to matter to people. In fact, it is not unusual that human consciences are engaged by precisely these issues.

Much attention has been given to controversies surrounding cultural norms in conflict with human rights. No doubt, these controversies are central to the multicultural debate. However, the present study suggests that there is value in analysing the nature of cultural rules and norms and their relationship to human rights in more general terms. An exclusive focus on a particular cultural norm and its adverse impact on the rights of a certain group, say, women or children, makes us oblivious to the potential worth of cultural norms in general. Even if it is concluded that some norms clearly legitimise wrongful conduct and for this reason ought to be abolished, a more thorough understanding of the role of cultural norms in action nevertheless informs us about the difficulties involved in inducing change through law. Above all, an exclusive focus on particular cases of abuse leaves us ignorant of the possibility of conscientious objections based on cultural norms which may generate legitimate demands for cultural accommodation from the standpoint of human rights. At present, the basis for considering these sorts of conscientious objections and their relevance to ensuring respect for human rights in a multicultural society remains largely unexplored. The objective of this chapter is to remedy this neglect.

ADIAPHORA

A persistent lack of attention to the sources of human preoccupation with dress codes, marriage ceremonies, dietary restrictions, production and reproduction, sexual relations, etc might depend on a faulty, or doubtful, yet persistent assumption as to how we best understand and explain behaviours in these realms of action. Among sociologists, there is a tendency to assume that behaviour—and difference in terms of behaviour—in these areas of life is best explained against the background of a human capacity for sociability.

In contemporary social thought, activities, such as manners of dress, diet, church-going, child-rearing, marriage, and family life, are often assumed to be matters of convention. Thus, for example, Jon Elster notes that some norms are a bit like conventions. According to him, norms of dress, rules of etiquette, and dietary rules fall into this category.[1] This understanding of how people think of their particular ways of going about their business is closely linked with claims about the possibility of establishing or maintaining common regulations, schemes of social co-operation, and shared public institutions and services (such as healthcare, education, and childcare) in spite of cultural differences in terms of how people solve issues that inevitably crop up in the course of life. If people think of their particular activities as conventional rather than as the expression of, say, God's will, they are obviously supposed to care less for them in the event that legislative initiatives require adjustment and revision of current behaviour.[2] Still, we should ask whether this is an accurate description of how people, in fact, perceive their activities in these realms.

No doubt, the institutional developments facilitated by the idea of the possibility of a common scheme of social co-operation in a plural society are great achievements. Perhaps the downplaying of individual perceptions of strict duties in relevant fields of legislative action was even warranted so as to facilitate such developments. At the same time, however, an exclusive focus on these accomplishments prevents the acknowledgement of the possibility of culture-based refusals to conform with generally applicable laws regulating matters of supposed moral indifference which arise relatively frequently today. These refusals may nevertheless raise issues of high principle. They require us to pay attention to the way in which these shared institutional arrangements

[1] J Elster, *Nuts and Bolts for the Social Sciences* (New York, Cambridge University Press, 1989), at 113.

[2] See eg J Locke, 'An Essay on Toleration' in M Goldie (ed), *Political Essays. Cambridge Texts in the History of Political Thought* (Cambridge, Cambridge University Press, 1997).

may, at times, create problems of conscience, and examine whether these problems undermine the supposition that the fact of cultural differences in these realms is morally irrelevant to the aim of securing respect.

The claim that manners, habits, and modes are essentially matters of convention or convenience is, at least in part, a *normative* claim: it tells individuals how they ought to think of their conduct in social life; still, there is no guarantee that this is, in fact, what they do. On the contrary, a more reasonable starting point for thinking about the conditions for the establishment and maintenance of common institutional frameworks and regulations of activities that are assumed to be morally indifferent is to assume that issues like dress, diet, prayer, child-rearing, family relations, healthcare, etc represent fields of action in which people's consciences are often and intensively engaged. This observation finds support in the lectures on ethics held by Immanuel Kant. Though Kant affirmed that conscience is an instinct to direct oneself to the moral law, he also recognised that the subjective affirmation of, and compliance with, the moral law may not be the only or perhaps not even the most fundamental concern for conscience.[3] Cases of conscience, Kant contends, commonly have to do, not with duties that we seek to determine, but with *adiaphora* which is made analogous to duties. Examples of this kind of doing are church-going, dress, diet, animal slaughtering, etc. In these fields, we *fabricate* morality. Unfortunately, instead of developing this claim further in his lectures, Kant only noted the bad consequences of having too many duties of this type since it may lead conscience astray. As he notes, such duties turn conscience into what can only function as introductory means of directing oneself to the moral law.[4]

Still, we may ask why we should expect problems of conscience concerning *adiaphora* to occur. Why are the difficulties associated with non-compliance with laws that regulate matters of *adiaphora* more likely to arise in a multicultural context than in a more homogeneous one?

The subsequent sections in this chapter examine and compare three different models used to explain human behaviour in social life and trace the idea of the presumed lack of ultimate relevance as to how things are done in social life from the standpoint of the individual to models emphasising the human capacity for sociability. These models explain the persistence of different kinds of behaviours concerning *adiaphora* in a multicultural environment as the result of having been socialised into differing social contexts. The sociability thesis, however, seems to predict that, once socialised into a certain manner of doing things, faced with multiple and conflicting norms, the individual will helplessly continue to observe the norms first acquired and internalised.

[3] I Kant, *Lectures on Ethics*, P Heath and JB Schneewind (eds), P Heath (trans) (Cambridge, Cambridge University Press, 1997), at 130 ff.
[4] *Ibid*, at 362–363.

In contrast alongside the sociability thesis, the present study considers the possible presence of constraining or coercive factors, such as social pressure or threat of sanction. The shift of focus onto social pressure indicates that, although a set of norms may eventually come to have a grip on the mind, it is by no means a painless process, ie a process that does not involve harm, suffering, or even abuse. A preoccupation with behaviour as such does not necessarily tell us anything about the oppressive dimensions of socialisation processes nor about inner feelings. In addition, the present study directs attention to the power of moral and religious instruction as yet another explanation for cultural norm observance.

Human Capacity for Sociability

Philosophers stressing human malleability usually do so out of mistrust of claims about the existence of independent moral norms and the subjective affirmation of such norms (and perhaps also out of disappointment that so many real events seem to attest to the absence of such norms). Evidently moved by the monstrosity of the war crimes in former Yugoslavia, Richard Rorty remarks that

> the only lesson of either history or anthropology is our extraordinary malleability. We are coming to think of ourselves as the flexible, protean, self-shaping, animal rather than as the rational animal or the cruel animal.[5]

Rorty seems to suggest that people adjust themselves, not because it is rational to do so, for example to avoid legal or other forms of sanction or to take advantage of opportunities, or out of sheer social pressure, but rather because human behaviour, including manners, habits, or gestures, would be influenced by whatever the prevalent norms in the immediate environment are, no matter how crazy or wicked they might actually be. Rorty propounds the view that we should stop thinking of people as rational and moral agents, but rather as fully conditioned by their social environment.

In an important sense, the multicultural phenomenon seems to indicate that the sociability thesis is mistaken inasmuch as people do not, in fact, necessarily assimilate their behaviour to established social and legal expectations prevailing in their place of residence. This is indicated by the behaviour of many first-generation immigrants. At the same time, however, the fact of multiculturalism does not seem to disprove the rationale behind the sociability thesis (or the assumption that social norm observance is rational).[6] In an important sense, a multicultural environment provides a range of *loci* for socialisation. Needless to say, it matters whether an individual arrives

[5] R Rorty, 'Human Rights, Rationality, and Sentimentality' in S Shute and S Hurley (eds), *On Human Rights: The Oxford Amnesty Lectures 1993* (New York, Harper Collins Publishers, 1993), at 115.

[6] S Lukes, 'Rationality of Social Norms' (1991) 32 *Archive Europée ne Sociologique* 142.

alone in a place whose inhabitants follow a different set of cultural norms compared with his native set, or if he arrives with a group of like-minded fellows. If an individual arrives alone, he is likely to do his best to assimilate his behaviour to the norms prevailing in his new environment so as to be able to communicate what he is (or aspires to be) to others through his manners, gestures, and habits. The lone individual would adjust to meet the minimum threshold of what is the rational thing to do (perhaps in an attempt to ensure his own survival). If his native community rapidly grows in size, however, he and his like-minded fellows may simply continue to conduct their affairs according to the norms with which they are already familiar in a deep sense and not let their way of going about their social business depend on how outsiders might judge them. On this account, cases of cultural resistance represent a rational response to the need to select between conflicting sets of cultural norms, each of which are already observed by others. The most rational thing to do seems to be to opt for the native set.

The sociability thesis offers a somewhat simplified account of what factors are at play and influence human behaviour on matters of moral indifference. The idea that behaviour can sometimes be explained as the outcome of the works of socialisation and malleability does not mean that all behaviour can reasonably be explained in this way. In particular, the thesis seems to be oblivious to a range of factors that are well known for their power to shape, inform, or even determine human action. For a start, an individual can be committed to the observation of a cultural norm in a more profound sense than the sociability thesis conveys. Whether people adjust their manners, habits, and gestures in confrontation with changing social and legal expectations depends, to some extent, on whether their current behaviour is moral or social in spirit, ie whether it is supported by moral or social norms. This distinction can be difficult to draw since a set of moral norms is (also) a subset of social norms if actually followed. As Elster states, 'everyday Kantianism' is a social norm (or perhaps a cluster of social norms) rather than a moral norm.[7]

Whether observance of a given norm is moral or social in spirit is not possible to know from the standpoint of the observer. It becomes more evident in the event that social circumstances change, for example, if a group of people moves to a different place where their habits, manners, and gestures are not appreciated by the local population. One case that illustrates the distinction in focus refers to the various motives for following the rule: 'do not eat meat.' Abstaining from meat consumption may depend on various reasons not all of which necessarily are of a compelling nature. Some people are vegetarians for reasons related to personal health while others are de facto vegetarians simply because they cannot afford to buy meat. Others are

[7] J Elster, *The Cement of Society: A Study of Social Order* (New York, Cambridge University Press, 1989), at 101.

vegetarians out of respect for the norm 'do not kill animals or in any way contribute to the killing of animals' (the *true* vegetarians, if you like). The actual motives for behaving in a certain way are crucial for understanding the possibility of different reactions to changing social and legal expectations. Unlike the purely sociable, the morally conscientious do not (primarily) care for what others happen to think about their commitment, ie if others disagree with them about the correctness of their moral judgement on the wrongs done in killing animals. In other words, the latter do not rely upon the supposition that the thing done by the majority is the thing to do. The sociable man, in contrast, is expected to adjust his conduct to what others do in his neighbourhood regardless of whether their activities are morally dubious if not outright wrong. That is to say, he will in all likelihood follow the meat taboo while mingling with the vegetarians. However, since vegetarianism is not the norm everywhere, the sociable person will change his habits to fit whatever is the local fashion with respect to meat consumption in the place where he resides. He will not be wary about respecting the norm taught by the vegetarian community as though it were a compelling one everywhere.

The morally conscientious person, in contrast, tries to act from independent moral norms and be less socially sensitive. However, if the social pressure is great, the morally conscientious person may also feel bound to succumb and assimilate his behaviour with the local standards prevalent in his surroundings. Unlike the sociable person, however, the latter will suffer guilt and anxiety as a result. Indeed, a violation of a food taboo may produce acute anxiety.[8] Due to the significance of social pressure in shaping human action, an attempt to act in accordance with independent moral norms, regardless of whether it means going against the crowd, is often thought of as heroic and as capturing the romantic side of individualism.[9] It is by no means a coincidence that the case of Socrates is often seen as a paradigm case of what an act of conscientious objection is (supposed to be) like.[10] Similarly, David Thoreau's defence of civil disobedience is often mentioned as expressing a similar kind of heroism.[11] The recognition of this fact directs attention to a second factor at play in explaining particular manners, gestures, and habits on matters of ultimate indifference: social pressure.

[8] ME Spiro, 'Some Reflections on Cultural Determinism and Relativism with Special Reference to Emotion and Reason' in RA Shweder and RA LeVine (eds), *Culture Theory: Essays on Mind, Self and Emotion* (New York, Cambridge University Press, 1984), at 341.

[9] EP Thompson, *The Poverty of Theory and Other Essays* (New York, Monthly Review Press, 1979).

[10] See eg H Arendt, 'Civil Disobedience' in H Arendt, *Crises of the Republic* (New York, Harcourt Brace Jovanovich, 1972).

[11] H Thoreau, 'Resistance to Civil Government (Civil Disobedience)' in N Rosenblum (ed), *Henry Thoreau: Political Writings* (Cambridge, Cambridge University Press, 1996), at 2.

Social Pressure

The significance of social pressure has not gone unnoticed by moral philosophers. As John Stuart Mill observed, social pressure can be a form of tyranny:

> Like other tyrannies, the tyranny of the majority was at first, and is still vulgarly, held in dread, chiefly as operating through the acts of the public authorities. But reflecting persons perceived that when society is itself a tyrant—society collectively, over the separate individuals who compose it—its means of tyrannising are not restricted to the acts which it may do by the hands of its political functionaries. Society can and does execute its own mandates: and if it issues the wrong mandates instead of right, or any mandates at all in things with which it ought not to meddle, it practices social tyranny, more formidable than many kinds of political oppression, since, though not usually upheld by such extreme penalties, it leaves fewer means to escape, penetrating much more deeply into the details of life, and enslaving the soul itself.[12]

There can be no certainty as to what makes people assimilate their behaviour to prevalent norms in their environment to the extent that they do. Suffice it to note in this context that a human tendency to succumb to social pressure is not the same thing as lacking personal integrity and conscience—aspects of the individual vastly neglected by the sociability thesis. Not only does the sociability thesis merely make it seem as though people do not care for their own conduct in social life beyond the threshold of rationality; it also fails to provide a basis for the argument about limits as to what it is reasonable to expect in terms of human adjustment to socially derived expectations. In particular, it fails to offer the backdrop against which a consideration of the sufferings and harms caused by social pressure makes sense.

Still, many people are subject to multiple sources of pressure and this circumstance is especially striking in a multicultural context. One case in point is that of immigrant children who are usually exposed to conflicting social pressure and sanctions imposed by their home cultures and school culture. Their circumstance is by no means insignificant. For example, it is not unusual that immigrant children are taught one set of norms at home governing, say, relations with the opposite sex (and supposed to apply to the sum-total of their conduct), while taught a different and often conflicting set of norms in school governing the same matters. While there is, in principle, a limited possibility to adjust to different sets of norms observed in different contexts, this type of situation often leads to great tension between different sets of norms. Furthermore, whatever set of norms the individual eventually may select as the right one, it involves rejecting one set of norms

[12] JS Mill, *On Liberty* (Cambridge, Cambridge University Press, 1989), at 8–9.

taught by, say, parents, peers, teachers, or priests. The recognition of social pressure—especially multiple social pressures—explains the harms and sufferings commonly experienced in socialisation processes. A recent interview with a Swedish lawyer reveals the enormous pressure imposed on female children of immigrants from Islamic cultures living in Sweden. The vast difference that exists in terms of dress and life-style between Swedish and Islamic cultures complicates the situation enormously for these girls who are often exposed to threats of punishment in case they should violate any set of norms, not least their home culture. Indeed, when the girls look for assistance, a lack of cultural literacy on the part of social agencies about the girls' home cultures may de facto worsen their situation.[13]

My criticism of the sociability thesis is not intended as a complete rejection of its power to explain why people assimilate or imitate the behaviour of others in their immediate environment to the extent that they do. What is doubtful is the simplistic presupposition that people do not care for conduct in the social realm beyond following the thing done by the majority. It presents us with an idea of man as ultimately plastic. The human capacity for sociability enables us to cope with social pressure to behave in accordance with established social expectations in direct competition with personal hopes and aspirations. However, what people cope with in ordinary life is obviously not a reliable indicator of the extent to which it is necessary to consider cultural norm observance on matters of *adiaphora* in the formulation of an account as to what is required to ensure a minimum provision of respect for freedom in a multicultural society.

For many of us, the particular mode of conduct on matters of ultimate indifference is seldom motivated by sheer voluntarism. For example, in the event that I should develop my thoughts about the right or perfect way of raising my children or moving about in everyday life, and supposing I should discover 'right' answers to a range of other matters of ultimate indifference, it remains doubtful whether I would, in fact, be able to do things 'my way', so to speak. I may criticise, secretly or openly, the prevailing practices in my environment, but then nevertheless behave in accordance with prevailing norms, perhaps out of sheer social pressure or to avoid sanctions imposed as a matter of law or by 'informal' authorities, such as parents, priests, or school teachers. Indeed, human affairs that are ultimately indifferent often exhibit a certain similarity in behaviour across individuals, in part, as a result of the various forms of coercive influence operating in these fields. Legal obligations and prohibitions are but one form of constraint. Another form is coercive influences depending on public opinion and social pressure.[14] While social pressure does not explain the link between cultural

[13] C Hagner, 'Flickförtryck i Traditionens Namn' (2001) 5 *Barn. Tidningen om Barns Rättigheter*.

[14] J Rawls, *Theory of Justice* (Cambridge Mass, Belknap Press of Harvard University Press, 1999), at 117.

norms and conscience, it makes it possible to address and take seriously the difficulties faced by individuals whose set of norms is in conflict with norms of others (whether in the home, among peers, in school or at the workplace).

The Details of Life

The mere recognition of social pressure and other tools of coercive influence common on matters of *adiaphora* does not consider the temptation to exert social control over matters that are ultimately indifferent. If these are realms of action that are themselves eventually morally irrelevant what, then, explains the widespread and intensive preoccupation with precisely these issues? For one thing, it may be precisely because dress, diet, sexual relations, health, hygiene, etc are matters of moral indifference that people, whether in their capacity as private persons or public officials or parliamentarians, take an immense interest in their own and one another's habits, manners, and gestures in these realms. As Robert Wuthnow suggests, uncertainties and ambiguities in the moral order are likely sources of rituals, ideologies, or other cultural productions.[15] In effect, empirical evidence supports the contention that *adiaphora* represents a realm of human affairs that is endowed with critical importance for private persons as well as religious and other public institutions. One simple reason for this seems to be that these affairs represent a significant part of what life is about for many people. Life, in the sense of ordinary life, is obviously not without meaning for people, quite regardless of whether they happen to have a secular, Marxist, Catholic, Protestant, or feminist outlook on how the various tasks and assignments which are part of ordinary life are supposed to be carried out.

What may usefully be defined as the 'small things in life' have not been given much attention by moral philosophers (unless, as we shall see, these things become matters of conscience). Alluding to the works of Aristotle, Charles Taylor explains that 'ordinary life' designates those aspects of human life concerned with production and reproduction, that is, the making of things needed for life, and our life as sexual beings, including marriage and the family. When Aristotle spoke of the aims of political association being 'life and the good life', he included these activities in the first of these terms. Taylor concludes that, in essence, this cluster of activities embraces what we need to do to continue and renew life. The maintenance of these activities must be distinguished from the pursuit of the good life. The former are necessary to be able to pursue the good life since they play an *infrastructural* role in relation to it. Aristotle employed this distinction to capture the idea that a mere association of families for economic and defence purposes is not a true 'polis' because of its narrow purpose. The proper life

[15] R Wuthnow, *Meaning and Moral Order: Explorations in Cultural Analysis* (Berkeley, University of California Press, 1987), at 342.

and the activities it connotes, Aristotle meant, are nevertheless made possible by this infrastructure.[16]

In his definition of the good life, Aristotle includes theoretical contemplation and participation as a citizen. These two elements of the good life find resonance also in contemporary philosophical thought as it usually stresses the values of participation and education. What is of special interest for us is the changing attitude towards the role of 'life'. Taylor explains that, while classical philosophers have tended to narrow their accounts of what the good life consists of (by stressing activities such as contemplation and participation) thereby almost excluding all matters of 'life', from the eighteenth century onwards a new model of civility was developed, one that places great value on sober and disciplined production.[17] Taylor continues by noting that this change marks the beginning of the 'bourgeois ethic' that has played a central role in constituting modern liberal society, with ideals of equality, a sense of universal right, work ethic, and emphasis on sexual love, and the family.[18]

What does it mean that human affairs are morally indifferent from a moral standpoint? If an act is morally indifferent, it means that there is no moral duty to perform it, nor to avoid it, although what we eventually do (or abstain from doing) might affect our general well-being. In this sense, a standard of conduct in this realm is more like a piece of advice or recommendation. For example, while we do not have a duty to preserve our own health, doing so is nevertheless advisable since it will contribute to our sense of well-being and improve our capacity for doing what is right.[19] Best described as pieces of advice, standards of conduct regulating matters that are ultimately morally irrelevant differ from what John Rawls refers to as 'natural duties'. The natural duties regulate conduct that affects others, and include duties to assist others when this can be done at small cost, the duty to show respect and courtesy, as well as duties to support just institutions, not to harm the innocent and not to cause unnecessary suffering.[20]

In spite of the presumed moral indifference of many activities, it is nevertheless possible—indeed, likely—that people perceive or experience their actions, recurrent in everyday life (habits, manners, and gestures), as being fraught with religious, moral, social, or political significance. John Locke, to mention one prominent philosopher, made the recognition of this

[16] C Taylor, 'God Loveth Adverbs' in C Taylor, *Sources of the Self: The Making of the Modern Identity* (Cambridge Mass, Harvard University Press, 1989), at 211. Taylor refers to Aristotle, *Politics* III, 1280b.

[17] *Ibid*, at 212.

[18] *Ibid*, at 215.

[19] FE Peters, *Greek Philosophical Terms: A Historical Lexicon* (New York, New York University Press, 1967).

[20] J Rawls, *Theory of Justice*, above n 14, at 98 ff. For a comment on these duties and their complicated relationship to freedom, see HLA Hart, 'Rawls on Liberty and its Priority' in N Daniels (ed), *Reading Rawls* (Stanford CA: Stanford University Press, 1989), at 238.

fact central to his defence of the right to toleration. While child-rearing, days of rest, marriage (polygamy and monogamy), divorce, slaughtering of animals, etc are activities that are ultimately indifferent from the standpoint of the moral legislator, this is by no means how these realms of human affairs are perceived from a religious standpoint. On the contrary, prayer, dress, and diet are aspects of religious worship which are usually of immense importance since they represent, as Locke puts it, what each person thinks is acceptable to God in worshipping him.[21]

Regulations on matters of *adiaphora* usually specify procedures and rituals, including what we ought to do and what we must abstain from. To follow conscientiously these kinds of regulations is not the same thing as making adequate use of moral powers for thought, reflection, and judgement. Indeed, as Kant despaired, having too many duties of this sort might even counter the development of moral faculties. All the same, these are human affairs where the free exercise of moral power is usually not encouraged. Most of us are caught up in established social frameworks regulating these themes. The particular shape and content of such frameworks at any given time tends to be inspired and informed by a social doctrine developed from, or as a direct criticism of, a stock of ethical or religious ideas. In effect, while moral philosophers tend to regard the mundane life (including freedom, health, life) as morally indifferent and as referring to those aspects of life that ultimately do not matter, the existing range of doctrines preoccupied with precisely these issues seem to reveal the contrary.

John Rawls refers to the various doctrines of moral or religious thought as 'comprehensive doctrines': each of these doctrines covers social ground in the sense of containing both rules for how to live and the ultimate purpose, if any, for which we live. A 'comprehensive' doctrine

> includes conceptions of what is of value in human life, and ideals of personal character, as well as ideals of friendship and of familial and associational relationships, and much else that is to inform our conduct.[22]

Thus, such a doctrine, whether moral, religious, or philosophical in character, is usually not restricted to epistemological or metaphysical issues; but it can (and often does) comprise detailed regulation of ordinary life, and the articulation of a range of values supposed to inform the performance of tasks that may ultimately be indifferent.[23]

However, apart from shaping a given individual's or family's life (ie function as a standard of conduct for individuals), such a doctrine might influence and flavour the common regulations of the entire population of a state (ie function as a standard of conduct upheld and enforced by public

[21] J Locke, 'An Essay on Toleration', above n 2, at 139–40.
[22] J Rawls, *Political Liberalism* (New York, Columbia University Press, 1995), at 13.
[23] *Ibid*, at 13 and 175.

institutions). The frequent use of such doctrines by public institutions is revealed by familiar classifications of types of states: for example, Islamic, Catholic, or Liberal. This kind of classification is misleading if what we are really interested in knowing is whether all people leading their lives in such states, in fact, find the doctrine informing standards of conduct for public institutions acceptable. Suffice it to note in this context that there are few, if any, places where all inhabitants endorse the doctrine (explicitly or implicitly) dominating their public institutions.

As suggested in the previous chapter drawing upon the work of Ann Swidler, a culture cannot be defined essentially or fundamentally in terms of shared ultimate ends since it attributes a faulty flavour of agreement to a given comprehensive doctrine among all the inhabitants of a place. Instead, we gain a better understanding of what it means to share a culture by focusing on the skills, styles, habits, and know-how we need to share to be able to interact, communicate, and resolve issues of common concern for society as a whole. However, this general understanding is not meant to downplay the dynamic aspect of culture, nor the need to distinguish between settled (culture as tradition and common sense) and unsettled periods (culture as ideology). As Swidler points out, whereas *settled* cultures are characterised in terms of low coherence, consistency, and encapsulation, *unsettled* cultures are defined in terms of high coherence and consistency and as direct competitors with other culture-specific views. In periods of stress and panic, the insiders of a culture (and often their political elite) seek to consolidate and define their shared norms and aims (even if not all insiders, in fact, agree about these aims). In the absence of threats (real or imagined), however, a culture is more ambiguous and open to outside influence as well as more tolerant of disagreements over shared ends.[24]

Since culture has a dynamic aspect, perceptions of strict duties concerning *adiaphora* might change and disappear. One illustration is the habit of church-going. In one period, this habit might rest on conscientious grounds and be generally understood as the manifestation of the will of God. However, it is also possible that the reasons for the habit change without rejecting the habit itself. The habit loses its original meaning. It may nevertheless persist as a habit if it takes on a new meaning. For example, it may instead provide an occasion to meet. The complication in a plural culture is that one and the same habit may be supported by some for many different reasons, while others may reject it all together. Thus, while some may think of the habit of church-going as a social event, others may think of it as representing 'the way of worshipping that is acceptable to God', and a third group might regard the habit as hypocrisy. Whatever we might think of

[24] A Swidler, 'Culture in Action: Symbols and Strategies' (1986) *American Sociological Review* 273, at 278 ff. (See especially table at 282).

these changes—we may endorse and encourage them or we may believe they are deeply regrettable—they are likely to occur in settled periods.

In a multicultural environment, it is possible that the actual commitments, values, or aims of the inhabitants are shaped or informed by differing comprehensive doctrines, sometimes in stark contrast with the comprehensive doctrine dominating the culture of public institutions. In the event that an individual's values or commitments seem to pose a threat to the official culture, it might well be the case that what was once merely regarded as common sense by most inhabitants in a given place becomes fraught with significance. These struggles may be unfortunate if they undermine, as contended in this study, the conditions for the adequate development of moral powers by directing attention to differences in manners, gestures, and habits among the inhabitants, ie differences in ways of doing things which are themselves morally irrelevant. At the same time, however, public ignorance may also result in oppression, and lead to a lack of trust, indignation, and even hatred on the part of those individuals whose differing cultural attachments continue to be neglected. This kind of ignorance may eventually unsettle the official culture, especially if the oppressed culture for some reason becomes more powerful.

The Power of Instruction

If cultural differences on matters of *adiaphora* are themselves morally irrelevant, why are they seldom so from the standpoint of individuals? This depends, in part, on the specific contents of comprehensive doctrines as well as the intensity of the story-telling, rituals, beliefs, art forms, and ceremonies surrounding them.[25] The likelihood that conscience surfaces in relation to these matters partly depends on the spirit in which a doctrine is being taught and transmitted to the next generation. A comprehensive doctrine may be taught in different ways. The selection of interpretative scheme for instruction may be independent of the specific content of the comprehensive doctrine as such. A more *orthodox* interpretative scheme approaches the cluster of conduct rules on *adiaphora* associated with a given doctrine as timeless, unchanging, and right (ie as the manifestation of the will of God or the word of the Prophet). A more *liberal* scheme, in contrast, recognises and encourages the capacity for independent thought, belief, and judgment on such rules. Thus, what is in one culture taught as true and non-negotiable standards of conduct may in other cultures be understood merely as pieces of advice or recommendations.

Disagreements about the correct interpretative scheme among the insiders of a culture are not unusual. One problem liberals seek to grapple with today has to do with the fact that, the more 'liberal' one is about the truth of the values and norms linked with a liberal doctrine, the less persuasive

[25] *Ibid* at 273.

they seem to be. One case in point is the disagreement between 'Kantian liberals' and 'political liberals' about the reasonableness or truth of the values of liberty and equality. Their disagreement seems to have its source in differing interpretations, but also in conflicting beliefs about the more efficient strategy to win allegiance from non-liberals.[26] An interpretative disagreement of a different kind refers to the possibility of adjusting the scope and content of comprehensive doctrines in the light of social changes and scientific discoveries. Such disagreements are common in several religions. One example is the ongoing debate in Muslim circles on issues such as whether or not to accept the premises of science, whether democracy and secularity are compatible with Islamic beliefs, and whether male-dominated practices such as polygamy are fair in relation to women.[27]

While recognising the importance of these sorts of disagreements to the field of moral and social inquiry, they do not necessarily undermine the claim that an educational institution at any given time seeks to present and transmit a coherent interpretation of a body of moral or religious thought as well as a cogent idea of whether or not the conduct rules on matters of *adiaphora* are matters of strict duty. Since it is reasonable to expect that there are many educational institutions (official and non-official) in a multicultural society, it is possible, indeed likely, to find that its inhabitants relate to the specific contents of different comprehensive doctrines in different ways. Some are likely to endorse a set of conduct rules associated with a particular doctrine and apply them in a strict and resolute manner. Others might engage in the crafting of responses to new matters of social concern that arise in their society by using the sources of moral or religious knowledge vested in such doctrines, but without thinking of themselves as bound by it. This difference, it is contended here, depends partly on the manner of instruction.

Individual differences, in terms of personal character and personality, also play a role. Quite regardless of particular schemes of interpretation several people take the content of instruction on trust. Thus, for example, Locke notes that 'several men whose business or laziness keeps them from examining, take many opinions on trust, even in things in religion.'[28] A similar observation is made by Rawls. He recognises that some may not examine their beliefs, but instead take them on faith or are satisfied with the response that these are matters of tradition. According to him, people should not be criticised for this (from the standpoint of political liberalism).[29] There are

[26] For evidence of this disagreement see eg J Raz, 'Facing Diversity: The Case of Epistemic Abstinence' in J Raz, *Ethics in the Public Domain: Essays in the Morality of Law and Politics* (New York, Oxford University Press, 1994).

[27] M Moaddel, 'Diversities and Discontinuities in the Islamic Response to Modernity' in M Cousineau (ed), *Religions in a Changing World: Comparative Studies in Sociology* (Westport, Conn, Praeger, 1998), 159.

[28] J Locke, 'An Essay on Toleration', above n 2, at 156.

[29] J Rawls, *Political Liberalism*, above n 22, at 313–314.

more critical accounts of cultural receptivity. The difference in cultural receptivity among people has received remarkable attention in liberal circles. More critical liberal scholars insist that people *ought* to make use of their moral and intellectual powers for independent thought, reflection, and judgment. It is in this spirit that John Stuart Mill advances his claim that people should not simply follow ideas of the good taught by others; instead, each should try to make ideas about the good their own.[30] Deborah Fitzmaurice, a contemporary liberal scholar, builds on his claim and articulates it even more forcefully. In her view, a commitment to autonomy as a good necessarily means that non-autonomy supporting forms of instruction ought to be treated as morally inferior. It is wrong to tolerate such institutions, she holds, since they harm those they have in their grip.[31]

Additionally, even if people have attended a particular form of instruction, they do not necessarily agree with either its form or content. On the contrary, they might regard their culture as oppressive if not directly destructive to the adequate development of their moral faculties, but find themselves de facto coerced, whether as a result of sheer social pressure or risk of legal sanction, to follow the rules taught by the cultural authorities. Alternatively, it is possible that the insiders of a culture come to view their conduct rules, once acquired and learned, as immensely important to them, and feel compelled to act in a certain way. While much attention has rightly been paid to the first category of people, not least in liberal circles, especially when the pressure toward conformity is supported by legal sanction in case of non-compliance, less attention has been given to the circumstance of the latter category of people whose motivational relation to their set of conduct rules may not be considered as having the same value due to its uncritical stance toward tradition. All the same, from the standpoint of human rights, it is fundamental that the difference between these categories of people is not viewed simply as a political struggle between radical and conservative forces. Such a move is unfortunate since it makes particular duties concerning *adiaphora* look like mere political (rather than conscientious) expressions which they are not necessarily.

Quite regardless of what we think of the proper manner of instruction by educational institutions with legitimate demands for space, recognition, and resources in a multicultural society, it hardly resolves the issues that public institutions must grapple with here and now as a result of diverse perceptions of duties on matters of *adiaphora*. Of particular concern in the present study is the circumstance of those who seek to lead a life in accordance with a range of specific rules stipulated by a comprehensive doctrine, some of which are in conflict with the official law. Although we may disagree about what moral or religious education ought to be like, the affirmation of our

[30] JS Mill, *On Liberty* (Cambridge, Cambridge University Press, 1989), ch 3, paras 2–9.
[31] D Fitzmaurice, 'Autonomy as a Good: Liberalism, Autonomy and Toleration' (1993) 1 *The Journal of Philosophy* 1, at 14.

disagreement hardly resolves the question how to understand, much less respond to, conscientious refusals to comply with the official law in conflict with cultural duties. That a person's educational institution has selected a method of instruction that does not seem to encourage independent thought can hardly determine the way in which we respond to his claim for respect in the form of accommodation of his cultural duty into the fabric of the official law.

As discussed earlier in this chapter, the problems of conscience in a multicultural society do not stem from an urge to follow the cosmopolitan moral law in the face of legal obligations. Rather, such problems of conscience amount to objections to conformity with a legal obligation that requires a person to act contrary to cultural rules whose development have been informed by a certain moral or religious doctrine as interpreted over a long stretch of time by like-minded fellows. Is it reasonable to characterise acts of non-compliance with the official law due to the conscientious observance of cultural duties as a 'case of conscience'? A case of conscience is usually defined as an instinct to direct oneself according to the cosmopolitan moral law.[32] Still, although the notion of conscience tends to be associated with moral content, it need not be. In fact, as Jean Hampton explains, conscience may operate in relation to different kinds of norms. What is decisive for an act to be defined as conscientious, Hampton suggests, is the agent's motivational relation to a norm. Accordingly, an act is conscientious when an agent is committed to a norm in such a way that, when its reasons are decisive, he conceives of himself as literally (and motivationally) unable to follow any other course of action. Since conscience can (and does) operate in relation to both moral and non-moral norms, both noble and wicked norms can be embraced in this way.[33]

Against this background, we may define a case of conscience as a condition where a norm has a grip on the mind. According to Jon Elster, that a norm has a grip on the mind means that it is followed even if a violation would be unobserved and even if the agent is not exposed to external sanctions (social pressure or legal sanction).[34] The grip in question consists of, or is supported by, an 'inner sanction'.[35] John Stuart Mill has described this inner sanction as:

> A feeling in our mind, a pain more or less intense, attendant on violation of duty, which in properly cultivated moral natures rises, in the more serious cases, into shrinking from it as an impossibility.[36]

[32] See eg I Kant, *Lectures on Ethics*, above n 3, at 130.
[33] J Hampton, *The Authority of Reason* (Cambridge, Cambridge University Press, 1998), at 87.
[34] J Elster, *Nuts and Bolts for the Social Sciences* (New York, Cambridge University Press, 1989), at 119.
[35] See eg J Elster, *The Cement of Society*, above n 7, at 104–105.
[36] JS Mill, *Utilitarianism* G Sheer (ed) (Indianapolis, Hackett Publishing Company, 1979), at 27.

From this standpoint, conscience operates in relation to different clusters of norms. One cluster is characterised as cosmopolitan moral norms (defined by Kant as the moral law). A second cluster refers to culture-dependent norms on matters of moral indifference. A third cluster, finally, is composed of norms that are wicked or abusive, that is to say, in conflict with the cosmopolitan moral law.

Notwithstanding the possibility of differentiating between different clusters of norms depending on their specific contents, it seems difficult to apply the distinctions when faced with practical questions as to whether a particular norm is morally indifferent or wicked from the standpoint of the moral law. Indeed, it is precisely these questions that are intensively debated in multicultural societies and for which there might not be a definite answer or an answer that everybody is likely to agree with. These questions will be dealt with in more detail in the eighth chapter in the discussion on the limits to excuse. Suffice it to note here that some norms are more likely to gain general acceptance as morally indifferent than others once their abusive impact has been discarded. The subsequent discussion proceeds on the assumption that it is possible to win such acceptance with respect to particular norms of moral indifference.

In the first instance, a decisive factor when determining which instances of cultural resistance against compliance with the official law amount to conscientious objections is whether or not the norm has a 'grip on the mind' of the person who observes it, ie whether his belief is *genuine*. However, it is not relevant whether a person's belief is the product of 'free' input or not. As Jeremy Waldron states, it is doubtful whether 'free' input ought to be accorded decisive relevance when determining what counts as genuine belief, ie for a belief to perform the functions it is expected to perform.[37] Additionally, and as Steven Lukes notes, it is in any case difficult to believe that a norm's grip on the mind could ever be the result of a blind process and not the product of a process of interpretation, selection, adhesion, and rejection.[38]

The affirmation of the power of instruction and its impact on conscience is meant to indicate that most of us do not pick ideas about proper, decent or acceptable social behaviour from 'nowhere', so to speak. More often, we have recourse to collections of moral or religious knowledge that are available to us in some form and dominate our immediate environment. While not determining our views, such collections nevertheless shape and inform particular processes of interpretation, selection, adhesion, and rejection of ideas. Also critics tend to centre their opinions on doctrines that have come to shape and dominate their lives. Still, is it reasonable to affirm that the power of instruction explains which norms particular consciences invoke in

[37] J Waldron, 'Locke, Toleration and the Rationality of Persecution' in J Waldron, *Liberal Rights: Collected Papers (1981–1991)* (New York, Cambridge University Press, 1993), 110.

[38] S Lukes, 'The Rationality of Norms,' above n 6, at 147.

their objections to compliance with the official law? In his lectures on ethics, Kant acknowledged two dimensions of conscience, namely, the *natural* conscience and the *acquired* (or instructed) conscience. He noted the practical difficulties of drawing a sharp line between what is natural (on the one hand) and what is acquired or learned (on the other).[39] Although Kant's philosophical writings proceeded by assuming the existence of a moral law that is universally binding on all rational beings he nevertheless acknowledged and took seriously the power of instruction in shaping and informing people by which rules they ought to lead their lives. As he noted, the instructed conscience might even come into conflict with the natural one.[40] Against this background, it is concluded that the power of instruction—and cultural differences in terms of the manner and content of instruction—is critical for understanding the sources of conscientious objections in multicultural societies.

ADEQUACY

Is the finding of a link between conscience and cultural norms regulating matters of ultimate indifference at all relevant to normative theorising about rights and justice in multicultural societies? I believe it is. More precisely, I believe that it directs attention to reasons for contending that a scheme of rights can be equal in the sense that it distributes the same set of rights to everybody while nevertheless failing to be *adequate* in the eyes of those supposed to benefit from those rights. The contention is that a government may distribute the same rights to everybody, but still fail to secure that the scheme of rights is adequate if people differ widely in their perception of cultural duties on matters of *adiaphora*.

The need to consider the 'adequacy' of a given scheme of rights is based on a deeper concern with the individual's development of personality and, eventually, moral personality, ie her moral powers for a conception of the good and a sense of justice. As John Rawls explains, while it is not a requirement of justice that all basic liberties are secured *equally* well, their 'central range of application' must always be protected. According to him, the institutional protection of this 'central range' is an essential condition for the adequate development of moral personality.[41] Rawls nevertheless believes that an equal distribution of basic liberties will secure the adequate development of moral personality including in a plural context. However, this is a

[39] I Kant, *Lectures on Ethics*, above n 3, at 18.

[40] *Ibid*, at 133. However, according to Kant, having been instructed contrary to the natural law is certainly not an excuse for wrong-doing.

[41] J Rawls, *Political Liberalism*, above n 22, at 297 ff. For a full elaboration of the claim that 'each person has an equal right to a fully adequate scheme of equal basic liberties which is compatible with a similar scheme of liberties for all' see 291. For an articulation of the idea of moral powers see 310–324.

contestable assumption. It has been forcefully objected to by Isaiah Berlin. In his view:

> There ought to exist a certain minimum area of personal freedom which must on no account be violated; for if it is overstepped the individual will find himself in an area too narrow for even that minimum development of his natural faculties which alone makes it possible to pursue, even to conceive, the various ends which men hold good or right or sacred.[42]

As Berlin argues, there is no guarantee that an exclusive focus on equality necessarily secures the minimum area of personal freedom deemed necessary for the adequate development of moral powers. However, because of the practical difficulties involved in determining what the requirement of adequacy involves in more concrete terms, contemporary political philosophers, such as Rawls, hope that an equal scheme will naturally also be adequate and, therefore, that no special attention need to be paid to the latter. As Jeremy Waldron explains:

> A concern for adequacy takes seriously the possibility that, in a crowded society, the equality requirement may squeeze the liberty of each person down to such a modicum that, at the individual level, it is scarcely worth having or fighting for. The algebra of modern liberalism rests on the hope that this will turn out not to be the case, and that the two constraints of equality and adequacy can be satisfied together.[43]

One reason for suspecting that a concern for equal protection does not necessarily ensure adequacy is the occurrence of what seem to be conscientious objections towards the official law regulating matters of *adiaphora* in the field of marriage law, public health law, traffic law, etc. The relative frequency of such objections by those who differ in cultural terms from the culture that dominates public institutions has not gone unnoticed by contemporary political philosophers; however, many believe that these sorts of objections do not raise new questions of justice and rights. This tentative conclusion might nevertheless be mistaken.

My account of the link between conscience and *adiaphora* suggests that a conscientious objection in this realm of life shifts the focus onto the importance of ordinary life issues. Such issues may not necessarily be what we have in mind when assessing the purposes for which we ought to exercise our moral powers. In classical thought, such purposes were confined to contemplation and participation. In addition, a focus on ordinary life issues fails to capture the question about the spirit in which people ought to approach, assess, and respond to them: not only are people expected to exercise their

[42] I Berlin, *Four Essays on Liberty* (Oxford, Oxford University Press, 1969), at 124.
[43] J Waldron, *Law and Disagreement* (Oxford, Clarendon Press, 1999), at 236–237.

moral powers for thought, reflection, and judgement in a *critical* manner; they are also supposed to use their reason to discuss matters of fundamental principle in their status as individual citizens and human beings. The present study does not contest the proclaimed superiority of activities such as contemplation and participation. What it does criticise, however, is the denigration of the role and significance of the many activities that constitute part of ordinary life and, in particular, the presumption that, having reflected upon what one perceives to be one's duties on matters of *adiaphora*, the norms underpinning them will eventually lose their grip on one's mind.

In his criticism of Rawls' understanding of liberty, HLA Hart asks Rawls for his view on the status of non-basic liberties, among them sexual freedom and the liberty to use alcohol or drugs, all of which apparently fall outside any of the roughly described basic liberties. Hart contemplates the suggestion that Rawls would regard these freedoms as basic liberties and, thus, as falling under his broad category of liberty of conscience, which is concerned not merely with religious but also with moral freedom. However, the Rawlsian understanding of the purpose of the liberty of conscience seems to be to ensure a person's freedom to fulfil his moral obligations. In other words, this liberty would only protect, say, sexual freedom if people see their activities in this realm as calls of moral duty. Others again have suggested that non-basic liberties would be protected by another Rawlsian category, namely freedom of the person. Hart rejects this proposition as well since, on Rawls' account, this freedom is connected with property.[44] Evidently, the object of the present analysis is not to find a place for activities that form part of ordinary life within a Rawlsian theory of rights. Still, Hart's criticism serves to indicate that this sphere of human activity tends to be forgotten when thinking about the scope of freedom that is necessary to ensure the adequate development of moral personality.

While the claim that human affairs that are governed by cultural norms directs attention to more general questions about the scope of individual freedom and about the role and significance of non-basic liberties, the present study is confined to cultural duties on matters of *adiaphora* and whether the possibility of performing these duties raises questions of fundamental principle. While not everyone conducts their affairs in these realms in a conscientious manner, some do, and their activities may deserve particular attention from a human rights standpoint. The purpose of freedom of conscience is not only to protect the human ability for moral thought, reflection, and (critical) judgement (freedom of expression and opinion) narrowly defined and in the abstract; it additionally requires a certain degree of sensitivity towards particular cultural duties (in part, protected by religious freedom). As Hersch Lauterpacht held in his comment on his draft to a

[44] HLA Hart, 'Rawls on Liberty and its Priority', in N Daniels (ed), *Reading Rawls* (Stanford Cal, Stanford University Press, 1989).

Universal Declaration of Human Rights in 1945, one fundamental purpose of human rights is to ensure that every individual is able to do what she conceives to be her duty (irrespective of whether that duty is religiously or morally derived).[45]

The authenticity of cultural duties has nevertheless come to be doubted by several contemporary scholars perhaps as a consequence of the conventional supposition that human affairs governed by cultural norms fall within the category of non-basic liberties. The sceptical outlook currently dominating much social thought should be contrasted with the spirit of the argument for toleration advanced by John Locke. Locke assumed that the individual may have religious duties that she must attend to and that such duties are not necessarily the same for all. At the same time, however, Locke believed that the reason why people want a right to toleration, and are capable of exercising that right responsibly, is their common interest in salvation. The foundation of his argument in favour of the right to toleration on matters of *adiaphora*, therefore, presupposes a belief in the existence of divine law, a law that in principle is accessible to all and may be interpreted independently by the same. Thus, unlike contemporary scholars, Locke did not have to consider the complications posed by the secularisation of conscience,[46] the development of a broader range of religious bodies of thought, and how to accommodate their respective differences into a single legal framework,[47] or discoveries such as psychoanalysis.[48] Today, theorists of conscience disagree about whether conscience is the voice of God, the product of social experience and taboo, the use of intellect and reason, or a biological instinct. The proliferation of sources have made the search for a generally acceptable basis for freedom of conscience all the more difficult to establish.

However, even if we were to admit that the cultural duties in focus are not like moral duties inasmuch as they do not refer to duties that everyone can be said to have regardless of location, creed, or ethnicity, the ability of individuals to carry out such duties may nevertheless be seen as a condition that is crucial to the adequate development of their moral powers. The ability to go about one's business on matters of *adiaphora* in the way one has become accustomed, in a profound sense, may be crucial in not having one's personality thwarted. This is the basis of the argument about the importance of being able to access and enjoy one's own culture. Such access and enjoyment are first and foremost individualistic in the sense that a person's particular activities on matters of moral indifference do not necessarily cease to

[45] H Lauterpacht, *An International Bill of the Rights of Man* (New York, Columbia University Press, 1945), at 17.

[46] H Arendt, 'Civil Disobedience', above n 10, at 64–65.

[47] See eg BA Shain, 'Individualism' in R Wuthnow (ed), *The Encyclopedia of Politics and Religion* (Washington DC, Congressional Quarterly, 1998), at 369; and JO Voll, 'Islam' in *ibid*, at 384.

[48] See eg A Bahm, 'Theories of Conscience' (1965) *Ethics* 128.

be meaningful to him in the event that the official laws by which he is expected to live change, such as if he moves to a different place or if his government is overthrown by radical forces or an intervening foreign power. On the contrary, such changes may lead to the reaffirmation of and preoccupation with matters of ordinary life because of the threat such changes pose to the very infrastructure on which his personality, a sense of who he is, depends. Lauterpacht recognised the existence of a deep link between culture and personality and defended a human right to access one's own culture on the basis of that link. In his view, the cultural dimension of human life must be taken seriously from the standpoint of human rights because of its relevance to the individual development of personality.[49] Although Lauterpacht focused on access to culture as a condition for the *development* of personality and did not discuss the importance of culture for the sake of *maintaining* personality throughout life, there is nothing in his argument that seems to contradict the argument about the need to consider that aspect of personality as well.

What does it mean to have access to culture? First of all, it may entail the ability to utilise the cultural sources of ethical, religious, or philosophical knowledge for the purpose of resolving matters of *adiaphora*, cultural sources that one is already familiar with in a profound sense. It may extend to a general freedom to carry out one's business in the way one is accustomed to, including the realms of life which Hart means are protected by non-basic liberties. Additionally, and more importantly in a human rights context, however, an individual's ability to access his culture may also be a component of freedom of conscience and regarded as a basic liberty. This is the case if what is at stake is an individual's ability to perform cultural duties, that is, strict duties on matters of *adiaphora* unless such conduct contradicts moral duties, such as the duty not to harm anybody else and the duty to contribute to the welfare of others. Even if a given individual's cultural duties are not necessarily the product of her deliberate and conscientious effort to interpret a particular religious, ethical, or philosophical body of thought in a critical and informed manner, her duties ought to be taken seriously by public institutions on the basis that cultural duties are of critical importance for the adequate development and maintenance of her personality. The circumstance characterised as an inability to observe a particular set of cultural duties because of public ignorance of them and their critical importance to those whose duties they are is a human rights concern.

[49] H Lauterpacht, *An International Bill of the Rights of Man*, above n 45, at 153. Lauterpacht states that a denial of the cultural needs of minorities has often resulted in conditions which are dangerous to international peace and that this is why the Bill of Rights would be deficient if it failed effectively to acknowledge the right of the individual not to be thwarted in his development by denial of his cultural rights. It is the object of the Bill of Rights to check the policies and practices that are inimical alike to the growth of human personality and to international peace.

Although others cannot be expected to know what it is like for *me* to have a particular duty, say, to baptise my child in a certain church, all should be able to understand what it is like to have a duty that is not necessarily shared by all. Similarly, all should be able to imagine what it is like to be motivationally related to a norm in such a way that the inability to do what is required by that norm will produce anxiety, guilt, or shame. Most of us are related to several norms—both moral and non-moral—in this compelling way. Although we may disagree about the ultimate source of duties, and so the source of conscience, most of us would probably agree that acting contrary to the norms that the conscience invokes produces anxiety and guilt.[50] Against this background, we may conclude that cultural duties ought to be respected as a matter of human rights. However, we may also contend that, if these are the effects of acting contrary to conscience, the individual with such duties will in all likelihood avoid situations or circumstances that could create problems of conscience. To avoid these kinds of problems must be an aspect of individual responsibility and not of human rights. However, as suggested here, there are limits as to what can reasonably be expected by individuals in terms of adjustment to conform with the official law quite regardless of how that law came into place or why a given individual is expected to live by it. While the question as to what the more precise limits are will always be a matter of dispute and controversy, it is nevertheless of utmost importance to seek to specify the absolute limits to adjustment from the standpoint of human rights. The link between cultural duties and individual well-being is a critical factor when working out what those limits are.

A concern with 'adequacy' when designing a scheme of rights for a multicultural society is motivated by a deeper concern about the need to be sensitive to the cultural conditions that are deemed critical for the development of personality and, ultimately, moral personality, and the realisation that these conditions are not necessarily the same for all. One implication of seeking to ensure universal access to one's culture in the sense of being able to observe one's cultural duties in a multicultural environment is that the implementation of this right inevitably requires the acknowledgement of cultural difference in this regard. To simply ignore the fate of those whose cultural duties are in conflict with the official law does not necessarily ignore their moral development; indeed, it may instead raise their consciousness of what it means to deal with one another in respectful ways in a multicultural society. An individual who is denied the right to observe his cultural duties will in most likelihood arrive at the conclusion that to have problems of conscience in relation to the official law drafted by the majority on the basis of 'better knowing' may not merely be oppressive, but also reveal that what the majority is appealing to is a competing stock of cultural knowledge which is not necessarily more convincing than his own. However, more

[50] See eg I Jenkins, 'The Significance of Conscience' (1954) *Ethics* 261, at 261–262.

common than a public defence of an official law that is objected to by a minority culture is the outright ignorance of its culture-based objection.

What has been presented is an individualistic interpretation of what a human right to access one's own culture could mean in a multicultural society based on the claim that a minimum provision of respect for freedom requires respect for the cultural dimension of children, men, and women. Such respect, it is suggested, is essential to the development and maintenance of personality and, ultimately, moral personality. The definition of a human right to access culture has been limited in this way, in part to demonstrate that, even if collective dimensions inhere in both the notion of culture and of conscience ('shared life-form' and 'knowing together'), it is important to emphasise that there are individual or subjective elements to those notions as well. Indeed, it is the purpose and basis of human rights to insist on the possibility of an individual perspective. At the same time, however, it must be noted that law, in this chapter mainly assessed by virtue of its function in restricting the scope of individual freedom, has the potential to be seen as a set of cultural norms and endowed with meaning instead of as a sheer imposition of force.[51] This is how Robert Cover understands the sources for the compelling nature of sectarian communities. These communities create and give meaning to law through their narratives, myths, and precepts. Indeed, in Cover's view, it is the multiplication of laws—too much law—created by 'communities of interpretation' rather than the lack of them that is the very problem for which the courts and the state are the solution.[52] From this standpoint, the human right to access one's own culture is not confined to a human ability to utilise the cultural sources of ethical, religious, or philosophical knowledge one is familiar with in a deep sense when resolving matters of *adiaphora*, or to observe cultural duties in this realm of life, but extends to sharing with others a system of values to interpret the laws by which we live. However, there is no guarantee that everyone will be able to live by laws whose scheme of interpretation they share with others in this pervasive way. It might be an aspiration, something to strive for, but cannot be required as part of what it means to ensure a minimum provision of respect for individual freedom. Therefore, a human right to culture does not extend to a right to be part of a 'community of interpretation' or to being assured the conditions for one's community to thrive in this way.

Even so, the claim about the need to consider the ability to access one's own culture as a condition that is crucial for the development and maintenance of one's personality may nevertheless contribute to the creation of communities of interpretation. As Cover notes, the interpretative engagement of some communities might even result in the development of an entire jurisprudence of cultural resistance to compliance with the official law. The law-creating

[51] RM Cover, 'Nomos and Narrative' (1983) 97 *Harvard Law Review* 4.
[52] *Ibid*, at 42.

processes of the Quaker, Amish, and other sectarian communities in the United States have made their relation to the official law and the state a critical normative question. Their resistance reveals the possibility that entire communities will insist on the primacy of their own laws in the face of conflicting prerogatives imposed by their state. The establishment of entire communities of interpretation and resistance within a state framework is a possible outgrowth of the exercise of individual freedom. However, not only the exercise of a human right to culture, but also the human rights to freedom of association and freedom of religion contribute to this end.[53]

THE LIMITED APPLICABILITY OF THE PRIVATISATION APPROACH

Notwithstanding the critical importance of the individual ability to access one's own culture, including the ability to observe one's cultural duties, we lack a conceptual and evaluative framework for addressing and responding to questions about justice and rights that arise as a result of the recognition of this fact. While the acknowledgement of pluralism has shaped, and continues to shape, much theorising about justice and rights, several theorists nevertheless proceed on the assumption that problems of conscience are private in nature and have no direct implications for legislative design nor for judicial supervision of this task. Although the motives behind the affirmation of the 'privatisation approach' in relation to problems of conscience have changed over time, it remains the common starting point in normative assessments of the relation between conscience and the official law. Indeed, from having been an approach defended on the basis of prudential considerations, it has come to be understood as the approach that is most consistent with, even required by, a commitment to equality.

Nevertheless, the claim considered in this section is that neither a concern for prudence nor equality exhausts the reasons for ignoring differing cultural duties on matters of moral irrelevance some of which are in conflict with the official laws in force. One reason is that the argument from prudence relies upon a doubtful understanding of the nature of conscience and, thus, of the nature of duties. A sceptical outlook towards the content of conscience has undermined any consideration of the importance of duties in the eyes of those whose duties they are. Additionally, the argument about the need to privatise problems of conscience has been developed in response to their adverse impact on democratic political discussion. However, the reasons for this stance do not seem equally compelling in the context of non-political public institutions associated with developed schemes of social co-operation (such as social security and health care services). Another reason for hesitating about the claim about the need to uphold the privatisation approach in the face of cultural duties is that it rests on a simplified understanding of what

[53] RM Cover, 'Nomos and Narrative', above n 51, at 52.

is required to ensure a minimum provision of respect for individual freedom in a multicultural society. The stance of public ignorance of particular cultural duties fails to consider the hardships suffered as a result. The subsequent subsections of this chapter advance this claim in greater detail.

Prudential Considerations

The most cogent articulation of the argument about the need for privatisation of matters of conscience for the sake of peace and stability is found in the writings of Thomas Hobbes.[54] While his response to pluralism on matters of conscience represents a radical version of the privatisation approach, it nevertheless sheds light on what sort of risks and dangers the approach seeks to counter.

Hobbes believed that living together in peaceful ways requires that everybody strive to harmonise their actions with those of others. Unless everybody is willing to adjust themselves to the rest there is a constant risk of social conflict that may escalate into violence. Hence, it is pivotal that each tries to figure out a way to behave that does not invade the freedom of others.[55] The imperative for peace demands that all of us abandon the items that are superfluous to us and only keep those things that are absolutely essential for our own survival. Thus, everyone must renounce the natural 'Right of man to every thing, even to one anothers body.'[56] The only inalienable right is the right to self-defence.[57] This right, argued Hobbes, is the sole right that is consistent with the fifth fundamental law of nature:

> A fifth Law of Nature, is COMPLEASANCE; that is to say, *That every man strive to accommodate himself to the rest.* For the understanding whereof, we may consider, that there is in mens aptnesse to Society, a diversity of Nature, rising from their diversity of Affections; not unlike to that we see in stones brought together for building of an Aedifice. For as that stone which by the asperity, and irregularity of Figure, takes more room from others, than it selfe fills; and for the hardnesse, cannot be easily made plain, and thereby hindereth the building, is by the builders cast away as unprofitable, and troublesome; so also, a man that by asperity of Nature, will strive to retain those things which to himself are superfluous, and to others necessary; and for the stubbornness of his Passions, cannot be corrected, is to be left, or cast out of Society, as combersome thereunto. For seeing every man, not onely by Right, but also by necessity of Nature, is supposed to endeavour all he can, to obtain that which is necessary for his conservation; He that shall oppose himself against it, for things superfluous, is guilty of the warre that thereupon is to follow; and

[54] T Hobbes, *Leviathan* R Tuck (ed) (Cambridge, Cambridge University Press, 1997).
[55] *Ibid*, at 92.
[56] *Ibid*, at 91.
[57] *Ibid*, at 93.

> therefore doth that, which is contrary to the fundamentall Law of Nature, which commandeth *to seek Peace.*[58]

According to Hobbes, the imperative for peace and stability legitimises an all together sceptical stance towards conscience and the full endorsement of the sociability thesis. In his view, those who are unable to fit their actions with those of the rest are 'Stubborn, Insociable, Froward, and Intractable' and must be expelled from society.[59]

Knowing, as contemporary scholars do, that the recognition, and at least a limited accommodation, of pluralism is not necessarily incompatible with peace, but may actually be necessary to establish or maintain common institutional arrangements, it is difficult to accept the reasons for Hobbes to draw these harsh conclusions. For example, as Richard Tuck contends, a sceptical position towards matters of conscience and the related privatisation policy does not automatically produce peace. The history of England in the 17th century illustrates how one powerful kind of scepticism had precisely the opposite effect.[60]

The Hobbesian reaction to pluralism was urged on the basis of a deep mistrust in the capacities of women and men to obey the official law in the event that it gave rise to problems of conscience. Therefore, recognition of pluralism would encourage disobedience, disobedience that would eventually undermine the conditions for peace. Hobbes was especially sceptical about the possibility of people being able to judge good and bad without automatically acting on their judgements in complete ignorance of what consequences their actions might have for society. The response to this supposed ignorance, Hobbes contended, was to think of the official law as the common and public conscience.[61] In addition, Hobbes argued at length with the clergy about the need to revise the requirements for salvation to the absolute essentials so as to avoid the occurrence of religious duties in conflict with the official law. For this, people must learn to separate what is necessary from what is not. According to Hobbes, what is:

> NECESSARY *to Salvation*, is contained in two Vertues, *Faith in Christ* and *Obedience to Laws*. The latter of these, if it were perfect, were enough to us.[62]

Thus, Hobbes believed the possible threats to peace provoked by conflicting and opposing consciences necessitated the reduction of what counts as the legitimate preoccupation of conscience to personal faith.

[58] T Hobbes, *Leviathan*, above n 54, at 106.
[59] *Ibid.*
[60] R Tuck, 'Scepticism and Toleration in the Seventeenth Century' in S Mendus (ed), *Justifying Toleration: Conceptual and Historical Perspectives* (New York, Cambridge University Press, 1988), at 35.
[61] T Hobbes, *Leviathan*, above n 54, at 223.
[62] *Ibid*, at 403.

Hobbes advanced a *normative* claim about the need to relegate matters of conscience to personal faith or inner belief for the sake of securing a peaceful and stable society. Apart from demanding that everybody give up their rights (except the right to defend their own bodies for survival), Hobbes also propounded a reinterpretation of what is required for salvation. The reality of a plurality of competing and conflicting consciences only served to reinforce a sceptical position towards the idea of conscience as a source of truth. At the same time, he noted a general 'stubborness' of people towards accepting and adjusting their activities to whatever the official law happens to command. Thus, while downgrading the importance of conscience as a source of truth, Hobbes recognised that peace nevertheless requires a consideration of private consciences in legislative design. As he put it, peace requires a very able architect who knows the art of making fit laws.[63] Thus, the consideration and, to some extent, accommodation of private consciences was warranted, if not out of respect for individual freedom, for the sake of peace and stability.

As the Hobbesian position on a plurality of consciences conveys, in its extreme version the privatisation approach might require the complete internalisation of those matters of conscience considered as inconvenient for the state, and render such matters 'invisible'. This position, which represents the most radical solution to pluralism, emerged as a result of a deep suspicion towards the human capacity to act responsibly when faced with conflicting duties. While admittedly it would be naïve to suggest that matters of conscience do not have the political implications that Hobbes suggests, it is likewise a mistake to disregard the bases for respecting acts of 'conscientious refusals' and 'disobedience'.[64] Such disregard ignores the individual capacity to develop a conception of the good and a sense of justice, capacities which are widely recognised and relied upon in contemporary social and political life.

A Concern for Equality

In his book *Culture and Equality*, Brian Barry argues at length about the need to privatise religion so as to neutralise religion as a political force.[65] However, as the present study suggests, the threat to peace and stability created by the politicisation of religion is a concern that must be dealt with separately from the issue as to whether official laws on matters of ultimate moral indifference and enforced by non-political public institutions, such as social security, health care, and unemployment services, might impose unreasonable burdens on individuals as a result of their cultural difference. The latter is a question that

[63] *Ibid*, at 221.

[64] For a comprehensive assessment of the distinction between an act of civil disobedience and an act of conscientious refusal, see J Rawls, *Theory of Justice*, above n 14, at 319 ff.

[65] B Barry, *Culture and Equality* (Oxford, Polity Press, 2001), at 24 ff.

deserves to be treated in its own right due to the direct relevance it has to ensuring respect for individual freedom.

To understand the background to this kind of hardship, it is necessary to consider the processes of modernisation and rationalisation undergone by many states and the impact of these processes on the nature of law and its administration. These developments have transformed the idea of the state into a scheme of social co-operation establishing agencies and services, whose task it is to enforce a host of social regulations, programmes, and policies. With the transformation of the state the nature of legislation itself has undergone a major change. As Edward Rubin explains:

> It no longer consists of rules that displace or supplement the common law: contemporary legislatures allocate resources, create administrative agencies, issue vague guidelines or general grants of jurisdiction to those agencies and enact a wide range of other provisions that bear little resemblance to our traditional concept of law. ... For these functions, we have no adequate theory, no general account of how such statutes should be designed and what makes them effective or ineffective, desirable or undesirable.[66]

The changing nature of legislation, above all, in its establishment and regulation of public social agencies and services, has far-reaching implications on the extent to which people interact with public institutions and the extent to which that interaction is regulated by official laws. The intensification of such interaction in multicultural societies directs attention to differing manners, habits, and routines as well as duties on matters of *adiaphora* that depend on cultural background and attachment.

Notwithstanding that the secularisation of conscience and the development of a broader range of religions deepen and complicate pluralism, these processes are often believed to necessitate very rough generalisations as to what people seek to be and do in their lives when theorising about justice and rights. Indeed, differences in life projects are believed to have no direct bearing on the legislative process. Instead, pluralism (except for political pluralism) frames that process by limiting the range of issues regarded as being of common concern. This understanding of the relation between pluralism and the legislative process is a critical characteristic in the political liberal approach to pluralism as developed by John Rawls. Having emphasised the importance of acknowledging the existence of a plurality of comprehensive doctrines and their aspiration to inform people's conceptions of the good, his discussion of the principles and values supposed to inform the legislative process is confined to interests and concerns that can reasonably be said to be shared by everyone. Thus, his account of the relation between pluralism and the legislative process does not entertain the plausibility of a more engaging

[66] EL Rubin, 'Law and Legislation in the Administrative State' (1989) 89 *Columbia Law Review* 369, at 369.

relation between particular interests and legislative outcomes. The hardships in the form of problems of conscience suffered by individuals whose cultures differ from the cultural framework informing the legislative process in their place of residence are ignored, not merely because of the supposed threat to peace and stability such problems give rise to, but also by virtue of a commitment to a particular understanding of equality.

The political liberal approach envisages a legislature whose members only enact laws and policies motivated by interests and concerns shared in common with all other members of their scheme of social co-operation. It thereby seems to effectively exclude the claim about the need to consider particular interests and concerns inasmuch as they do not represent common ground. The common interests and concerns refer to the values of equal political and civil liberty, equality of opportunity, the values of social equality and economic reciprocity, values of the common good as well as the various necessary conditions for all these values.[67] Thus, one common reason for membership in a scheme of social co-operation is the critical importance of individual freedom (civil liberty). The actual implementation of that freedom in a multicultural society requires the direct consideration of actual differences in terms of particular commitments, duties, and values. However, in its exclusive focus on points of common interest and concern, the political liberal approach tends to gloss over such differences.

The basic idea of the political liberal approach is that each political decision, irrespective of whether it refers to a certain law, allocation of a resource, the abolition of a benefit, and so on, must be justified on the basis of a common stock of reasons. However, this basic idea is not necessarily contradicted by the direct consideration of difference in terms of particular cultural duties in the legislative process insofar as it can be motivated by a common concern. That concern, it is suggested, is to ensure respect for individual freedom. Nevertheless, although Rawls recognises that particular duties can come into conflict with the laws in force, he does not believe that this sort of conflict calls for consideration and even accommodation of duties into the fabric of the official law. Instead, he only notes that it is regrettable if legislative action—unintentionally—comes into conflict with particular religious commitments.[68]

The political liberal account of justice does not require particular attention to the circumstance of people whose cultures differ from the cultural framework dominating their public institutions and legislative action. Their circumstance is not seen as a reason for legislative change to alleviate the unreasonable burdens imposed on those whose duties conflict with official laws regulating matters of moral indifference. If a piece of legislation can be motivated by a common reason, say, social equality, it is regarded as just

[67] J Rawls, *Political Liberalism*, above n 22, at 224.
[68] *Ibid*, at 197.

from the standpoint of political liberalism, quite regardless of how people fare as a result of the legal obligations it imposes. All the same, it is my contention that a commitment to securing respect for individual freedom requires us to take note of the fact that all individuals who are members of co-operative schemes are also private persons. An individual is related to such a scheme both in her capacity as a member (citizen) and as a human being (private person). This claim is developed in the subsequent subsection on 'hardships'.

The political liberal supposition that adequate respect for individual freedom is automatically guaranteed by looking to the 'legislative intention' assumes, not only that it is practically possible to discern what the 'intention' for each and every piece of legislation actually is, but also that it is the 'intention' behind a piece of legislation which is the exclusive concern from the standpoint of justice. No attention is paid to the effects of a piece of legislation on people whose cultures differ from the cultural framework informing the legislative discussion. Another reason for hesitating about 'legislative intention' as a measure of the justice of a given piece of legislation was alluded to by Justice O'Connor in the Supreme Court of the United States. In the case *Employment Division v Smith*, O'Connor remarked that if states actually sought to suppress a religion, few states would be so naïve as to enact a law directly prohibiting or burdening a religious practice as such.[69]

However, in spite of the serious shortcomings inherent to an exclusive focus on the motive behind a law, the judgment by the majority of judges in that case followed the line of reasoning developed in the spirit of political liberalism, as it has also done in subsequent case-law.[70] The same line of argument has persuaded staff at the European Court of Human Rights that its current case-law is based on a sufficiently refined understanding of what respect for human rights requires in a multicultural environment.[71]

Hardships

Is avoidance of evaluating the impact of regulations on individual freedom plausible? At present, and as we have seen, the response to the question as to whether difference in terms of particular cultural duties ought to be given direct consideration in legislative design is dominated by the idea that the state is a scheme of social co-operation with the aim of protecting values of

[69] *Employment Division v Smith* 494 US 872 (1990), at 885.

[70] See eg *City of Boerne v Flores* 521 US 507 (1997). The case concerns a complaint by an archbishop who had been denied a building permit by local zoning authorities to enlarge a church in Boerne, Texas. The authorities denied the permit relying on an ordinance governing the historic preservation in a district that, they argued, included the church.

[71] S Stavros, 'Freedom of Religion and Claims for Exemption from Generally-applicable, Neutral Laws: Lessons from Across the Pond?' in Council of Europe, *Religion and the Integration of Immigrants* (Strasbourg, Community Relations, Council of Europe, September 1999).

equality, including social security, health, safety, and welfare. From this standpoint, people are primarily viewed as members in an ongoing scheme of social co-operation or as otherwise aspiring to membership in such a scheme due to the benefits it promises to provide. This understanding of the purpose of the state has influenced our impression of the relevance of problems of conscience to the realisation of that purpose. A growing mistrust of the authenticity of conscientious objections on matters of *adiaphora* coincides with a sustained shift of focus onto the human capacity for a sense of justice. This capacity is not first and foremost defined in terms of an individual's ability to reason about issues of fundamental principle as much as it signifies a capacity to willingly submit and be loyal to the more specific legal obligations generated by such a scheme.

The processes of rationalisation coupled with a belief in the primacy of equality have resulted in a radically simplified understanding of what people might seek to be and do in their lives apart from being members of a co-operative scheme. The temptation to simplify complicated issues, exacerbated by a sceptical outlook on conscience, has undermined the likelihood that contemporary liberal theorists would pay special attention to the hardships experienced by those whose cultural duties are in conflict with the laws in force. The public ignorance of problems of conscience concerning *adiaphora* implies that the subjective standpoint is effectively denied, and thus the very basis for being concerned with adequacy in the first place. The same processes of rationalisation have led to an excessive trust in the potentiality of ideas about equality as both framing and informing common discussions about legislation.

Much contemporary political philosophical thought assumes that ideas about equality are critical to the multicultural debate whether it is in an attempt to object to propositions involving unequal treatment, or to justify such unequal treatment. One example is Bhikhu Parekh's defence of exempting Sikhs from the requirements imposed by the British crash helmet law:

> As for the complaint of inequality, there is a prima facie inequality of rights in the sense that Sikhs can do what others cannot. However, the alleged inequality grows out of the requirements of the principle of equal respect for all, and it is not so much inequality as an appropriate translation of that principle in a different religious context.[72]

Parekh defines the situation for Sikhs as a cultural inability.[73] In a response to Parekh's defence of cultural exemptions, however, Brian Barry points out,

[72] B Parekh, 'Equality in a Multiracial Society', in J Franklin (ed), *Equality* (London, Institute for Public Policy Research, 1997), at 235.

[73] B Parekh, *Rethinking Multiculturalism: Cultural Diversity and Political Theory* (Cambridge Mass, Harvard University Press, 2000), at 241.

I think correctly, that the claim about the need to take note of cultural difference in legislative action is not a justice-based argument, but motivated by a concern with alleviating *hardships* imposed on an individual as a result of conflicting duties giving rise to problems of conscience. John Locke also endorsed this understanding of the basis for caring about problems of conscience and pleaded for compassion and relief for those who suffer these sorts of hardships.[74]

The reason for paying attention to people's differing cultural duties some of which may be in conflict with legal requirements cannot be understood with reference to equality alone since it ignores the subjective standpoint in the light of which a commitment to ensure a minimum provision for individual freedom makes sense; it ignores the hardships imposed on individuals because of their duties. Barry contends that

> if it is true that a law bears particularly harshly on some people, that is at the very least a reason for examining it to see if it might be modified so as to accommodate those who are affected by it in some special way. Prudence or generosity might support such a move.[75]

In spite of his initial argument, however, Barry pulls back from the assertion that some may suffer hardships under a law due to their conscience even if others do not. Instead, he continues by stating that either the case for regulation (or some version of it) is strong enough to rule out exemptions; or alternatively, the case that can be made for exemptions is strong enough to suggest that there should be no law at all.[76]

According to Barry, nobody can suffer hardships because of regulations of matters that are ultimately indifferent (including health, safety, security, and welfare) since such regulations do not *coerce* anybody. Nobody is coerced to ride a motorbike, to work in the construction industry, or to eat the meat of animals slaughtered in accordance with 'humane' slaughter regulations. In defence of equal treatment before the British helmet law, Barry argues that riding a motorbike is an entirely voluntary act, and that a person who tries to lead his life in conformity with a Sikh conception of the good is not forced to ride a motorbike. Nor does a law regulating slaughter practices force Jews or Muslims to eat meat. Finally, British law does not coerce people to accept jobs that require them to adjust their particular duties of prayer, diet, and dress. Conscientious objection in relation to these regulations (and most conscientious objections in multicultural contexts are of this character), Barry concludes, simply lacks the requirement of being an objection against a coercive act.[77]

[74] J Locke, 'An Essay on Toleration', above n 2, at 152.
[75] B Barry, *Culture and Equality*, above n 65, at 38–39.
[76] *Ibid*.
[77] *Ibid*, at 44. On job discrimination, see 54 ff.

Barry applies a narrow interpretation of coercion which is similar to that examined by Robert Nozick. On Nozick's account, a person cannot be regarded as coerced into performing an action if he performs it simply because someone has *offered* him something in exchange. However, a person is normally considered to have been coerced into performing an action if he does it because of a *threat* that has been made against him if he would act otherwise. A threat is coercive in a way that an offer is not.[78] Even so, Nozick does not settle the issue of what counts as a threat. What is decisive, he contends, is what constitutes the 'baseline', ie what a person can expect in terms of personal integrity and goods that nobody must deprive him of lest it be considered as a threat. There are obvious difficulties in specifying what constitutes the 'baseline'. At the same time, however, it is unclear whether conscientious objections occurring in multicultural societies depend on the want of goods that clearly go beyond that baseline. It is unclear, that is, whether Barry's understanding of the situation for those whose cultural norms come into conflict with common regulations can reasonably be characterised as a pure choice situation.

Quite regardless of how one wants to characterise conscientious objections in relation to regulations of matters of *adiaphora*, it must be noted that such objections cannot always be avoided by cultural minorities. While it seems correct to suggest that, generally speaking, it is only reasonable to expect that people take responsibility for their convictions and shoulder the burdens, there may nevertheless be instances where the hardships involved become too great to ignore.[79] Thus, the assumption about the non-coercive character of regulations of morally irrelevant activities is not entirely correct. For a start, it fails to appreciate the reality of individual dependency on non-political public institutions, eg health care services, child care, state schools, unemployment agencies, welfare institutions, etc. Some of these institutions are coercive in a way that others are not. One category of institutions of a coercive character includes prisons, military service (in the case of universal conscription), compulsory treatment of mentally ill persons and compulsory education. These institutions do not treat their inmates, soldiers, patients, and pupils as being in a position to choose whether or not to be bound by their respective regulations. The coercive element of those regulations may be justified on the basis of a common interest in health, national security or social equality, but this is not the point. The point is that the obligations imposed by such institutions may be far more burdensome for some than for others, in part, due to their difference in terms of cultural makeup.

[78] R Nozick, 'Coercion' in S Morgenbesser and P Suppes (eds), *Philosophy: Science and Method* (New York, St Martin's Press, 1969), at 458.

[79] J Raz, *The Authority of Law: Essays on Law and Morality* (Oxford, Clarendon Press, 1979), at 282–284.

The presence of a coercive element of some regulations on matters of moral indifference, such as dress codes in public schools or prisons, is of direct relevance when responding to conscientious objections on these matters. One example is the conscientious objection by the Sikh prisoner in an Austrian prison who complained to the European Commission of Human Rights on the basis that the prison rules do not permit him to observe his dress code and dietary restrictions.[80] While conceding that the shift of focus onto the hardships suffered by the subject and imposed by the public institution may not settle the question of how to respond to the conscientious objection by the prisoner, it does place additional justificatory burdens on the relevant authority once his case has been brought to its attention. As Parekh affirms, although the unequal impact of a prohibition does not *mandate* exemption, there should be strong additional reasons for maintaining the prohibition.[81] Still, it is not sufficient to simply refer to common interests in, say, safety or hygiene, if these interests can be reconciled with the alleviation of hardships faced by prisoners whose particular cultural duties are ignored. In other words, when it is possible to reconcile cultural duties with the basic function of a given regulation in a coercive institutional context, such reconciliation should be made. Such reconciliation is required to ensure a minimum provision of respect for individual freedom.

A second category of public institutions lacks a coercive element, at least formally speaking, and from the standpoint of observers (as opposed to beneficiaries). This category includes civil registrars, health care services, public universities, child care, elderly care, social security agencies, unemployment agencies, etc. These kinds of institutions have been set up in order to respond to educational needs, ill-health or chronic disease, maltreatment of children, unemployment, poverty, homelessness, and so on. Public institutions that have been established to protect the welfare, social security, and health of people are not coercive in the way prisons, universal conscription, and compulsory education are; in principle, people may choose whether or not to utilise the services, programmes, and opportunities provided by health care services, public universities, elderly care, and so on. Still, if no other agency or service is available for a person who suffers from any of the involuntary conditions that these institutions are expected to alleviate, or who otherwise wishes to make use of opportunities that in principle are available to everybody, such as university education, it nevertheless means that he or she is de facto dependent on the public institutions in focus. Thus, even if at first glance it seems to be a matter of choice whether or not to utilise the services, programmes, and opportunities provided by such institutions and, thus, to conform one's behaviour to their respective regulatory frameworks,

[80] Appl 1753/63, *X v Austria*, Yearbook VIII (1965), 174 at 184.
[81] B Parekh, *Rethinking Multiculturalism: Cultural Diversity and Political Theory*, above n 73, at 242.

the dependency situation of many beneficiaries nevertheless renders such regulations coercive from their standpoint.

Against this background, it must be concluded that, similarly to the first category of public institutions, this category is not free to regulate matters of *adiaphora* as they please as long as their regulatory frameworks protect a common interest in, say, health or safety. Since the situation of their intended beneficiaries can hardly be characterised as a choice situation, it becomes equally important for these institutions to reconcile particular cultural duties of intended beneficiaries with their respective regulatory frameworks to the extent that it is possible and to the extent that such reconciliation does not undermine the function of these regulations. Such reconciliation becomes especially critical when the cultural duties of intended beneficiaries render it impossible for them to make adequate use of these institutions. However, it is also of relevance in relation to actual beneficiaries who suffer hardships as a result of their usage of a given service, programme, or facility, especially if they are meant to alleviate an involuntary condition.

One case that illustrates what I have suggested is the problem of conscience faced by the Hmong community living on Rhode Island in the United States in dealing with the local health care service. A Hmong couple brought a suit against Rhode Island's chief medical examiner in response to an autopsy of their son's body without their consent. The couple, originally from Laos, believe that autopsies constitute mutilations of the body. As a result of their son's autopsy

> the spirit of Neng [their son] would not be free, therefore his spirit will come back and take another person in his family.[82]

Though regretful, the district court in the United States that judged on the matter held that the couple's conscientious refusal to accept an autopsy did not constitute a valid reason for not having it done. In this way, it did not recognise the hardships suffered by the Hmong couple as a result of the act of the chief medical examiner, nor did it regard the conscientious objection in relation to the autopsy regulations as indicating the need for reconciliation and accommodation of differing conceptions of autopsy into the fabric of the law in a multicultural society.

Nevertheless, given the hardships suffered by the Hmong couple as a result of the coercive nature of the post-mortem rules regulating matters of *adiaphora*, it is my contention that the district court should have ruled in favour of the Hmong couple. It is well known that death and the disposal of the dead, especially close family, are fraught with significance, rituals, and story-telling in all cultures even if cultures differ in their conceptions about right and wrong in this realm of life. From a scientific standpoint, it may be

[82] *You Vang Yang, Ia Kue Yang v William Q Sturner* (750 F Supp 558) (1990).

difficult to accept the credibility of these kinds of stories. Even so, it may seem to be beside the point what scientists happen to think about the contents of such stories as long as believing in them does not harm anybody. If cultural beliefs give rise to conscientious objections to official regulations on matters of moral indifference they ought to be considered as raising legitimate claims about toleration, compassion, and even accommodation. At the same time, it seems unreasonable to hold a public official or servant or any other person accountable for having acted in accordance with official regulations on matters of moral indifference even if his action gives rise to problems of conscience. Thus, the point is not that the Hmong couple should be able to sue a person and get compensation for the hardships suffered as a result of their problem of conscience, but that the occurrence of conscientious objections in relation to official regulations provides a motive to review those regulations.

Public unemployment agencies constitute a somewhat different institutional context which, at first sight, seems non-coercive, but where conscientious refusals occur. While it is correct, as Barry argues, that nobody is *forced* to accept a job if the regulations of that workplace would make it impossible to observe one's cultural duties, not accepting it may involve the deprivation of unemployment benefits. Indeed, the unreasonableness of being de facto coerced to accept a job that creates problems of conscience as a result of cultural duties has been the catalyst for legislative review and revision in the United States. Thus, the United States unemployment agencies no longer require people to accept jobs in contravention of their religious duties in order to receive unemployment benefits.[83] Nevertheless, the Supreme Court has been reluctant to extend this recognition of the importance of cultural duties in the eyes of those whose duties they are to other public institutional contexts. Thus, for example, it has refused to accommodate a refusal of a parent to provide a social security number for their daughter to enjoy benefits from a federal statutory scheme.[84] Nor did it consider an appeal by a Jewish man to be released from the military dress regulations so as to be able to wear his yarmulke.[85] However, the Supreme Court has mandated revision of prison rules regulating hours of work in order to accommodate prisoners who need to attend worship services.[86]

In summary, a more careful assessment of the circumstance of people whose cultures differ from the culture informing the specific contents of a range of

[83] See *Sherbert v Verner*, 374 US 398 (1963); *Thomas v Review Board of Indiana Employment Security Division*, 450 US 707 (1981); and *Hobbie v Unemployment Appeals Commisson of Florida*, 480 US 136 (1987).

[84] See *Bowen v Roy*, 476 US 693 (1986). In this case, it was decided that no consideration should be given to problems of conscience experienced by parents obliged to obtain and provide a social security number for their daughter in order for her to benefit from a federal statutory scheme.

[85] *Goldman v Weinberger*, 475 US 503 (1986).

[86] *O'Lone v Estate of Shabazz*, 482 US 342 (1987).

regulations in different institutional contexts is warranted in the light of the hardships suffered as a result of problems of conscience. It is a mistake to regard all interaction with public institutions as voluntary; rather, there is often a coercive element involved in such interaction which renders it all the more important to ensure that the laws regulating that interaction do not give rise to conscientious objections. Even so, at present, it is not unusual that the decision rules addressed to public servants and professionals in these institutions are insensitive to the cultural differences that exist among the people they are interacting with.

There is a widespread belief that equal treatment is the proper translation of what it means to ensure a minimum provision of respect in these kinds of institutional contexts. Nevertheless, as Harry Frankfurt notes, treating everybody equally is not necessarily the same as treating them with respect.[87] While ideas about equality have been the concern of many of the institutions in focus, the same ideas do not necessarily capture the hardships suffered by those whose cultural differences are ignored, that is, those for whom stories, myths, and rituals which in themselves are morally indifferent nonetheless attribute meaning and significance to ordinary life issues and, at times, result in conscientious objections. To consider these objections does not necessarily undermine ideas about equality nor the possibility of implementing those ideas in multicultural societies. Rather, the fact of multiculturalism alerts us to the possibility that the public institutions in focus have been designed to meet the particular interests, needs, and commitments associated with a single culture or a similar range of cultures. From this standpoint, it is precisely an expression of equality to be similarly attentive to the particular needs, interests, and concerns of minority cultures. Thus, while the present study argues that cultural sensitivity is required by virtue of a commitment to ensuring a minimum provision of respect for individual freedom, it also recognises that ideas of equality do not work against such sensitivity, but provide additional support for it.

THE ALTERNATIVE OF CULTURAL ACCOMMODATION

An increasing number of scholars who are preoccupied with the hardships suffered by people whose cultural duties remain ignored in the development of law and policy have sought to advance an 'accommodationist' approach in response to conscientious objections on matters of *adiaphora*. The approach has been developed in response to a criticism of the privatisation approach for its ignorance of the extensive services, programmes, and facilities set up and administrated by many states today. In an important sense, it is believed to be able to reconcile the values motivating common regulations with the demand for respect and consideration on the part of those

[87] H Frankfurt, 'Equality and Respect' (1997) 64 *Social Research* 3.

whose cultures differ from and come into conflict with those regulations. At the same time, however, while the accommodationist approach represents a more favourable treatment of cases of cultural resistance towards compliance with common regulations, it is a matter of serious dispute and controversy as to what could possibly motivate such treatment. In addition, there is a heartfelt reluctance to support this approach since it is inevitably bound up with a somewhat different set of practical issues that may be impossible to resolve in a satisfactory way. Above all, there is a fear that claims for special treatment of different cultures will proliferate, and that it will not be possible to treat such claims in a consistent manner.

Earlier on in this chapter it was suggested that the ability to observe one's cultural duties on matters of *adiaphora* may be critical for the adequate development and maintenance of personality and that, in a multicultural context, these duties are obviously not the same for all. In other words, the present study defends a claim about the need to consider cultural difference on the basis of a deeper concern about the conditions for personality and, ultimately, moral personality. The purpose of this section is to defend this claim against a fear of inconsistencies and arbitrariness in the practical implementation of this proposition. To this end, it first delineates a scheme for sorting out when special consideration of a person's cultural duties is warranted on the basis of this concern. In this context, it distinguishes between different sorts of conflicts between a person's cultural duties and official laws in force. (Of particular significance is whether the law in question seeks to regulate *malum in se* or *malum prohibitum*). Thereafter, it seeks to specify the limits to cultural accommodation. This discussion centres on the relevance of the moral duties not to harm others and to contribute to the welfare of others.

Conduct Rules in Conflict

A classification of the possible cases of conflicting sets of conduct rules at stake in conscientious objections towards compliance with the laws in force may assist in disentangling various sorts of conflicts, each of which requires a different response. It also serves to sharpen our understanding of the nature of the cultural norms involved in conflicts giving rise to more serious controversies about the limits to cultural accommodation. The table below distinguishes between the different conflicts that may exist between an individual's cultural norms and rules (on the one hand) and the laws in force (on the other).

The term *mala prohibita* refers to laws regulating fields of action which are themselves morally indifferent from the standpoint of the individual and/or the sovereign legislator.

The term *mala in se*, in contrast, refers to laws regulating fields of action believed to be warranted by compelling norms. Such norms can be either independent moral or culture-dependent norms.

	Mala prohibita	*Mala in se*	No rule
Mala prohibita	Co-ordination	Over-regulation	Legislative initiatives
Mala in se	Conscientious objection	Criminal law	Conscience politicised
No rule	Over-regulation	Over-regulation	No law

The conflicts defined in the first row are not necessarily more frequent in a multicultural context than in less plural environments. As to the first conflict (*mala prohibita–mala prohibita*), the individual agrees about the need for regulation on matters of *adiaphora*, but disagrees with the sovereign legislator about what the best regulation would be. Neither the individual subject nor the state perceives the relevant field of action as involving problems of conscience whether in relation to independent moral norms or culture-dependent compelling norms. Therefore, the conflict in question does not give rise to conscientious objections on matters of *adiaphora*.

The conflicts specified in the third row direct attention to the sources of emancipation in fields of action that are protected by non-basic liberties. The individual subject does not necessarily think of his activities in these fields as being rightful or good, but neither does he think of them as wrongful, that is, as being contrary to a compelling norm. Rather, he believes that it is part of his non-basic liberties to engage in activities such as gambling, drinking, or drug-use freely without legal interference. Thus, over-regulation in these realms may provoke resistance and non-compliance by individuals who are attached to cultures whose members are accustomed to drink, gamble, or use drugs. If it seems difficult for cultures persuade the sovereign legislator about the need for review and revision of regulations in these fields of action, a somewhat different method with the potential to bring about legislative change is to encourage ignorance of such regulations and, in this way, raise the costs for law enforcement. This sort of disobedience has a strategic dimension that is lacking in the case of conscientious objection.[88]

The conflicts specified in the second row become more frequent in multicultural societies and elucidate the background to the occurrence of conscientious objections in those societies. The conflicts that give rise to objections to compliance with official laws and are the most difficult to deal with have their roots in the existence of a plurality of differing and conflicting compelling cultural norms. Neither the official rule nor the private rule is mandated by an independent moral norm, but instead by compelling culture-dependent ones.

[88] For a distinction between 'integrity-based disobedience' and 'justice-based disobedience', see R Dworkin, *A Matter of Principle* (Cambridge, Mass, Harvard University Press, 1985), at 109. According to Dworkin, the former is defensive in the sense that the actor does not do something his conscience forbids. The latter, in contrast, is instrumental and strategic since it aims at an overall goal, ie the dismantling of an immoral political programme.

A case that has come before the European Court of Human Rights amply illustrates the sorts of conflicts between individuals and sovereign legislators that may occur as a result of this sort of pluralism. In this case, two citizens who had been elected to the Parliament of San Marino refused to refer to the gospels when taking the oath laid down in a decree from 27 June 1909. As a result, their oath was declared invalid and they were obliged to retake it in order to avoid losing their parliamentary seats. While the government of San Marino sought to defend the oath as part of its cultural heritage, the court decided that a reference to cultural heritage fails to count as an acceptable justification of the legal obligation that citizens elected to the San Marino Parliament must take a religious oath.[89]

The first and the third conflicts specified in the second row are expected to be more frequent in multicultural places whose inhabitants purport to regulate their mutual affairs in a liberal spirit. Both conflicts involve an individual whose convictions about the wrongs inherent in a certain action have their root in a culture-dependent compelling norm. In the first case, he objects to an official law for its treatment of the action in question as being morally indifferent, that is, as not being a matter of conscience. In the second case, in contrast, he objects to the lack of any regulation whatsoever of the relevant action and insists, on the basis of his cultural norm, about the need to prohibit it as a matter of law.

As the present study suggests, conscientious objections to compliance with official laws on matters of *adiaphora* (in focus in the first conflict in the second row) ought to be taken seriously by the sovereign legislator since they indicate that the scheme of rights in place may fail to be adequate. Before assessing this conflict in greater detail in the subsequent subsection, it is necessary to focus on the second and third conflicts in focus in the second row.

To begin with, in the second conflict in the second row, the individual whose conscience is informed by a compelling culture-dependent norm has his convictions reflected in the official law. In other words, both the individual and the sovereign legislator agree on the need to criminalise the action. The official law may rely upon an independent moral norm or a compelling culture-dependent norm that happens to converge with that of the individual. The British law prohibiting blasphemous conduct exemplifies the possibility of convergence on what constitutes *mala in se* in a multicultural society. Similarly to Christian believers, the practising Muslims living in Britain also believe that blasphemous conduct is wrongful and ought to be prohibited as a matter of law.

[89] *Buscarini and Others v San Marino*, no 24645/94 ECHR 1999–I. The oath reads: 'I, (...) swear on the Holy Gospels ever to be faithful to and obey the Constitution of the Republic, to uphold and defend freedom with all my might, ever to observe the Laws and Decrees, whether ancient, modern or yet to be enacted or issued and to nominate and vote for as candidates to the Judiciary and other Public Office only those whom I consider apt, loyal and fit to serve the Republic, without allowing myself to be swayed by any feelings of hatred or love or by any other consideration' (para 8).

The third conflict in the second row finally, is that for which the privatisation approach has been designed. It seeks to safeguard the potential risks posed to peace and stability in a plural setting if consciences enter political life by urging a 'de-politicisation' of conscience. The standard example of how consciences can enter political life is when a group of people tries to use the coercive powers of law in order to impose its culture-dependent norms on others who do not agree with its members about the wrongs committed by a certain action. Alternatively, the group may seek to impose a controversial interpretation of an independent moral norm in the face of ferocious disagreement about the correctness of its interpretation. The value of human life and its supposed relevance to abortion is but one example of a particularly controversial interpretation of an independent moral norm. Such disagreements may best be understood as having their source in competing moral judgements.[90] The conflict involving the urge of a group of people to impose a culture-dependent norm or a controversial moral judgement on others who disagree cannot be resolved by way of cultural accommodation; instead, it directs attention to the potential powers of democratic discussion in the management of such conflicts. The importance of democracy and participation for the realisation of human rights in a multicultural society will be discussed in chapter seven of this book.

Accommodating Conscientious Refusals

The vast majority of conscientious objections in relation to laws regulating matters of *adiaphora* originate as a result of a plurality of cultural norms, some of which are more compelling than others from the standpoint of the individual. From a moral standpoint, perhaps the most problematic conflict involves an individual whose culture-dependent norms compel him to act in a certain manner even if his action is contrary to a state regulation (that is, the first conflict in the second row in the table above). The state regulation is motivated by a value associated with viewing the state as a scheme of social co-operation, such as health, safety, or welfare. It regulates behaviour in fields of action which are useful if a sufficiently large number behave in the ways prescribed by it, but which is without value if nobody or only a few people follow it.[91] Thus, it prohibits certain behaviour, not because it is wrong as such (*mala in se*), but because doing so would promote a value associated with a scheme of social co-operation (*mala prohibita*).

How should we distinguish between these two types of prohibitions in practice? Let us consider the discussions surrounding the nature of three legal prohibitions that tend to provoke conscientious objections in multicultural

[90] See generally R Dworkin, *Life's Dominion: An Argument about Abortion, Euthanasia, and Individual Freedom* (New York, Knopf, 1993).
[91] See J Raz, *The Authority of Law*, above n 79, at 247–248.

societies, namely, those prohibiting the slaughtering of animals, carrying knives in public, and the intentional possession of drugs.

Brian Barry suggests that the British regulation of slaughtering practices prohibiting slaughter before stunning necessarily prevails over the Jewish and Muslim conduct rules requiring that animals be slaughtered without prior stunning. In support of his position, he argues that the state regulation is more humane and protects animal welfare.[92] While not contesting the need for regulation of this field of action for the sake of animal welfare, I contend that there is something suspect about limiting that regulation to ritual slaughtering practices and not taking into account the entire meat industry. In my view, the argument that the British regulation adequately protects the welfare of animals while the Jewish and the Muslim regulations do not fails to be persuasive. The animals still suffer. Indeed, regardless of how animals are slaughtered a significant degree of animal suffering is inevitable. Therefore, it is at best an argument that the British regulation *reduces* animal suffering. It does not seek to abolish slaughtering practices universally and categorically on the basis that such practices are morally wrong (*mala in se*). From this standpoint, the British regulation only seeks to make an altogether cruel practice 'less cruel'. Since it does not consider all practices of slaughtering animals as morally wrong, the state regulation is best characterised as *malum prohibitum*. This understanding of the nature of the regulation in question influences the way Britain (and all other states with similar regulations) ought to respond to refusals to observe it on conscientious grounds.

What about a regulation prohibiting the carrying of a knife in public? Such a regulation really seems to be warranted on the basis that carrying a knife in public is morally wrong in that it presents a threat to life (*malum in se*). Nevertheless, there are cultures that permit, indeed, compel their members to do so. Some Sikhs believe it is a strict duty to carry a sword or a dagger (*kirpan*). Because of this, British Sikhs are given special treatment under the Criminal Justice Act 1988 which penalises those who carry knives and other sharply pointed objects. It specifically states that if an accused can prove that he had the knife with him in a public place for religious reasons he is exempted from punishment.[93] The general prohibition against having 'articles with blades or points and offensive weapons' in a public place is not generated by a duty to protect the welfare of others which a scheme of social co-operation ultimately is founded upon; instead, it is motivated by the need to outlaw threatening acts in civil society that induce fear in inhabitants. It is a precondition of civil society that people do not fear for their lives. A knife

[92] B Barry, *Culture and Equality*, above n 65, at 40 ff.

[93] Criminal Justice Act 1988, s 139(5)(b) as amended by the Offensive Weapons Act 1996. The Criminal Justice Act states that 'it shall be a defense for persons charged with an offence [of having an article with blades or points and offensive weapons] to prove that he had the article with him for ... (b) religious reasons'.

will generally be perceived as a threat by others. If it cannot reasonably be expected that everybody is familiar with the variety of reasons for having a knife or similar article in a public place, not all of which necessarily amount to an intention to threaten others, the special treatment of Sikhs seems unjustified. However, this conclusion also brings into question the other exemptions from the general prohibition in question, notably that which allows people to carry a knife or similar article if it is 'part of any national costume.'[94] The decisive question is whether it can reasonably be assumed that every subject of UK law is familiar with one another's religious or national costumes and the fact that knives or similar articles may simply be a decorative part of such costumes. It is doubtful whether this assumption is sustainable in societies that are multicultural as a result of immigration.

Another regulation that has provoked debate is that which prohibits the intentional possession of drugs. For example, the State of Oregon in the United States criminalises such possession. Notwithstanding the criminalisation, however, it is my contention that the regulation cannot be classified as *malum in se*, but must be *malum prohibitum*. While it may well constitute a moral wrong to provide others with drugs likely to lead their eventual destruction, personal possession and ingestion can hardly be considered as such. Although it is advisable that the individual cares for his health by abstaining from drug-use, it is not his strict duty to do so from the standpoint of cosmopolitan moral law. In the case that brought this piece of regulation into the multicultural debate, two Native Americans had ingested peyote as part of a religious ceremony in their church and were accused and punished for their activity.[95] At first sight, the criminalisation of drug possession and ingestion seems to amount to an unreasonable restriction of individual freedom to observe cultural norms. In this particular case, however, the men accused of drug possession were employed in a private drug rehabilitation centre where drug-use—especially drug-use by employees—is fraught with significance given the function of the centre. The context renders their misconduct as employees more serious than it might otherwise have been. More importantly, however, it is uncertain whether the Native American religion sees drug-use as a matter of strict duty or as merely advisable. If it is only advisable, it could not be argued that their abstention would create problems of conscience in the first place.

The argument in favour of cultural accommodation advanced in this study does not cover cases where an individual's culture-dependent conduct rules are not compelling, but merely specify the outer limits of *permissible* conduct. One case in point is that of a 21-year-old man living in England who married a girl aged fourteen and a half years. The couple undertook a Muslim

[94] Criminal Justice Act 1998, s 139(5)(c); Offensive Weapons Act 1996, s 4(4)(d). Other exemptions include 'use at work'. It must be noted that the Offensive Weapons Act extends the number of exemptions from punishment to include people who carry a weapon for 'educational purposes.'

[95] *Employment Division v Smith*, 494 US 872 (1990).

marriage ceremony, without the permission of the girl's father, in contravention of British law. They lived together for four months until the man was convicted and sentenced to nine months in prison for under-age sex, as prohibited under the British Sexual Offences Act 1956. The man sought to defend himself by invoking an Iranian interpretation of Islamic conduct rules according to which it is *permissible* to marry minors from 12 years old without parents' consent. The interpretation had been adopted after the Islamic revolution.[96] In other words, the man only argued that his conduct is considered *acceptable* in his culture, but not that such conduct is advisable or recommended, and certainly not a duty.[97] Another case that amply illustrates the occurrence of objections on the basis of different cultural understandings of permissible conduct is the specific amount of maintenance owed in divorce cases. In this case, an Indian Muslim was accused of having violated an Indian law requiring that he pay such maintenance to his former wife.[98] He sought a legal advantage by invoking Islamic law according to which he would pay less maintenance to his former wife than he would in accordance with Indian law.[99] While both laws suppose that some allowance is required, the exact amount differs somewhat between the two legal systems. For this reason, it cannot be said that the refusal of the Muslim man to pay the maintenance he owes his former wife according to Indian law, and his reliance on Islamic law in this regard was conscientious (unless he saw himself as compelled to follow the Islamic law as a matter of principle).

Although culture-dependent compelling norms do not necessarily correlate with an independent moral norm, but are in principle subject to drift and change, such norms at any given time may compel an individual in the same way as a moral norm. Indeed, culture-dependent norms may be transmitted from generation to generation in a way that attributes them with a flavour of 'timelessness'. As suggested earlier on in this chapter, the air of 'timelessness' may be deliberately maintained through conscientious instruction by parents, schools, priests, and other cultural authorities. Norms regulating mode of dress, diet, and prayer are not thought to be part of the moral conscience, but

[96] Appl No 11579/85, *Khan v the United Kingdom*, D&R 48 (1986), 253.

[97] See generally R Gleave, 'Elements of Religious Discrimination in Europe: The Position of Muslim Minorities' in V Konstadinidis (ed), *A People's Europe: Turning a Concept into Content* (Aldershot, Dartmouth, 1999), at 100 ff.

[98] See generally V Das, 'Cultural Rights and the Definition of Community' in O Mendelsohn and U Baxi (eds), *The Rights of Subordinated Peoples* (Bombay, Oxford University Press, 1994). The *Shah Bano* case is about the right to maintenance, ie the obligation of a husband to provide maintenance to the divorced wife, and whether this right was applicable to Muslims (Judgment by the Supreme Court of India on 25 April 1985).

[99] *Ibid*, at 127–128. Shah Bano's maintenance was raised from Rs. 70 to Rs. 130. The reason why this protection is in the Criminal Code is somewhat surprising. The original reason for the provision was not to protect the security of women, but to function as a 'mode of preventing vagrancy or at least preventing its consequences.' Its concern is not with individual rights but with vagrancy as a threat to public order. Not supporting indigent relatives is criminalised.

originate and develop as a result of human creativity, engagement, and curiosity about ordinary life issues. Still, such norms may come to have a grip on the mind and compel people to act in certain ways. Thus, it is possible that an activity prohibited by a certain regulation may be classified as *malum prohibitum* from the standpoint of the state, thus, possibly, subject to change and revision while, at the same time, be perceived as *malum in se* in the eyes of some people given their different cultural background and attachment.

The reason for accommodating particular cultural perceptions of duties on matters of moral indifference is not that we care for the survival of a given culture or religion. Instead, it is motivated by a deeper commitment to ensuring a minimum provision of respect for individual freedom. One part of what that commitment involves is the securing of the crucial conditions for the adequate development of personality, a precondition for the actual exercise of moral faculties. The requirement of respect is obviously not without significance for the sustainability of the co-operative scheme itself insofar as it depends on the actual exercise of such faculties. The strains imposed on the individual as a result of extensive regulation on matters of *adiaphora* that come into conflict with particular duties risk undermining the conditions for this exercise. From the standpoint of the cosmopolitan moral law, observing these duties only an introductory means of directing oneself to the moral law. Still, the legislature ought to take these duties seriously and accommodate them in the fabric of regulations, since doing so will safeguard the personal infrastructures that are essential for the development of moral personality.

To recognise the human capacity for a conception of the good is to affirm the individual's ability to reason about various factors that she is supposed to consider in deciding what to do and to assume that she will be able to form reasonable judgments. For example, when riding a motorbike, an individual must consider the risk of head injuries as well as her duty, if any, to observe a particular dress code. While legislatures are often tempted to interfere in this process of reasoning and might do so with efficacy and success, such interference may also provoke conscientious objections if the individual has arrived at a different conclusion as to what she ought to do. Objections of these kinds are not embarrassments for the claim about the possibility of developing or maintaining a scheme of social co-operation as societies become increasingly diverse. At most, they indicate the need for careful judicial supervision of regulations in multicultural societies, regulations that can often afford to be sensitive towards problems of conscience. This conclusion seems to be supported by Joseph Raz. As he notes in relation to the Sikh objection to the British crash helmet law, although the regulation in question is not paternalistic insofar as it is motivated, in part, by a public interest, ie to avoid the cost imposed on the public for injured motorcyclists, it nevertheless constitutes a 'pathetic example of bureaucratic insensitivity'.[100] The circumstance of Sikhs and others whose dress codes are not always consistent with the various legal requirements regarding dress is a contemporary problem in Western societies. Raz explains that increasingly the state is thought to have an obligation to care for the victims of various misfortunes and has, consequently, a duty to prevent such misfortunes. The measures taken by the state are often excessive since they create problems of conscience and provoke conscientious objections.[101] Even so, the recognition of this fact has not led to the development of a comprehensive account of the moral limits to individual compliance with such regulations.

An exclusive focus on values associated with a scheme of social co-operation makes it seem as though conscientious objectors must offer something in exchange for 'concessions' in the form of accommodations made by the other members of the scheme. Such an accommodation must be of value for everybody. At the same time, in the event that an objector cannot find reasons for others to consider his exemption, such as in the proclaimed value of cultural diversity, this failure can hardly mean that his cultural duties do not warrant consideration. Unless others believe in the value of cultural diversity and accept his exemption as a manifestation of that value, they will obviously not benefit from his exemption. However, it must be sufficient that the individual's observance of his cultural duties do not harm others and that the duties are consistent with the purpose of a scheme of co-operation, that is, to contribute to the welfare of others. Each and every individual's participation in each and every regulation can hardly be necessary to achieve that purpose.

The prevailing understanding of what rights and freedoms individuals have in relation to legislation regulating matters of moral indifference should be compared with that of John Locke who suggested that the *starting point* for thinking about legal restrictions of personal duties must be that particular manners, gestures, and habits are entitled to toleration. Locke delineated three fields of action according to their degree of relative importance from the standpoint of the individual as well as the sovereign legislature. These fields of action are: (1) speculative opinions and divine worship; (2) practical opinions and actions on matters of indifference; and (3) moral virtues and vices.[102] According to Locke, the first cluster of actions is entitled to absolute toleration, and covers place, time, and manner of worship (including prayer, dress, and diet). These are fields where people of religious faith tend to have religious duties. In Locke's view, these actions are to be tolerated insofar as they are done sincerely and out of conscience and to the best of the knowledge and persuasion of the subject.[103] While admitting that the legislature in principle has legislative competence over these matters,

[100] J Raz, *The Authority of Law*, above n 79, at 283–284.
[101] *Ibid.*
[102] J Locke, 'An Essay on Toleration', above n 2, at 136.
[103] *Ibid*, at 140.

Locke argued that the legislature ought to keep in mind that in religious worship nothing is indifferent.[104]

The second set of opinions and actions are also entitled to toleration, and entail what Locke defined as matters of indifference. These practices include child-rearing, polygamy, and divorce. Variations among people in these fields are to be tolerated unless a particular practice leads to disturbances or causes more inconveniences than advantages to the community. The sovereign should recognise the risk of fallibility on these matters. Legislative actions and administrative initiatives are legitimate insofar as they are intended to preserve the welfare, safety, and peace of his subjects. The laws must suit the good of all subjects.[105] Locke's approach is a general one. As such, it does not explain how we are to respond to particular cases of conscientious objection occurring in liberal democratic societies today. Even so, his claim conveys the spirit in which we should engage in these issues and seek to find answers to them given a commitment to ensure adequate respect. More importantly, it seems to give us additional reasons for taking these cases seriously and responding to them favourably.

The Limits to the Accommodationist Approach

The purpose of the analysis in this chapter has not been to discuss the specifics of accommodation, but to develop an argument about what sorts of concerns urge an accommodationist move in the case of conscientious objections against regulations that are associated with a scheme of social co-operation. However, it is necessary to consider that there may be limits as to what is practically possible to achieve in terms of cultural cases of accommodation. First of all, there might be economic constraints involved, especially if a culture demands the establishment of separate institutions (say, for educational purposes or health) as a possible solution. More importantly, however, is that an overly sensitive political climate tends to undermine the prospects of mutual respect for one another's settlement on matters of *adiaphora*.

As Locke notes, the right to toleration is not absolute, but may be restricted. The right is supposed to be exercised in the spirit of duty, sincerity and out of conscience. For example, it does not protect attempts to use religious habits, gestures, and manners in an attempt to gain power and dominance and to force or compel others to be of one's mind. However, Locke carefully pointed out that political ambition is not the fault of worship, but the product of depraved, ambitious human nature making use of all sorts of religions.[106] Thus, the modern idea of toleration was not developed—at least not originally—as a right to do what one pleases, but as a

[104] J Locke, 'An Essay on Toleration', above n 2, at 139.
[105] *Ibid*, at 140–141.
[106] *Ibid*, at 139.

right to be able to do what one believes is one's duty. That said, however, contemporary cases of conscience indicate that a religious habit may become fraught with political significance regardless of what the agent intended it to be. The politicisation of a habit does not exclusively depend on those whose habit it is, but also on the perceptions of others (whether well-founded or not) as to what the habit means.[107]

Several publicly funded school systems have been confronted with what appear to be pressing problems of conscience created by multiculturalism. While *prima facie* trivial, difference in mode of dress, diet, and prayer is not always easy to accommodate, not merely due to the practical difficulties involved in changing existing regulations, but also because of actual political climate. The French headscarf affair is an obvious example, although it should be noted that by now virtually all European states have their own headscarf affairs.[108] The question posed in these cases is whether or not to accommodate the religious dress code of a child learned from the culture at home if it is in conflict with school regulations informed by secular ideas. In France, the principle of secularity is supposed to shape the spirit of French public institutions and this commitment seems to legitimise enormous social pressure when anybody seems to be acting in a way that contradicts that principle. The debates surrounding the permissibility of Islamic headscarves in French schools focus on the possible pressure exerted by the Islamic minorities on their children and less on the pressure exerted by the French public culture in relation to these minorities. Thus, in 1989, the French *Conseil d'Etat* held that

> *dans les établissements scolaires, le port par les élèves de signes par lesquels il entendent manifester leur appartenance à une religion n'est pas par lui-même incompatible avec le principe de laïcité, dans la mesure où il constitue l'exercice de la liberté d'expression et de manifestation de croyances religieuses, mais que cette liberté ne saurait permettre aux élèves d'arborer des signes d'appartenance religieuse qui, par leur nature, par les conditions dans lesquelles ils seraient portés individuellement ou collectivement, ou par leur caractère ostentatoire ou revendicatif, constitueraient un acte de pression, de provocation, de prosélytisme ou de propagande, porteraient atteinte à la dignité ou à la liberté de l'élève ou d'autres membres de la communauté éducative, com-*

[107] I thank Steven Lukes for alerting me to this problem.

[108] See generally WAR Shadid and PS van Koningsveld, *Religious Freedom and the Position of Islam in Western Europe* (Kampen, Kok Pharos Publishing House, 1995), esp 86 ff for a comparative analysis of headscarf affairs in several countries (France, Belgium, England, and the Netherlands).

> *promettraient leur santé ou leur sécurité, perturberaient le déroulement des activités d'enseignement et le rôle éducatif des enseignants, enfin troubleraient l'ordre dans l'établissement ou le fonctionnement normal du service public.*[109]

While the council did not rule out the possibility of accommodating the Islamic dress code in state schools, the issue became heavily politicised. This politicisation led the French Parliament to adopt a legal provision to be incorporated into the French educational code according to which:

> *Dans les écoles, les collèges et les lycées publics, le port de signes ou tenues par lesquels les élèves manifestent ostensiblement une appartenance religieuse est interdit.*[110]

If the headscarf is instrumentalised and used for purposes other than religious ones, for example as a symbol of resistance, the right to observe one's dress code may be legitimately restricted. If others in one's environment perceive one's act as political, it may be impossible to avoid politicisation, no matter how sincerely and conscientiously the right is exercised. Still, the argument that the right to toleration is affected by the actual political climate in one's place of living is not a legitimate ground for restricting its exercise. Though it can be difficult to ensure respect for this right in all places and at all times precisely because it purports to protect freedom on matters of *adiaphora*, matters which people, quite paradoxically tend to care most about, this complication does not render the right less significant. On the contrary, the difficulties related to the actual implementation of the right to toleration necessitate a reaffirmation of this right and an explanation of its meaning and implications in multicultural societies where particular conditions for adequate development and maintenance of personality are in risk of being so

[109] *Avis No* 346893 *du* 27 Novembre 1989. *Assemblée générale plénière* (1990). *L'actualité juridique - Droit administratif* (AJDA) 39 (1990). For a translation of the legal opinion into English, see K Boyle and J Sheen (eds), *Freedom of Religion and Belief: A World Report* (London, Routledge, 1997), 299. The translated paragraph reads: 'Freedom of expression and freedom to manifest religious beliefs stated under the Constitution do not allow students to wear religious symbols which, by their nature, by the conditions under which they are worn either individually or collectively, or by their ostentatious or assertive character, amounts to acts of pressure, provocation, proselytism, or propaganda, which could affect the dignity or freedom of the student or of other members of the educative community, thus compromising their health or security, disturbing teaching activities and the educational role of teachers, finally, upsetting the order in the school or the smooth running of the public sector.'

[110] *Loi no* 2004–228 *du* 15–3–2004 (JO du 17–3–2004) *Texte adressé aux rectrices et recteurs d'académie; aux inspectrices et inspecteurs d'académie, directeurs et directrices des services départementaux de l'éducation nationale* (2004) 21 *Bulletin Officiel* 1043. For a translation of the legal opinion into English, see K Boyle and J Sheen (eds), *Freedom of Religion and Belief: A World Report*, above n 109, at 300. The translated paragraph reads: 'Students must not wear any ostentatious distinguishing sign, in clothing, or otherwise, which aims to promote a religious belief; also proscribed is any proselytising behaviour which goes beyond simple religious convictions and aims to convince other students or members of the education community and to serve as an example to them.'

blatantly thwarted. The same difficulties also urge an account of the duties that flow from this right; these duties are not addressed to public institutions alone, but also to citizens as participants in political life.[111]

The French national prohibition of the headscarf in state schools should be compared with a recent German case where the administrative court in Lüneberg permitted a Muslim woman to follow her dress code in her role as schoolteacher. The court emphasised the importance of exercising her right responsibly, and that whether it is practically possible for her to make use of the right depends on how others perceive her act. Furthermore, it stressed the value of viewing educational institutions, not only as institutions of learning, but also as performing a mediating role between the public realm and civil society.[112] The German understanding that the state school system is not part of the public realm, but constitutes a shared institutional context between public and civic life seems better suited for cultural accommodation of conscientious objections by pupils, teachers, and other staff on matters of *adiaphora*.

Notwithstanding the recognition of freedom of conscience and its relevance for state schools in multicultural societies, its implementation might be difficult. Another German case amply illustrates this point. It concerns the use of Christian symbols in state education in Bavaria, regulated by a law requiring that the crucifix should be displayed in every state school class room. A parent objected to the presence of a crucifix with an image of the bleeding body of Christ in his three daughters' classroom. Although the local priest agreed to replace the crucifix with a plain wooden cross, the parent pursued his campaign against the Bavarian law and its administration in the face of considerable opposition. In 1995, the German Constitutional Court ruled that the Bavarian regulation violated freedom of conscience.[113] Even so, local public campaigns to keep the crucifixes or crosses, fuelled by memories of their removal during the Nazi era, led to a new draft law affirming the requirements to display the crucifix or cross but also to the establishment of an appeal system. Hence, the issue remains unsettled; in the meantime, no crucifixes or crosses are displayed in the classroom of the three children.[114] The case indicates that conscientious objectors tend to bring about social changes though they may be difficult and take time.

[111] For an account of tolerance as an attitude of citizens as participants in formal and informal politics, see T Scanlon, 'The Difficulty of Tolerance' in D Heyd (ed), *Toleration: An Elusive Virtue* (Princeton, Princeton University Press, 1996).

[112] VG Lüneburg Urt. v. 16. 10. 2000–1 A 98/00, *Neue Juristische Wochenschrift*, 3/2001, 767. See also E Böckenförde, '"Kopftuchstreit" auf dem richtigen Weg?' (2001) 3 *Neue Juristische Wochenschrift* 723.

[113] BVerfG 16.05.1995–1BvR 1087/91, *Neue Juristische Wochenschrift* Ausgabe 38/1995 (2477–2482).

[114] K Boyle and J Sheen (eds), *Freedom of Religion and Belief: A World Report* (London, Routledge, 1997), at 309.

One issue that has not been discussed so far is how to respond to the problems posed by conscientious observance of wicked or abusive norms that are in conflict with state regulations. This is so since the present study is limited, for the most part, to culture in action which is neither right nor wrong according to independent moral norms, but whose observance is fraught with significance for the individual whose culture it is. While possibly equally important in the eyes of the individual, wicked and harmful norms are obviously not morally indifferent. The fact that observance of some norms harms others is a reason for not accommodating them. The insistence on limits to what is permissible for any culture to do is not meant to encourage public neglect and ignorance of cultural norms that harm others. Rather, national public institutions should give them attention and adjust their own cultural equipment so as to be able to protect those who are abused and maltreated in the name of culture. While practices involving maltreatment and violence are accepted in several cultures, they are rarely advisable, and seldom conscientious in spirit. However, they might be, and this reality must be taken into account. Female circumcision amounts to such a practice. The recognition that this practice is a matter of conscience in the eyes of those who circumcise and support circumcision explains the difficulties involved in eradicating the practice through the use of the coercive powers of law.[115] While the criminalisation of female circumcision may be important to indicate a state's official position on the unacceptability of that practice due to the serious harms it causes, criminalisation may have but a marginal effect in terms of eradicating the practice or bringing the perpetrators to justice.[116] As Parekh explains, a more effective and respectful way of responding to harmful norms may be through inter-cultural dialogue.[117] Thus, it is not sufficient to criminalise the practice; additional measures are necessary, usually non-coercive methods consisting of discussion, dialogue, and dissemination of information about the practice's effects on one's health, to efficiently eradicate the practice.

CONCLUSION

The purpose of this chapter has been to explain the importance of cultural differences on matters of *adiaphora*, in particular, if there are cultural duties involved, from the standpoint of the individual. To this end, it developed an

[115] For John Locke's argument about the irrationality to compel others by force to be of one's mind, see J Locke, 'An Essay on Toleration', above n 2, at 155–156. For doubts about the irrationality of persecution and the need for substantive moral argument to explain what is wrong about persecution, see J Waldron, 'Locke, Toleration, and the Rationality of Persecution' in J Waldron, *Liberal Rights*, above n 37, at 113.

[116] See 'Comments to the Swedish government Proposition 1998/99:70: Female Circumcision—Abolishment of the Requirement on Double Criminal Liability'.

[117] B Parekh, *Rethinking Multiculturalism*, above n 73, at 268 ff.

argument about the inadequacy of an exclusive focus on the human capacity for sociability in a variety of environments to explain these differences, and alluded to the importance of considering other factors at play as well, notably social pressure and instruction, to explain the roots of these differences.

In multicultural societies, these differences can give rise to conscientious objections to state regulations that conflict with particular cultural duties. These kinds of objections are particularly frequent in relation to mode of dress, diet, and prayer. It was suggested that the human conscience is not solely concerned with activities such as contemplation and participation as a citizen in political life, but often preoccupied with ordinary life issues. Indeed, it is not unusual that ethical, religious, and philosophical doctrines entail views on how to raise one's children, how to relate to the other sex, to one's parents and the elderly, how to dress, and so on. These views have developed as a result of a human capacity for a conception of the good exercised in a certain context and informed by a particular stock of ideas. They may be interpreted as uncompromisable rules that compel their observers to act in a certain way in any environment regardless of consequence. This is the upshot of cultural duties on matters of *adiaphora*.

Why do cultural duties matter from the standpoint of human rights? The argument for caring about problems of conscience confronted by individuals whose cultures have not been considered in the adoption of state regulations is based on a commitment to ensure an adequate provision of respect for individual freedom. This commitment requires that a scheme of rights is not merely the same for all, but that it is adequate from the standpoint of any given individual in the light of the sort of life he or she seeks to lead. In a multicultural society, it is only reasonable to expect that the actual exercise of a human capacity for a conception of the good will result in a plurality of life-ways especially when considering the reality of different educational institutions whose instructional programs are informed by different schemes of interpretation and comprehensive doctrines. Neither the schemes of interpretation nor the doctrines are necessarily liberal in spirit or content. Nevertheless, quite regardless of whether we favour a liberal outlook on matters of *adiaphora* and seek to develop educational policies in that direction, an account of conscientious objections and their relevance for human rights must consider that by no means everybody is liberal about their particular habits, manners, and gestures. What ultimately matter are the hardships a conscientious individual suffers as a result of an inability to observe his cultural duties without, at the same time, breaking the official law.

While specific settlements on issues of *adiaphora* are irrelevant from the standpoint of cosmopolitan moral law, they nevertheless matter immensely for people in their ordinary lives. Such settlements constitute infrastructures that are essential to the development and maintenance of personality, and, ultimately, moral personality. It may be difficult for an individual whose cultural infrastructure is at stake to try to convince others with whom she shares a diverse society to care about her way of life in the name of, say, cultural diversity; indeed, others may find her practices offensive, wrongful, or threatening. However, if we instead explain the need for cultural accommodation on the basis of what we know about the relationship between cultural infrastructure and personality, including moral personality, it is not necessary to seek to persuade others about the more general value of this or that way of life as such.

7

Conflict, Participation, and the Risk of Exclusion

THE ACCOUNT OF culture developed so far gives the impression that multiculturalism does not necessarily have any political significance. Evidently, vast differences in terms of suitable cultural equipment and cultural duties on matters of *adiaphora* among the inhabitants of a state are directly relevant to its legislative process. The circumstance faced by those lacking suitable cultural equipment, or whose compelling culture-dependent norms on matters of moral indifference are in conflict with state regulations, calls for collective action, including legislative revisions and, possibly, the distribution of legal exemptions. I do not intend to dwell on the moral reasons behind such actions, but only note that, contrary to what the privatisation approach indicates, issues related to multiculturalism may enter the legislative process in an obvious and welcoming sense. From this standpoint, the legislative process is a critical device for ensuring that a scheme of rights is effective as well as adequate in the eyes of those who are supposed to benefit from it.

This chapter shifts the focus onto a different function of the political process in a multicultural context, namely its potential capacity for resolving cultural conflicts. The shift of focus is urged by the relative frequency of conflicts that allegedly have their source in the social and, as the case may be, universalistic aspects inherent in several conceptions of the good. Even if far from all cultural conflicts escalate to the point where a political settlement is warranted, some of them do, and it is the recognition of this fact that constitutes the starting point for this chapter. There is a second motive for paying attention to cultural conflicts and their relevance to the political process and this has to do with their impact on individual rights and freedoms. It is not unusual that such conflicts involve attempts either to impose a culture-specific prohibition universally and categorically, regardless of disagreement, or to maintain such a prohibition as a matter of law irrespective of how unreasonable it may appear in the eyes of those whose aims it seriously frustrates as a result. It is necessary, therefore, to discuss whether it is reasonable to exclude some conceptions of the good from the ambit of political life.

The analysis undertaken in this chapter is not meant to indicate how specific cultural conflicts ought to be resolved. Instead, it examines the usefulness of two framework models for resolving any such conflict. These models are defined as the 'liberal' and 'democratic' ones. While conceding that democracy and participation seem superior in the light of the indeterminacy that plagues the liberal model, there are allegedly also difficulties with the democratic model, not least because of the inherent risk faced by those whose cultures differ from the majority culture of being excluded from the ambit of legislative discussion. Of particular interest in this respect is the usefulness of the criterion of reasonableness developed in political liberalism as a measure of what sorts of issues may or may not be discussed in the legislative process in a diverse society. It is suggested that the idea of considering 'unreasonableness' as a legitimate ground for excluding issues from that process should be treated with caution from the standpoint of respect, not merely because of the risk of abuse of that option in confrontation with offensive or threatening claims or demands, but also because the right to take part in political affairs must reasonably entail a right to criticise, dissent from, and protest against the current political settlements of cultural conflicts.

RESPONDING TO CULTURAL CONFLICTS

The relative frequency of conflicts having their source in cultural differences indicates the need to consider suitable models for conflict-resolution in multicultural societies. This section is devoted to an analysis of the principles behind two models. It seeks to answer the question of by what principle cultural conflicts are to be resolved. To this end, it assesses the meanings of the principle of equal freedom and the principle of equal participation as well as their practical implications on fair and efficient conflict resolution. The approach advanced should be compared with that of Simon Caney who articulates three solutions to the problem in focus. Apart from the liberal and the democratic solutions, he also analyses the perfectionist solution. In this study, however, the third solution is not an alternative since it takes seriously the fact of disagreement about principle.[1]

Cultural Conflicts

There are at least three different types of conflicts having their source in cultural differences. One type of conflict occurs when people seek to exercise their rights (or what they think are their rights) in a place inhabited by others with different cultural attachments. In an important sense, such conflict may be inevitable if those seeking to make use of their rights have vastly different

[1] See S Caney, 'Diversity and the Lexical Priority of the Right to Equal Freedom' (1997) 17 *Oxford Journal of Legal Studies* 147.

ideas of what they wish to use their rights for. Thus, one class of conflict has its source in the sheer diversity of ways in which rights-holders try to take advantage of their rights. The conflicts occur by default, so to speak, and are due to incompatible aims. This is how theorists of rights usually depict the root of conflicting rights-uses. As Joseph Raz asserts, conflict is endemic to value pluralism in all its forms; in a multicultural society this pluralism is manifested as a conflict between competing and incompatible ways of life.[2] For the purpose of the present analysis, what is relevant about this type of conflict is that the agents are not—at least not initially—interested in one another's particular exercises of rights. For example, imagine a group of people leading a life in accordance with religious prescriptions. They believe that rightful worship requires the performance of a ritual every Friday night. After some time, their weekly gatherings are totally ruined by an entrepreneur who has opened a club next door that turns out to be immensely popular. The sect would not pre-eminently be interested in stopping what is going on next door were it not for its serious disturbance of the calm and serenity necessary to their ritual.

Compare this conflict with that between the proselytising Jehovah's Witness and the Greek Orthodox woman dealt with by the European Court of Human Rights in 1993.[3] Unlike the sect in the previous example, Jehovah's Witnesses take an active interest in the belief and actions of others, and so do the Greek Orthodox. The former are in the business of converting people, while the latter perceive this type of activity as an insult to their beliefs and seek to curb them through law. This conflict is exacerbated by rival beliefs about rightful conduct in a plural society. The point is that both the Witnesses and the Orthodox could argue that respecting their beliefs is a crucial condition for them to be able to pursue their understanding of the good. It is as much part of a Witness's conception of the good to proselytise as it is part of a Greek Orthodox conception of the good not to be put under pressure to convert to a different faith. This conflict really seems more complicated than the first type of conflict discussed in the previous paragraph. Unlike that conflict, the second type of conflict is aggravated by a deeper disagreement about decent conduct in a plural society.

A third kind of conflict, at the intersection with the second, is that between, for example, those whose conceptions of the good entail a commitment to secularist ideology (on the one hand) and practising female Muslims (on the other). These conflicts are currently present, for example, in Turkey and, in a less aggressive form, in France.[4] The secularists affirm a view of the ideal society free from religious symbols without consideration for those practising Muslim women who believe it is their duty to cover

[2] J Raz, 'Multiculturalism: A Liberal Perspective', in J Raz, *Ethics in the Public Domain* (New York, Oxford University Press, 1994), at 179–180.

[3] *Kokkinakis v Greece* Series A no 260–A (1993) 17 EHRR 397.

[4] See chapter six of this book.

their head wherever they happen to be, including in state-run facilities.[5] The conflict between the British mainstream culture and a faction of British Muslims similarly captures the character of the third type of conflict. The British Muslim Parliament expresses its concern with what it perceives as signs of serious moral decay in Britain.[6] The Parliament declares that Muslims cannot lead a decent life nor raise their children properly in a place that accepts gambling, drug use, and sexual promiscuity.[7]

The difference between these types of conflicts has to do with the degree of sensitivity towards the activities of others as well as the degree to which a given conception of the good has articulated a more general standpoint on what society ought to be like in response to its discontent. The sensitivity does not necessarily play an essential role in explaining the *source* of the conflict. As the first example conveys, this sentiment can be a *consequence* of the conflict that occurs between mutually disinterested individuals. As conceded here, however, that conflict is usually less problematic to resolve than those having their source in conflicting conceptions of the good, both of which are (extremely) sensitive to the actions of others.

The second and third types of cultural conflicts draw attention to the fact that far from every conception is necessarily individualistic in spirit and content. That is to say, it is a mistake to assume that the vast majority of people lead their entire lives without any opinion whatsoever on the more general permissibility of certain activities. On the contrary, a more careful consideration of the specific contents of actual conceptions of the good reveals that several, if not most conceptions, include an account of the social environment. Indeed, as Peter Jones notes, most conceptions are social in

[5] See generally Bureau of Democracy, Human Rights and Labor, US Department of State, *Turkey Country Report on Human Rights Practices for 1997* (Bureau of Democracy, Human Rights and Labor, US Department of State, 1998). The Turkish Government periodically enforces a 50-year-old ban on the wearing of religious head garments in government offices and other state-run facilities. According to human rights monitoring groups, some women wearing the hijab—the scarf worn by Muslim women—have lost their jobs in the public sector as nurses and teachers. 99% of the population are Muslim. The Constitution establishes Turkey as a secular state.

[6] It should be noted that not all British Muslims support this institution. Michael King informs us that: 'it is clear that many, and probably the majority of Muslims in Britain would largely dissociate themselves from these separatist ambitions and from the more extreme statements that emerge from time to time from the Muslim Parliament.' At the same time, however, 'it would be a mistake to discount those grievances of Muslims over their past treatment and the anxieties for the future that have given Siddiqui his support and guidance.' See M King, 'Introduction' in M King (ed), *God's Law Versus State Law: The Construction of an Islamic Identity in Western Europe* (London, Grey Seal, 1995), at 8. The Muslim Parliament of Great Britain originated from a study into the Muslim situation by the Muslim Institute, London, under the leadership of Dr Kalim Siddiqui, during the Rushdie affair in 1989–90. It declined rapidly following his death in 1996, and is now defunct to all intents and purposes. See the Institute of Contemporary Social Thought, 'Short Introduction to the Muslim Parliament' [available at: http://www.islamicthought.org/mp-intro.html#intro] last visited on 12 January 2005.

[7] See *The Muslim Parliament: Building a Better Future for Muslims in Britain* (London, May 1995) [available at:<http://ummah.net/mp/mp-doc.htm>]. Last visited on 27 January 2000.

character and bound up with a conception of the right society.[8] John Rawls expresses a similar position in his articulation of what a conception of the good consists of; that is,

> a more or less determinate scheme of final ends, that is, ends we want to realize for their own sake, as well as attachments to other persons and loyalties to various groups and associations. These attachments and loyalties give rise to devotions and affections, and so the flourishing of the persons and associations who are the objects of these sentiments is also part of our conception of the good.[9]

The claim about the social character of conceptions of the good is true for both religious and secular conceptions of the good. It is also true for communal conceptions.

The social dimension can be restricted to a concern for behaviour of like-minded people (and others *expected* to be like-minded by virtue of their ascribed membership). However, the same dimension may also have inherent *universalistic* tendencies or, as contended here, develop such tendencies in reaction to external pressure to assimilate or convert. For example, even if an individualist is not essentially in the business of telling others what to think and do, to the extent that her environment is dominated by communitarians, she, too, is likely to develop opinions about the ideal social environment. In the event that communitarians and individualists are brought into relation with one another under the same set of laws, it is only reasonable to expect that these differences will create incentives for the like-minded to cluster together and that both parties will pay attention to—even try to compare and evaluate—how the other goes about its social business (eg household, child-rearing, family relations, business organisation, etc). If the circumstances so warrant, the communitarians may seek to assimilate the individualists to their way of life, since, from their standpoint, all people may be expected to behave in the way prescribed by their authority. Such a move is likely to be met with great resistance since it is in direct competition with the essence of an individualistic outlook, assuming, as it does, that the subordination of feelings and aspirations to a social authority would be wrong and amount to self-denial. Hence, it is likely that not only communitarian conceptions of the good, but also individualistic conceptions, will have views of what the ideal social environment ought to be like in a plural society.

One reason for assuming that several conceptions have universalistic tendencies has to do with the existence of the diverse bodies of ethical, religious, or philosophical thought discussed at length in chapter six of this book.

[8] P Jones, 'The Ideal of the Neutral State' in RE Goodin and A Reeve (eds) *Liberal Neutrality* (New York, Routledge, 1989), at 28.
[9] J Rawls, *Political Liberalism* (New York, Columbia University Press, 1995), at 19.

Such doctrines cover social and, as Jeremy Waldron points out, political concerns and aspirations. As he puts it:

> if a religious or philosophical tradition has nurtured a rich and resourceful conception of the good, it would be odd to expect its priests, ideologues, or philosophers not to have developed that conception also in a social and political direction. Social and political concerns are, after all, among the most pressing concerns we have: it would be odd if a tradition had views about what made life worth living, but no views at all about the basis on which we ought to live our lives together.[10]

The claim that the conduct rules generated by a certain doctrine are currently observed only by a few is not necessarily a sign that the doctrine is parochial. Its universalistic tendencies may be held back by other factors, for example, a disadvantageous balance of power or a sudden loss of adherents who have converted to a different religion or philosophy. It may also depend on a deliberate commitment to limit the scope of application of the conduct rules prescribed by the doctrine on the basis of respect for the right to toleration.

It is not unusual (and the previous chapter sought to make this point clear) that doctrines (often religious) tend to be associated with a list of acts *mala in se* (eg abortion, gambling, proselytising, apostasy, drug use, etc). Such doctrines lend support and affirmation to the belief that one's convictions about wrongful conduct are true for everybody. Therefore, attempts may be made to enforce these prohibitions universally and categorically. Undeniably, many religions have a historical record of seeing themselves as guardians of truth:

> Each religion has a tendency to consider that it is the sole guardian of truth and is duty bound to behave accordingly, an attitude which is not always conducive to inter-religious tolerance. What is more, each religion may be tempted to fight against whatever it defines as deviant either within its own faith or at its boundaries, which is equally unlikely to encourage internal religious tolerance.[11]

However, the temptation or urge to fight against wrongs done in the world is not a feature exclusive to religious conceptions of the good, but also shared by those whose conceptions are secular in spirit and content. It is an urge similarly shared by environmentalists, feminists, pro-life activists, human rights promoters, pacifists, and adherents to the anti-globalisation movements. In radical cases, these movements make their own good depend on accomplishing what they believe is the good for all.

[10] J Waldron, *Law and Disagreement* (Oxford, Clarendon Press, 1999), at 161.
[11] K Boyle and J Sheen (eds), *Freedom of Religion and Belief: A World Report* (London, Routledge, 1997), at *xv*.

To tolerate actions while knowing (or believing that one knows) that such acts are not merely idiotic, but outright sinful can be difficult.[12] It may be felt unbearable to tolerate what is going on in society, whether it be prostitution, gambling, heavy pollution, the destruction of a historic monument or, much more seriously, torture, starvation, ethnic cleansing, and so on. Moreover, as Susan Mendus explains, sometimes we may simply feel without reason that an activity simply cannot continue:

> The intolerable is the unbearable. And we may simply feel, believe, conclude without reason, that something is unbearable and must be stopped.[13]

It may be irrelevant whether the actions in question take place in one's neighbourhood or elsewhere. As Immanuel Kant contends, a violation of human rights is 'felt everywhere'.[14] The idea of what is tolerable is obviously not the same for all, but depends, in part, on one's degree of moral, religious, or social consciousness and, in part, on one's perception of one's ability to make a difference. The point of the principle of toleration is to moderate the temptation to take measures to change the behaviour of others, whether it involves disrespect for what are believed to be the requirements of divine or moral law or simply something felt to be 'unbearable'. At the same time, however, many of us maintain that unrestricted toleration is itself a crime.[15]

The choice of avenues for shaping the social environment in a way that better accords with particular convictions about right and wrong obviously depends not merely on the strength of one's conviction, but also on what one believes to be the more effective method for influencing the conduct and belief of others. A belief about what is the 'true belief' creates incentives for proselytising, missionary, or promotional activities on the marketplace of ideas. It may also create incentives to take part in, and seek to influence, the political process. Thus, from having been characterised in terms of diverse attempts to exercise individual rights to freedom or religion and freedom of conscience, the aspiration to shape or control the behaviour of others might be transformed into political aims.

This is, in broad terms, the background to the occurrence of cultural conflicts in social and political life in multicultural societies. Each of these

[12] T Scanlon, 'The Difficulty of Tolerance' in D Heyd (ed), *Toleration: An Elusive Virtue* (Princeton, Princeton University Press, 1996).

[13] S Mendus, 'Introduction' in S Mendus and D Edwards (eds), *On Toleration* (New York, Oxford University Press, 1987), at 2–3.

[14] I Kant, 'To Perpetual Peace. A Philosophical Sketch (1795)' in I Kant, *Perpetual Peace and Other Essays,* T Humphrey (trans) (Indianapolis, Hacket Publishing Company, 1983), sec 360. According to Kant: 'because a (narrower or wider) community widely prevails among the Earth's peoples, a transgression of rights in *one* place in the world is felt everywhere.'

[15] But see C Kukathas, 'Cultural Toleration' in I Shapiro and W Kymlicka (eds), *Ethnicity and Group Rights. Nomos XXXIX* (New York, New York University Press, 1997).

conflicts obviously raises questions about respect for individual freedom and, more precisely, directs attention to the possible need to impose legal restrictions on rights-uses. However, as the conflicts indicate, what counts as necessary or reasonable restrictions on the exercise of rights is something that the rights-bearers are likely to disagree about. This is not to say that these kinds of disagreements necessarily become politicised. Whether they do depends, in part, on the extent to which the rights-bearers are able and willing to tolerate one another's activities even if they consider them to be outright sinful and amount to serious wrongs. Nevertheless, if a conflict becomes imbued with political significance it is of the utmost importance to resolve it. The contention that cultural conflicts can become politically relevant is indicated by the existence of state regulations that are best understood as settlements of such conflicts. The laws may have been considered legitimate in one period, but are no longer so. While many of us believe that the conflicts and disagreements in focus are unfortunate given their adverse impact on individual freedom and, for this reason, should remain outside the ambit of political life, it may be necessary all the same to admit that this is a normative claim about the ideal relation between cultural conflicts and the political process. There is no guarantee that this is how every subject of a legal system reasons about this matter. The belief in the need for political settlements of cultural conflicts is manifested by the Turkish ban on headscarves in government offices and state-run facilities.[16] The Greek prohibition of proselytising is yet another example.[17] The specific contents of these state laws obviously do not represent what all inhabitants of Turkey and Greece in principle can agree upon; instead, such laws are controversial official positions of multicultural societies in the face of difficult conflicts and disagreements. These laws—unfair or not—represent authoritative settlements of such conflicts. The settlements are not final, but can change in

[16] See K Boyle and J Sheen (eds), *Freedom of Religion and Belief: A World Report*, above n 11, at 389–390. Political parties, trade unions and associations may be closed down if they are held to violate the principle of secularism. According to the Turkish Constitutional Court, 'from a legal point of view, in the classical sense, secularism means that religion may not interfere with the state [affairs] and the latter not with religious affairs.' Turkish secularism is defined as follows: (1) religion is not to be effective and dominant in state affairs; (2) secondly, in such parts of religion as relate to the spiritual life of the individual, a constitutional guarantee recognises unlimited freedom, without any discrimination; (3) *in such parts of religion as go beyond the spiritual life of the individual and as relate to actions and behaviours which affect societal life, restrictions may be imposed*, and abuse and exploitation of religion may be prohibited, with a view to protecting public order, public safety and the public interest; and (4) as the guardian of public order and public rights, the state may be given a power of control and supervision with respect to religious rights and freedoms [author's emphasis].

[17] Law no 1672/1939. In section 2.2 of that law the term 'proselytism' is defined as: 'any direct or indirect attempt to intrude on the religious beliefs of a person of a different religious persuasion (*eterodoxos*), with the aim of undermining those beliefs, either by any kind of inducement or promise of an inducement or moral support of material assistance, or by fraudulent means or by taking advantage of his inexperience, trust, need, low intellect or naïvety.' *Kokkinakis v Greece* Series A no 260–A (1993) 17 EHRR 397.

response to, say a change in public opinion, international political pressure, or a judgment of an international court.

The Principle of Equal Freedom

By what principle are the cultural conflicts outlined in the previous section supposed to be resolved? Let us begin with the first example of conflict that is familiar to theorists of rights, namely the example of the sect *versus* the club owner. It originates as a result of the fact that two aims are incompatible with one another. As Hillel Steiner explains, 'several pursuits can and do obstruct one another. We unavoidably restrict one another's freedom.'[18] He continues by noting that an exclusive focus on rights fails to provide an answer to the question of what constitutes a fair settlement of such conflicts. Instead, when rights are in conflict with one another, it is necessary to shift the focus onto justice; justice addresses how a set of restrictions on diverse rights-uses ought to be arranged.[19]

One liberal proposition on how to resolve this conflict is to apply the principle of equal freedom.[20] This principle stipulates that a set of constraints on conduct must satisfy two conditions:

1. no two actions are permitted by the set of constraints to conflict with one another; and
2. for each individual who is subject to the set of constraints, the range of actions permitted by it must be adequate for the pursuit of his ends.[21]

According to Jeremy Waldron, the first condition may usefully be referred to as the requirement of *compossibility*[22] and the second as that of *adequacy*. He explains that, by itself, compossibility concerns the relation between actions, and is not directly a relation between ends.[23] That is to say, compossibility pays no attention to the worth of a particular settlement on matters of *adiaphora* in the eyes of a given individual, but is solely concerned with the compatibility of the activities involved in that settlement with the activities of all other settlements that may come into conflict with them. Compossibility does not indicate whose activities ought to be constrained in order to secure that compatibility. Thus, for example, it does not tell us how the conflict between, say, the religious sect and the club owner is to be resolved. Nor does it tell us how to resolve, for example, the conflict between the secularists and the practising Muslims. In other words, the condition of

[18] H Steiner, *An Essay on Rights* (Cambridge Mass, Blackwell Publishers, 1994), at 2.
[19] *Ibid.*
[20] My discussion of the liberal solution is heavily indebted to Jeremy Waldron's analysis in J Waldron, 'Toleration and Reasonableness', in D Castiglione and C McKinnon (eds), *The Culture of Toleration in Diverse Societies: Reasonable Tolerance* (Manchester, Manchester University Press, 2003), 13–37.
[21] *Ibid*, at 14.
[22] See generally H Steiner, *An Essay on Rights*, above n 18, at 86–101.
[23] J Waldron, 'Toleration and Reasonableness', above n 20, at 16.

compossibility yields indeterminate results. In an important sense, the approach is similar to that of Hobbes as articulated in the *Law of Compleasance* (cited in the previous chapter) except for the fact that, unlike contemporary liberal rights theorists, Hobbes took seriously the lack of natural fit. Well aware of the fact that actions are not always compossible with one another, Hobbes propounded that each must strive to accommodate himself to the rest. Otherwise, we are in constant risk of endangering peace. Each must square his actions so as to fit the actions of all others. Who, in the end, is to give way when actions are in conflict with one another is irrelevant; what is crucial is that *somebody* does.[24]

Does the second criterion of adequacy indicating the significance of a certain action from the standpoint of the individual performing that action yield a determinate answer as to how a conflict ought to be resolved? Adequacy stipulates that a given constraint must be adequate to the pursuit of one's particular ends. As suggested in chapter six, this requirement may call for revisions of state regulations in the light of changes in the cultural make-up of subjects, especially when such regulations give rise to conscientious objections. Even so, that argument essentially focuses on individualistic understandings of the good; such conceptions are obviously more hospitable to accommodation. This is so because an individual with a truly individualistic conception of the good does not challenge the justice of the regulation which he fails to comply with, but only refers to his (moral or instructed) conscience. As also suggested in chapter six, the criterion of adequacy requires us to pay attention to state regulations that seriously undermine the minimum conditions necessary for the development and maintenance of personality. However, it does not take account of the fact that some conceptions entail the belief that the realisation of certain aims presupposes a certain behaviour by others. As the second illustration of the type of cultural conflict in focus indicates, the Greek Orthodox population has prohibited proselytising on the basis that this activity seriously undermines the possibility of realising a Greek Orthodox conception of the good. As Waldron points out, these sorts of complications in real life cannot simply be ignored in the formulation of principles of justice for a plural society. Thus, it is necessary to consider more carefully what sorts of conflicts occur in a multicultural society and advance a 'second-best' principle stipulating how they ought to be resolved.[25] The principle of equal freedom plainly fails.

Are there any more specific liberal accounts available? John Rawls introduces the criterion of reasonableness as a measure for taking account of the worth of a conception of the good from the standpoint of a given

[24] T Hobbes, *Leviathan* (Cambridge, Cambridge University Press, 1997), at 106. See also chapter six of this book.

[25] J Waldron, 'Toleration and Reasonableness', above n 20, at 34.

individual. On his view, some conceptions are 'unreasonable' and ought to be given no weight in the resolution of conflicts with 'reasonable' conceptions. The distinction between 'reasonable' and 'unreasonable' conceptions may help an arbitrator to resolve a conflict between incompatible aims. Still, how do we know what is a 'reasonable' as opposed to a 'unreasonable' conception? According to Rawls, to be 'reasonable' means, first of all, a willingness to share the social world with others. One's willingness to do so influences one's actual formulation and pursuit of the good. Indeed, it is this claim that lies at the heart of the idea of the priority of the right over the good. According to Rawls:

> The principles of right, and so of justice, put limits on what satisfactions have value; they impose restrictions on what are reasonable conceptions of one's good. In drawing up plans and in deciding on aspirations men are to take these constraints into account.[26]

Jeremy Waldron makes a similar claim. In his view,

> people must be prepared to tailor and discipline their conceptions of the good so they fit together into a just and practicable social structure.[27]

Besides being willing to adjust and revise one's conception of the good so as to fit others, Rawls' notion of 'reasonable' requires that an individual's conception of the good must be intelligible in the light of what he defines as the 'burdens of judgement'.[28] The 'burdens of judgement' explain differing judgements among reasonable people as the outcome of

> the many hazards involved in the correct (and conscientious) exercise of our powers of reason and judgement in the ordinary course of political life.[29]

The burdens refer to the difficulty of balancing claims against one another, against common practices, and institutional arrangements. The difficulty involves prioritising among cherished values. It is also created by conflicting and complex empirical and scientific evidence which is hard to evaluate. We may agree about what sorts of considerations are relevant when discussing a given issue, but we nevertheless disagree about their relative weight, and arrive at different judgements about what to do. Furthermore, most concepts are vague and subject to hard cases and this indeterminacy means that it is necessary to rely on judgements and interpretations (and judgements

[26] J Rawls, *Theory of Justice* (Cambridge Mass, Belknap Press of Harvard University Press, 1999), at 27.

[27] J Waldron, 'Toleration and Reasonableness', above n 20, at 21.

[28] *Ibid*, at 10. For a full articulation of the 'burdens of judgement', see J Rawls, *Political Liberalism* (New York, Columbia Univesity Press, 1995), at 54–58.

[29] *Ibid*, at 56.

about interpretations) within some range.[30] Finally, our assessment of evidence and the weighing of moral and political values are shaped, at least in part, by our total experience (in the whole course of life).

In the light of this definition of 'reasonable' is it possible to judge conceptions of the good involved in the cultural conflicts in focus as 'unreasonable' and for this reason give them no weight when seeking to resolve such conflicts? For example, should the Turkish and French secularists be considered unreasonable? Alternatively, should the Turkish and French Muslims be regarded unreasonable in their insistence on conveying religious symbols in public institutions? Are Jehovah's Witnesses unreasonable given their mission to try to convert others to be of their mind? Are the Greek Orthodox believers unreasonable in their demands that others respect their beliefs? Are the British Muslims unreasonable when they protest against activities in their society, such as gambling and prostitution, which in their view are signs of moral decay? More generally, is it unreasonable to take an active interest in the activities and beliefs of others and seek to curb what one deems to be wrongful, if not downright sinful? If this is the case, a significant number of conceptions of the good would be unreasonable and excluded from consideration. This can hardly be what Rawls had in mind when he introduced the notion of 'reasonableness', though. It would simply leave too many conceptions, too many people, without rights to pursue what they view as the good life.

The Right to Equal Participation

In his book *Law and Disagreement*, Jeremy Waldron suggests that a focus on justice alone is not likely to be the final answer to conflict-resolution bearing in mind that people disagree about what justice means; that is to say, they disagree about whose pursuits should be restricted and on what basis. According to him, this is a circumstance of political life in a plural society. Against this background, a theory of rights must be complemented, not by a particular theory of justice, but by a theory of authority that takes seriously the conflicts of rights that arise in a crowded plural society.[31]

The claim about the need for authority to deal with conflict and disagreement about justice may have been a critical feature of the mature political philosophy of Immanuel Kant. In Kant's view, in a situation of disagreements and conflicts occurring when each is doing what seems right and good to him, it is necessary to emphasise the capacity of law and of the legislature to issue authoritative determinations to settle disagreements and

[30] But see G Gaus, *Justificatory Liberalism: An Essay on Epistemology and Political Theory*. (New York, Oxford University Press, 1996), at 154. Gaus disagrees with Rawls about 'indeterminacy'; instead, he suggests that the basic problem is 'inconclusiveness'.

[31] See J Waldron, *Law and Disagreement*, above n 10, especially chapter eleven.

in this way avoid violence from breaking out.[32] Thus, it is in the light of a consideration of people's sense of righteousness that the claim about the need for positive law should be understood. Indeed, the reality of disagreement about justice is critical to understanding the point of the concept of positive law and the philosophical doctrine of legal positivism. According to this doctrine

> law must be such that its content and validity can be determined without reproducing the disagreements about rights and justice that it is law's function to supersede.[33]

If people fail to 'agree to disagree' about the permissibility of some conception of the good, some authoritative position must be forthcoming. Alternatively, as Waldron explains,

> we can agree to differ in our *opinions*, but it is necessary, all the same, that we arrive at some position on the issue to be upheld and enforced as the *community's* position.[34]

In addition, since people disagree about which position should be upheld and enforced in the name of their community, it is necessary to establish a political process to determine what that position is.[35]

Thus, if it cannot reasonably be argued that everybody has a right to enjoy their culture to the full because the universal exercise of such a right would inevitably lead to conflicts and disagreements some of which must be resolved through legislative actions, the least to be expected is that everybody has an opportunity to take part in the political process preceding those actions. The right to participation may be a second-best alternative in the light of the indeterminacy that plagues the principle of equal freedom and the notion of reasonableness. However, the right to participation may also be, as Waldron suggests, a 'rights-based' response to the question of who is to decide about fair settlements of cultural conflicts. As he explains, the special role of participation in a theory of rights

> is the upshot of the fact that participation is a right whose exercise seems peculiarly appropriate in situations where reasonable rights-bearers disagree about what rights they have.[36]

[32] I Kant, *The Metaphysical Elements of Justice*, John Ladd (trans) (Indianapolis, Bobbs-Merrill, 1965), sec 44.
[33] J Waldron, 'Kant's Legal Positivism' (1996) 109 *Harvard Law Review* 1535 at 1540.
[34] *Ibid*, at 1538.
[35] *Ibid.*
[36] J Waldron, *Law and Disagreement*, above n 10, at 232.

The right to participate is evidently not a right to decide oneself what rights one has, but a right to take part in discussions on this matter. As John Rawls declares:

> Taking part in political life does not make the individual master of himself, but rather gives him an equal voice along with others in settling how basic social conditions are to be arranged. Nor does it answer to the ambition to dictate to others, since each is now required to moderate his claims by what everyone is able to recognize as just. The public will to consult and to take everyone's beliefs and interests into account lays the foundations for civic friendship and shapes the ethos of political culture.[37]

According to Rawls, then, the right to participation is supposed to give each an equal voice along with others in settling how social life is to be arranged.

There are several reasons for distributing the right to participation to all subjects of law without qualifying the enjoyment of that right with something like a criterion of reasonableness. One reason is prudential. The right to participation functions as a channel of communicating dissent. By giving people an opportunity to have a say about the contents of the legal system, the right facilitates adjustments of that system in the light of social changes in the cultural make-up of the individual subjects who are expected to comply with its rules, codes, and regulations. Even Thomas Hobbes who opposed a democratic response to the issue of who should be the political authority recognised the need to consider, and to some extent, accommodate within the fabric of law, what people, in fact, do. The importance of paying attention to actual activities is warranted, Hobbes declared, out of a basic concern for peace.[38] A conception of justice—settled once and for all—risks leading to alienation and estrangement inasmuch as it fails to accommodate new claims and concerns not considered at the time of its original formulation. As Rawls explains, without inclusive sentiments,

> men become estranged and isolated in their smaller associations, and affective ties may not extend outside the family or a narrow circle of friends. Citizens no longer regard one another as associates with whom one can cooperate to advance some interpretation of the public good; instead, they view themselves as rivals, or else as obstacles to one another's ends.[39]

Additionally, Rawls continues by noting that equal participation is critical for the maintenance of stable and just institutions inasmuch as it fosters the development of intellectual and moral sensibilities and a sense of duty and obligation. Against this background, it may be concluded that an inclusive

[37] J Rawls, *Theory of Justice*, above n 26, at 205.
[38] T Hobbes, *Leviathan*, above n 24, at 221.
[39] J Rawls, *Theory of Justice*, above n 26, at 206.

democracy is imperative for securing stable institutions as societies become more diverse.

However, a defence of the right to equal participation on prudential grounds alone fails to be convincing inasmuch as democratic participation represents but one possible channel of communication. There may be other methods to ensure communication. Thus, a vindication of the right to participation as the most appropriate response to the issue of who is to decide on matters of common concern may have to be defended on substantive moral grounds.

One substantive idea is that the right to participate is a claim to a right to share in power; it is an individual's right to play his part '*along with the equal part played by all other individuals*, in the government of the society.'[40] The basis for equal distribution of participatory rights, Waldron suggests, may be the

> peculiar insult, to an individual, A, of A's being excluded from political power [which] has to do, first, with the impact of political decisions on A's own rights and interests, and, second, with A's possession of the capacity to decide responsibly about those issues (even granted that A's own rights and interests are not the *only* rights and interests involved). Because A is affected (along with B, C, D, ...), A can think of himself as having standing in the matter (...) And because A has a sense of justice, A may think of himself as having what it takes to participate in decisions where others' rights are also involved.[41]

Thus, what is asked for, in the distribution of the right to participation to all subjects of the law, is that everybody is treated as equals in matters affecting their interests, their rights, and their duties.[42]

There are several forms of participation, ie various strategies for taking part in the political process of one's society. Waldron focuses on the right to vote in his analysis of the right to participation. However, apart from voting in periodically held elections, the right to participation entails that every citizen is to have equal access, at least in a formal sense, to public office, including eligibility to join political parties, to run for elective positions, and to hold positions of authority. In addition, it entails the rights to protest and demonstrate as well as, under certain conditions, a right to disobedience.

PROBLEMS OF EXCLUSION

If the right to participation is the correct response to the issue of who should decide in cultural conflicts it is necessary to take account of the reality of cultural difference as a vehicle for political exclusion. Even if everybody in

40 J Waldron, *Law and Disagreement*, above n 10, at 236 [emphasis in original].
41 *Ibid*, at 238–239.
42 *Ibid*, at 239.

principle has a right to take part in political affairs, not everybody might be able to actually do so. Indeed, a commitment to ensuring that everybody is treated as equals in resolving conflicts is more complicated to realise as society is becoming more culturally diverse, especially with respect to difference in terms of ability to take advantage of the various avenues available.

Universal participation is a real democratic aspiration. As Rawls states, a focus on the worth of political liberty emphasises fair opportunity to take part in, and influence, the political process. If the public forum is to be free and open to all, and in continuous session, everyone should be able to make use of it. They should also have the means to be informed about political issues and a fair chance to add alternative proposals to the agenda for political discussion.[43] However, there are many obstacles—or even barriers—that may get in the way and inhibit the ability to make use of this right, especially for those whose culture differs from those in government. The cultural barriers or obstacles to the enjoyment of the right may be created as a result of ideological difference or depend on a difference in terms of cultural equipment. While the present study is limited to a concern with these sorts of differences and their adverse impact on the individual's ability to take advantage of the right to participation, it must be noted that there are additional cultural barriers or obstacles that similarly reduce the worth of the right to participation in the eyes of its holders. For example, a cultural barrier to participation may be experienced by those who are simply denied political rights for reasons related to their cultural difference.[44] Another example of a cultural barrier is that established in societies that tolerate a hierarchical relationship between knowledge bases, sexes, or ethnic groups because the voice of the people is thereby truncated. As a result, specific segments of society are likely to be viewed as inherently inferior and as unworthy of public attention. An unwarranted stigma may be imposed on people who are viewed as inferior, a stigma that is almost impossible to overcome since proposals originated by them are likely to be excluded on the basis that they lack intelligence or cannot be trusted.[45] The serious conditions imposed on people as a result of these sorts of cultural barriers are a critical concern for Iris Marion Young. Young develops an argument about the need to recognise, and work towards the inclusion of, different groups of people into the ambit of political life, who are not necessarily organised along ideological lines, but who form interest groups protesting against ingrained discriminatory practices on the basis of colour, sexual orientation,

[43] *Ibid*, 197–198.

[44] See generally R Bauböck, 'Changing the Boundaries of Citizenship: The Inclusion of Immigrants in Democratic Polities' in R Bauböck, *From Aliens to Citizens: Redefining the Status of Immigrants in Europe* (Aldershot, Avebury, 1994). See also YN Soysal, *The Limits of Citizenship: Migrants and Postnational Membership in Europe* (Chicago, The University of Chicago Press, 1994).

[45] JM Choi, KA Callaghan and JW Murphy, *The Politics of Culture: Race, Violence, and Democracy* (Westport Conn, Praeger, 1995), at 123.

or ethnicity. For Young, the politics of difference is a necessary step towards redress of years of repression and exclusion under the politics of assimilation.[46]

Reasonableness

The Canadian philosopher Charles Taylor remarked recently:

> Democracy, particularly liberal democracy, is a great philosophy of inclusion. Rule of the people—by the people, for the people—and where 'people' is supposed to mean, unlike in earlier days, everybody, without the unspoken restrictions of yesteryear against, peasants, women, slaves, etc this offers the prospect of the most inclusive politics in human history. And yet there is also something in the dynamic of democracy that pushes to exclusion ... Exclusion is a by-product of something else: the need, in self-governing societies, for a high degree of cohesion. Democratic states need something like a common identity.[47]

Thus, although all in principle have an equal right to participation, Taylor alerts us to a variety of conditions imposed on the exercise of that right, especially in relation to the contention that people in government are supposed to rule. It is against this background that Taylor propounds that the members of government make up a decision-making unit, ie a body that takes joint decisions. To form such a decision-making unit, it is not sufficient for a vote to record the fully formed opinions of all their members. These units must not only decide together, but must deliberate together. A decision produced from joint deliberations does not merely require everybody to vote according to his or her opinion, but also requires that each person's opinion should have been able to take shape or be reformed in the light of the discussion that took place. Meeting these expectations requires a degree of cohesion. According to Taylor, to some extent the members must know each other, listen to one another, and understand one another. These must be the very conditions of the legitimacy of democratic states.[48]

Apart from conditions of understanding and acquaintance, Taylor adds trust and commitment. As he declares, apart from a high level of participation and commitment, free societies presuppose a significant level of mutual trust. Such societies are vulnerable to mistrust especially that some may not really fulfil their commitments, eg tax-paying.[49] Hence, while there is a drive in modern democracy toward inclusion in the fact that government should be by all the people, at the same time,

[46] IM Young, *Justice and the Politics of Difference* (Princeton NJ, Princeton University Press, 1990).

[47] C Taylor, 'Democratic Exclusion (and Its Remedies?). The John Ambrose Stack Memorial Lecture' in AC Cairns *et al* (eds), *Citizenship, Diversity, and Pluralism: Canadian and Comparative Perspectives* (Montreal, McGill-Queen's University Press, 1999), at 265.

[48] *Ibid*, at 270.

[49] *Ibid*, at 271.

> there is a standing temptation to exclusion, which arises from the fact that democracies work well when people know each other, trust each other, and feel a sense of commitment toward each other.[50]

The conditions associated with a supposed need for cohesion would seem to come into conflict with the claim for equal participation, since those who differ, culturally speaking, may not be perceived as meeting these requirements.

Are the conditions enlisted by Taylor—understanding, acquaintance, trust, and commitment—what Rawls has in mind when introducing 'reasonableness' as a criterion for taking part in political life? In an important sense, the criterion of reasonableness advanced by Rawls seems to correspond, at least roughly speaking, to the conditions listed by Taylor. According to that criterion, an individual must be reasonable not only when developing his own conception of the good, but also when exercising his right to political participation. It purports to shape and guide the manner and spirit of deliberation on matters of common concern for society as a whole and, above all, when such deliberations involve individual rights. Rawls explains that the general idea of reasonableness is inclusive: most persons are assumed to be reasonable in the sense of affirming a reasonable comprehensive doctrine, that is, an ethical, religious or philosophical view of the good that does not reject the fundamentals of a democratic regime.[51] An unreasonable doctrine rejects one or more democratic freedoms.[52] From this standpoint, his understanding of what it means to be reasonable is substantive inasmuch as it considers the affirmation of his political conception of justice as a measure of reasonableness. However, it is not necessary that everybody actually agrees about the reasonableness of his proposition of using his conception of justice as a measure of inclusion/exclusion. Rather, what is decisive is that there are reasons for affirming that conception of justice which are 'sufficient to convince all reasonable persons that it is reasonable.' Thus, holds Rawls:

> To say that a political conviction is objective is to say that there are reasons, specified by a reasonable and mutually recognizable political conception (satisfying those essentials), sufficient to convince all reasonable persons that it is reasonable.[53]

The practical implication of his claim is that people who oppose his conception will be understood as unreasonable. As Rawls notes, no assent is required from people who are mad, irrational, or unreasonable.[54]

[50] *Ibid* at 274. See also RD Putnam, *Making Democracy Work: Civic Traditions in Modern Italy* (Princeton NJ, Princeton University Press, 1993), especially chapter six on social capital and institutional success.
[51] J Rawls, *Political Liberalism*, above n 28, at *xviii–xix*.
[52] *Ibid*, at 64.
[53] *Ibid*, at 119.
[54] *Ibid*, at *xviii–xix*.

Rawls is aware of the difficulties involved in judging the reasonableness of a comprehensive view. He predicts that such judgements are likely to be particularly controversial.[55] In fact, he contends that there are inherent risks in specifying criteria for inclusion/exclusion. Therefore,

> we avoid excluding reasonable comprehensive doctrines as unreasonable without strong grounds based on clear aspects of the reasonable itself. Otherwise our account runs the danger of being arbitrary and exclusive. Political liberalism counts many familiar and traditional doctrines—religious, philosophical, and moral—as reasonable even though we could not seriously entertain them for ourselves, as we think they give excessive weight to some values and fail to allow for the significance of others. A tighter criterion is not, however, needed for the purposes of political liberalism.[56]

Against this background, it nevertheless seems suspicious to regard the comprehensive views of the Jehovah's Witnesses, Greek Orthodox, secularists, practising Muslims, etc, involved in the cultural conflicts in focus, as unreasonable and, on this ground, exclude them from the ambit of political life.

An alternative approach may be to consider only some forms of participation as unreasonable irrespective of which comprehensive view triggered them. Rawls recognises the unreasonableness of two forms of participation. First of all, he suggests that it is unreasonable to seek to enforce a comprehensive view through legislative action in a plural society.[57] Secondly, it is unreasonable to take advantage of political power to proclaim and insist on the truth of one's views on matters involving justice.[58] On this basis, it is possible to conclude that, irrespective of what anybody might think of the reasonableness of their comprehensive views, the Greek Orthodox as well as the French and Turkish secularists are unreasonable in insisting on their controversial laws in the face of cultural opposition. Nevertheless, since it cannot be assumed that everybody will agree on these criteria as grounds for inclusion/exclusion—and the position of the Greek Orthodox as well as the French and Turkish secularists indicates this—it may be necessary to open up a political discussion on these issues as well.

Cultural Equipment

While the right to participation is a right that in principle is to be enjoyed by everyone, a range of conditions is nevertheless imposed on the exercise of that right. To begin with, the idea of an inclusive democracy—the possibility of everybody's involvement in discussions of matters of common concern—presupposes that suitable cultural equipment is already on hand.

[55] J Rawls, *Political Liberalism*, above n 28, at 63.
[56] *Ibid*, at 59–60.
[57] *Ibid*, at 138.
[58] *Ibid*, at 61.

Apart from being willing to share the social world with others, a political actor must also be able to signal that he or she is committed to doing so. Whether the actor is capable of that depends, in part, on his culture's previous experience with pluralism. The extent to which a culture entails views on how to relate to other cultures is shaped by its history. Some cultures have developed a range of views and practices on how to deal with 'outsiders' as a result of intensive confrontation and interaction over long stretches of time, and may have settled on a tolerant outlook. Relatively isolated cultures, by contrast, may largely lack such views and practices in the field of 'external' relations. What is more, even if a given culture comprises norms and rules to be applied by its members leading their lives in a multicultural society where they constitute a minority, members who have just arrived may nevertheless lack experience of observing such norms.

Apart from having previous experience of pluralism, the ability of a culture to adjust itself to other cultures depends on the character of the beliefs its members uphold. Obviously, a culture affirming more fundamentalist or orthodox beliefs has greater difficulties in adjusting than others, since it regards any trade-off or concession as involving an unbearable loss. As a result, some religiously inspired cultures demand an increase in the influence of their principles of conduct in public life. The trouble with these cultures is not necessarily their lack of experience of pluralism, but their experience of being oppressed and persecuted. At the same time, however, many cultures recognise the importance of finding a way of living together with others—whether they like it or not—and develop different sets of conduct rules for their members, the application of which depends on where they live. The reality of pluralism has led cultures to distinguish between core-principles and peripheral ones. The conduct rules of many Islamic cultures illustrate this phenomenon. Such cultures embody elaborate and detailed rules regulating how Muslims are supposed to lead their lives in a non-Islamic and plural context. Similarly to many other religious cultures, the Islamic systems of norms and values are not confined to 'faith' and 'rituals' only, but encompass sets of social rules regulating, for example, family structure, economy, trade, penal system, etc.[59] The issue of the strict duties of Muslims as a minority in a non-Islamic context is often accorded special significance by several Muslim religious scholars. In a publication entitled *Muslim Minorities in the World Today*, the Moroccan scholar M Ali Kattani expresses his views on the way Muslim minorities should try to maintain their religious tradition within a non-Muslim society.[60] According to him, it is quite acceptable for a Muslim to live in a non-Muslim society as long as he is allowed to adhere to the essential aspects of the Islamic faith. Should a Muslim

[59] WAR Shadid and PS van Koningsveld, *Religious Freedom and the Position of Islam in Western Europe* (Kampen, Kok Pharos, 1995), at 60.

[60] M Ali Kettani, *Muslim Minorities in the World Today* (London, Mansell, 1986).

be unable to defend and maintain his faith, however, he is obliged to emigrate. The obligation to emigrate does not apply in cases of failure to ensure official recognition of, say, Islamic family law by the non-Muslim state in which a Muslim lives. What is necessary is that Islamic core-principles ('articles of faith' and 'devotional rules') are observed, including rules concerning prayer, charity, fasting, and the performance of the pilgrimage to Mecca, if possible, once in a life-time. The social rules, in contrast, do not constitute core-principles.

Apart from being accustomed to pluralism more generally, political participation in a multicultural society presupposes that a culture is expected to be accustomed to the specific context of which it is a part. The members of a culture might otherwise not succeed in advancing their demands in an effective way. As a result, their aspirations risk being misunderstood. It is an essential aspect of the cultural equipment suitable for a plural context to have the know-how and skills necessary to engage in discussions with others who might disagree. It requires familiarity with one another's schemes of interpretation of behaviour. It may also presuppose acquaintance with one another's doctrines. New cultures tend to adjust to the political language in use since it is crucial to advance one's particular claims and concerns. For example, as Yasemin Soysal observes, the Islamic communities in Europe have come to adopt human rights rhetoric, thereby drawing upon the host country and world-level repertoires of claim-making.[61]

Rawls and Taylor's respective accounts indicate the importance of shared cultural equipment for the sake of ensuring the background conditions for effective communication. The barriers created by lack of shared equipment are more evident in a society where different cultures have only recently been brought into relation with one another, and thus, are unfamiliar with the meaning of one another's language, manners, behaviour, etc. Though the principle of familiarity is not a necessary condition for communication (but is perhaps itself a reason for engaging in communication), it nevertheless requires that each makes an effort to ensure that the basis for, and the point of, particular proposals, counter-arguments, objections, etc are understood by others whose rights, interests, and duties are in play. One reason for stressing the importance of being concerned with mutual familiarity is that it enables effective communication in a culturally diverse population. It obviously makes a difference whether the range of cultural sources commonly referred to is familiar to everybody or if some have only recently been introduced.

In a society where one culture has dominated a place for stretches of time and established a range of public institutions, it is not unusual that a new

[61] Y Soysal, 'Changing the Parameters of Citizenship and Claims-Making: Organized Islam in European Public Spheres' (1996) 4 *European University Institute Working Paper European forum* 3–4.

culture with different cultural equipment fails to take part in political life due to its members' lack of the know-how that is crucial for being able to use existing avenues in an effective way. This know-how is not confined to knowledge about the acceptable ways of taking part in political discussion, but is also relevant for the use of other more informal (and usually non-argumentative) avenues. It is sometimes thought that it is easier to use these avenues for minority cultures; I believe this is a mistake. Additionally, the ability to use these avenues effectively presupposes familiarity with the context. Moreover, while it may not be necessary to develop a rich and refined vocabulary to be able to articulate one's claims, demands, and concerns in order to employ these avenues, having recourse to them may result in the risk of serious reprimands, including expulsion, as in the case of non-citizens. Prior to articulating the basis for this claim in somewhat greater detail, however, it is necessary to explain the centrality of these avenues in a multicultural society.

In spite of being formally or de facto excluded from access to the public forum, there are other more informal ways of taking part in the political process. These avenues include protests, demonstrations, open resistance, strikes, and civil disobedience. Protests and demonstrations entail making use of symbolic means such as the gathering of a great number of people in the main square or similar public place.[62] It is not unusual that cultural groups have resort to these avenues in efforts to change laws and policies that, in their view, are grossly unjust. They are used by a range of moral dissenters, including anti-racists, anti-globalisation advocates, environmentalists, pacifists, animal welfare promoters, and so on. In effect, as Claus Offe's essay on challenging the boundaries of institutionalised politics indicates, the frequent use of such avenues may call for a change in attitude on the marginal importance of such avenues for political theory. In his view, these actions are also forms of political participation in spite of their unconventional and non-institutional character.[63] Offe asks us to consider that the use of such avenues is not the expression of parochialism or unintelligibility, but depends on a range of reasons often not appreciated by those who continue to conduct their affairs in the spirit of the distributive paradigm. For example, there are religious movements aspiring to place issues on the political agenda that have nothing to do with the fair distribution of rights, opportunities, and welfare. Therefore, there is a tendency in liberal theory to exclude them.[64] Obviously, to act upon what one believes is a true cause

[62] C Offe, 'Challenging the Boundaries of Institutional Politics: Social Movements Since the 1960s' in C Mayer (ed), *Changing the Boundaries of the Political: Essays on the Evolving Balance Between the State and Society, Public and Private in Europe* (New York, Cambridge University Press, 1987), at 71.

[63] *Ibid*, at 63.

[64] But see R Grundmann and C Mantziaris, 'Habermas, Rawls, and the Paradox of Impartiality' (1990) 1 *European University Institute Working Paper Department of Political and Social Sciences*.

without consideration for others may be regarded as unreasonable inasmuch as such behaviour contravenes democratic values of reciprocity, exchange, and compromise. A perceived unwillingness to co-operate, therefore, can provoke strong reactions from established political actors. In a Western political context dominated by the distributive paradigm, it is not unusual that actors with a single moral or religious cause are depicted as passionate, unintelligible, politically incompetent, and irresponsible. The established actors thereby fail to acknowledge that unconventional actors with a moral or religious cause are unable to negotiate since they have nothing material to offer in exchange for the concessions made by others.[65]

Another problem faced by unconventional actors is that they often lack a position on other problems faced by society that may also require attention and consideration. Nevertheless, a 'single-issue' approach may be an effective method for organising and mobilising a group sharing a particular experience or characteristic while not others.[66] This is the way in which, for example, Islamic associations in Europe organise themselves in the light of the fact that their members do not necessarily share views on all issues faced by society as a whole.[67] This manner of organisation has the potential to transcend political and economic divisions by classifying political conflicts according to parameters such as age, ethnicity, humanity, and so on. However, a difference in moral outlook hardly means that actors operating outside the ambit of the public forum are unintelligible. As Offe notes, from their standpoint, the rationality of political institutions and collective action involves implicit selections and non-decisions on issues that nevertheless have a deep impact on society in its entirety.[68]

As already noted, the successful employment of these avenues depends on a variety of factors not all of which are necessarily confined to the persuasiveness of the actual cause, but are also influenced by know-how, skills, and familiarity with the context. This variable is especially striking with respect to disobedience where the fluidity of what counts as disobedience, conscientious objection, and unreasonable or unwise behaviour is most striking. The avenue of disobedience is of particular importance as a channel of communication when considering the many cases of non-compliance with the law that occur in multicultural societies. Whether they are acts of conscientious objection or disobedience is not always clear. George Kateb refers to a range of forms of non-compliance used to protest against laws in force. Among them are passive resistance, conscientious objection, selective law-breaking,

[65] C Offe, 'Challenging the Boundaries of Institutional Politics: Social Movements Since the 1960s', above n 62, at 71–72.

[66] *Ibid.*

[67] J Nielsen, *Muslims in Western Europe*, 2nd edn (Edinburgh, Edinburgh University Press, 1995). See chapter 4.

[68] C Offe, 'Challenging the Boundaries of Institutional Politics: Social Movements Since the 1960s', above n 62, at 71–72.

civil disobedience, disobedience of an order, and massive non-violent endeavours.[69] Although none of these terms lend themselves to unambiguous use, conscience seems to be the common element. In addition, though conscience is an ambiguous term, Kateb suggests that we would all probably agree that

> the solitary individual, or the succession of like-minded individuals, or the organized group, or the spontaneous group, or the movement, who of which engages in any of these modes is saying no, is refusing to go along with public authority, or public officials on the basis of some overriding or especially compelling moral reason.[70]

Kateb concludes by noting that, while it is a peaceful way of refusing to go along with the public authority, it nevertheless requires a response by the public forum.

Rawls presents a more formal definition of civil disobedience. In his view, it is a

> public, non-violent, conscientious, yet political act, contrary to law usually done with the aim of bringing about a change in the law or policies of the government.[71]

It differs from acts of conscientious refusal insofar as disobedience is political in a way the latter is not. An act is *political*, then—it is an act of civil disobedience rather than conscientious objection—if it is addressed to those in power and believed to be justifiable by political principles (ie principles regulating the constitution and social institutions more generally).[72] It is a *non-political* act, in contrast, if it is not a form of address and appeal to the sense of justice of the majority.[73] Even so, what may ultimately be decisive to the question of the political significance of an act of non-compliance may involve not solely the motive, but also other factors, such as the number of

[69] G Kateb, *Hannah Arendt: Politics, Conscience, Evil* (Totowa, NJ, Rowman & Allanheld Publishers, 1984), at 97.

[70] *Ibid.*

[71] John Rawls, *Theory of Justice*, above n 26, at 320.

[72] For a definition of 'civil disobedience' see *ibid*, at 321. According to Rawls, an act of civil disobedience is a 'political act not only in the sense that it is addressed to the majority that holds political power, but also because it is an act guided and justified by political principles, that is, by the principles of justice which regulate the constitution and social institutions generally. In justifying civil disobedience one does not appeal to principles of personal morality or to religious doctrines, though these may coincide with and support one's claims .... Instead one invokes the commonly shared conception of justice that underlies the political order.'

[73] *Ibid*, at 323–324. According to Rawls, an act of conscientious objection is 'noncompliance with a more or less direct legal injunction or administrative order. It is refusal since an order is addressed to us and, given the nature of the situation, whether we accede to it is known to the authorities.... Conscientious objection is not necessarily based on political principles; it may be founded on religious or other principles at variance with the constitutional order.'

people involved, the importance of the law in question, as well as mistrust (well-founded or not) as to the ultimate loyalty of those who disobey. As Hannah Arendt points out, if a significant number of people are bound in their conscience and agree to act contrary to law, the conscientious act *becomes* politically significant. Conscientious dissenters, she notes,

> are in fact organized as a minority, bound together by common opinion, rather than by common interest, and the decision to take a stand against the government's policies even if they have a reason to assume that these policies are backed by a majority; their concerted action springs from an agreement with each other, and it is this agreement that lends credence and conviction to their opinion, no matter how they may have originally arrived at it.[74]

The act of conscientious objection becomes politically significant when a plurality of consciences happen to coincide and enter the marketplace of ideas to make their voice heard in public. At this point, Arendt contends, we are no longer dealing with individuals, one-by-one, so to speak. What was once decided in *foro interno* has now become part of public opinion. Once in the marketplace, the fate of conscience is not so much different from the fate of philosophers' truth: it becomes an opinion indistinguishable from other opinions.[75] Thus, even if the refusal to obey the law is not meant to be a political act, it can nevertheless come to have political significance and raise issues of common concern for society as a whole.

What Rawls and others are ignorant of in their account of legitimate forms of disobedience, however, is the small likelihood that a marginalised voice taking advantage of the right to disobey will be considered reasonable, intelligible, and trustworthy. Thus, if disobedience is the only option available for minority cultures to communicate their dissent, the circumstance of the excluded must be regarded as severe. Additionally, the right to disobey presupposes know-how, skills, and familiarity with context. For example, Rawls lists a number of factors that dissenters are expected to consider in deliberating about whether or not to disobey, all of which evidently presuppose more than superficial familiarity with context. First of all, those planning to disobey must act rationally and consider alternative avenues (except in cases of extreme injustice).[76] Furthermore, the act must be directed against a public wrong incorporated into the fabric of law or social arrangements. In addition, the dissenters must have reasons to believe that their act is likely to be effective and will not undermine the conditions for stability of

[74] H Arendt, 'Civil Disobedience' in H Arendt, *Crises of the Republic* (New York, Harcourt Brace Jovanovich, 1972), at 56.

[75] *Ibid*, at 68.

[76] J Rawls, *Theory of Justice*, above n 26, at 319. Note that Rawls' account of restraints on action is limited to a society that is well ordered for the most part, but in which violations of justice nevertheless occur. A state of near justice is defined as a democratic regime.

arrangements that are just, or as just as it is reasonable to expect them to be in the circumstances. Those planning to disobey must also consider that others similarly situated have the same right to disobey. Rawls concludes with the observation that the right to disobey must, like any other use of right, be rationally framed so as to advance one's aims or the aims of those one wishes to assist.[77]

While deficient cultural equipment inhibits people's ability to take part in political discussion in effective ways, it is hardly a legitimate ground for exclusion. It is obviously necessary to develop a shared political language between people from different cultural backgrounds, and newcomers and others similarly situated, culturally speaking, are expected to acquire such a language. This acquisition does not ensure that everyone agrees on the meaning of different concepts and notions. Since the specific meaning of vague and general concepts differs from culture to culture, it is only reasonable to expect that a given language will be used to express a variety of concerns some of which seem to be in conflict with the values that the language was originally introduced to secure. The reality of different motives for having recourse to, say, human rights rhetoric is not necessarily unfortunate, though. As Waldron notes,

> we can profit rather than suffer from sharing a vocabulary with opponents. To share a vocabulary means that it is possible to talk to one another, and in framing the ideas of those who disagree with us, they may contribute, even if unintentionally, to the shared endeavors of developing concepts and apparatus of political argument.[78]

The introduction of new ideas into the debate about what a given concept means may also contribute to the furthering of the good for which the concept was introduced.

Expectations of cultural adjustment may lead to 'symbolic' refusals concerning the selection of vocabulary, concepts, and terminology, not necessarily on the basis of their quality, but because of their associations with a particular range of cultures and their conceptions of law and justice. A Muslim commentary to the Universal Declaration of Human Rights is expressed in this spirit:

> Why do we not simply put into practice our own Islamic laws? Indeed, why do we not put them forward at the United Nations and at its various Commissions and Conferences? Why do we not orientate the compasses of the nations of the world by the pole-star of Islam, and publicly glory in our possession of laws

[77] *Ibid*, at 328, 330.

[78] J Waldron, 'Rights and Needs—The Myth of Disjunction' in A Sarat and T Kearns (eds), *Legal Rights: Historical and Philosophical Perspectives* (Ann Arbor, University of Michigan Press, 1996), at 109.

> that so exactly fit the human condition? Why do we not demonstrate the values of those laws, and illustrate their excellence in our words and our practice? Why do we not invite the United Nations to express their Conventions in the terms already laid down in the Islamic Canon?[79]

In spite of these and similar protests, however, and perhaps due to the importance of taking part in political processes that affect one's rights, duties, and interests, most political actors—whether sub-cultures or governments—who would like to use a different vocabulary in addressing issues of right and justice are nevertheless active participants in relevant forums for common discussion. Their demands, claims, and concerns cannot be excluded from consideration on the basis that their unconventional behaviour in the form of protests, demonstrations, or sheer refusals to comply with regulations in conflict with their cultural norms is unintelligible or unreasonable without taking due account of the many difficulties involved in taking part in the political process due to deficient cultural equipment. The lack of suitable equipment is not a legitimate ground for exclusion.

REASONABLENESS AND DISAGREEMENT

According to David Hume, conflict is an inevitable aspect of political life. If resources were abundant and people more generous than they usually are, conflicts would not occur. As Amy Gutmann and Dennis Thompson affirm, however, apart from the circumstances of moderate scarcity and limited altruism, there may be additional circumstances not considered by Hume, but which must nevertheless be accounted for. One such circumstance is that of disagreement about justice and right.[80] According to them, moral disagreement ought to be considered as a circumstance of democratic political life. As they explain,

> while the locus and content of particular disagreements shift over time, moral disagreement is a permanent condition of democratic politics.[81]

Though Gutmann and Thompson's position may be considered to be controversial, the charges against the idea of acknowledging moral disagreements as a circumstance of political life fail to be convincing. A notorious charge refers to the risk of undermining the conditions for social justice and moral disagreement as a source of incomprehensibility. Another charge is

[79] S Tabandeh, *A Muslim Commentary on the Universal Declaration of Human Rights* (Guildford, FJ Goulding, 1970), at 57. Cited by AE Mayer, *Islam and Human Rights: Tradition and Politics* (Boulder, Westview Press, 1999), at 169.

[80] J Waldron, *Law and Disagreement* above n 10, especially chapter eleven.

[81] A Gutmann and D Thompson, *Democracy and Disagreement* (Cambridge, Mass, Harvard University Press, 1996), at 9.

based on the contention that the political process is capable of mediating between conflicting interests between groups, but can hardly hope to resolve disagreements in any satisfactory way. Not only are there stability considerations for avoiding disagreements; above all, there may be no substantive solution to cultural conflicts that would be deemed acceptable from the standpoint of everyone. Therefore, the political process must be limited to conflicts that can actually be resolved in the framework of distributive politics.[82] The subsequent sections respond to these objections.

The Distributive Objection Unwarranted

The perceived urgency of reaffirming the distributive paradigm often overlooks the fact that the paradigm presupposes the existence of agreement about what goods are to be distributed, to whom, and on what grounds. If such agreement is lacking, it is necessary to address and resolve not only the distributive issues, but also the more fundamental question about what goods are to be distributed.[83] The contention that the 'interest' issue may not be settled in a multicultural society indicates that conventional goods said to be valued by everybody regardless of cultural background and attachment (rights, opportunities, income, and wealth) may not fully capture all that people care for. Even so, the reality of disagreement is seldom taken seriously by theorists of justice when formulating their own substantive account of what justice requires. As Waldron explains, however, the kinds of disagreements we are familiar with in democratic politics is not limited to issues about the fair distribution of goods wanted by all, but also covers disagreements that are the direct upshot of disagreements about the goods. Such disagreement differs from, and cuts across, disagreement about justice. For example, it is not the case that people who share a religious identity naturally share a political view on, say, the socio-economic structure:

> Conceptions of justice ... are viewed as rival attempts to specify a quite separate set of principles for the basic structure of a society whose members disagree about the good. The rivalry between competing conceptions of justice is seen as independent of (and cutting across) the rivalry between competing conceptions of the good. Thus among Catholics there are socialists and libertarians, who, although they agree about ultimate values, disagree fundamentally about the principles that should govern the economic structure of a modern plural society.[84]

Thus, the issue of moral disagreement is separate from the issue of disagreement concerning the fair distribution of rights, opportunities, income, and

[82] See eg 'The Limits of Cultural Politics' (1998) 24 *Review of International Studies* 307.
[83] C Offe, 'Challenging the Boundaries of Institutional Politics: Social Movements Since the 1960s', above n 62, at 65–67.
[84] J Waldron, *Law and Disagreement*, above n 10, at 150.

wealth. Why, then, do many theorists of justice not take moral disagreements seriously?

Incomprehensibility

Rawls is reluctant concerning the possibility of accommodating the deeper kind of political pluralism that Waldron considers an inevitable circumstance of modern political life. In an important sense, Rawls' posture is motivated by the supposed irreconcilability and incommensurability that plague disagreements having their source in the existence of diverse bodies of ethical, religious, or philosophical thought.[85] It is in the light of this contention that he develops the idea of a political liberalism, that is, the idea that it is possible to find a shared liberal basis for political discussion by drawing upon publicly recognised ideas and principles that are part of the public culture. He affirms that his theory of justice, 'Justice as Fairness', with its two principles of justice, represents such common ground. The limitation to publicly recognised sources appears to be the only solution available as 'citizens realise that they cannot reach agreement or even approach mutual understanding on the basis of their irreconcilable comprehensive doctrines.'[86]

Thus, one concern is that moral disagreement is a source of incomprehensibility. To tolerate moral disagreement that has its source in the existence of diverse religious, ethical, and philosophical bodies of thought will inevitably undermine the conditions crucial for having an intelligible discussion between people with different cultural backgrounds and attachments. In Rawls' view, a necessary requisite for such a discussion is that the participants share a set of background values in the light of which the discussion can go on. Hence, a discussion about issues in the field of justice can only be successful if the parties already share a substantive conception of justice. From this standpoint, conscientious dissent generated by a particular conception of the good is unintelligible to others with a different conception of the good since the latter fail to understand the basis of that dissent. Others involved in discussions on matters of common concern must understand what one is trying to do when applying a particular norm or value in an attempt to resolve a particular conflict. If this activity is unintelligible, that is, if others fail to understand the norm or value informing a participant's attempt to contribute to the discussion, it is impossible for them to make an intelligible and informed judgement about the quality of his demands, objections, and legislative proposals.[87]

[85] J Rawls, *Political Liberalism*, above n 2, at 133.
[86] J Rawls, 'The Idea of Public Reason Revisited' (1997) 64 *University of Chicago Law Review* 765 at 766.
[87] For a contemporary analysis of the neo-Wittgenstenian position, see eg S Lovibond, *Realism and Imagination in Ethics* (Minneapolis, University of Minnesota Press, 1983).

The assumed correlation between agreement and intelligibility is controversial and has been challenged by Gerald Gaus who contends that there is no inherent correlation. As he affirms, irreconcilable disagreement is not always a source of unintelligibility.[88] Nevertheless, the political liberal approach is restricted, for the most part, to disagreement about justice, ie disagreement about the fair terms for co-operation. Rawls thereby excludes consideration of questions such as how to cope with disagreement about the permissibility of blasphemy, proselytising, euthanasia, cloning, prostitution, pornography, drugs, gambling, etc. These disagreements that can and do surface in political life are the result of a plurality of comprehensive conceptions of the good. Though we may want to argue that arguments in favour of prohibiting these kinds of activities are unreasonable, few would avow that the arguments, defences, objections, and counter-proposals would be unintelligible. If, for example, a community of *A*s demands that the *B*s stop gambling on the basis that gambling is wrong, and the *B*s happen to enjoy gambling, the latter will not necessarily demand an explanation as to why gambling is wrong, but will instead signal that they refuse to discuss their gambling by stating that it is none of the *A*s' business what they do as long as they do not harm anybody. In other words, the *B*s demand that the *A*s privatise their opinion about gambling. The *B*s may continue to disagree. However, though there are quite different strategies of reasoning at play, nobody would say that the parties have failed to understand the basis for one another's positions or what their disagreement is about.

Still, some disagreements are serious inasmuch as they really seem irreconcilable, and insofar as they centre on the need for legislative action that seems to challenge the very idea of a rights-based approach to cultural conflict, ie an approach that gives everybody a right to take part in the resolution of that conflict. Once again, this reality does not render such disagreements unintelligible. One way of making sense of disagreement is by way of abstraction. Although this method does not *resolve* the disagreement as such, it assists in sorting out what is not in dispute and may clarify what lies behind a certain disagreement. For example, this is how Ronald Dworkin suggests we should approach disagreements about the permissibility of abortion, euthanasia, and cloning.[89] Though we agree about the sacredness of life, we disagree—ferociously and intensively—what this means in the context of these issues, and who is to decide about that. However, while liberals suggest that an endorsement of individual freedom is the reasonable solution to this sort of disagreement, there may be others who nevertheless continue to disagree with them.

[88] G Gaus, *Justificatory Liberalism*, above n 30, at 117.
[89] R Dworkin, *Life's Dominion: An Argument About Abortion, Euthanasia, and Individual Freedom* (New York, Knopf, 1993).

The Right to Disagree

Even though, as Mark Tushnet argues, abstract rights get specified in political contexts and do not provide determinate answers for what rights we have on the ground, it is still important to say something about the way in which rights-bearers are supposed to approach, assess, and resolve conflicts about rights.[90] Rawls pleads for reasonableness in the sense of limiting the range of sources drawn upon to resolve a cultural conflict to those recognised in the public culture of one's society. This limitation seems unacceptable in a society composed of individuals with different cultural backgrounds and attachments. As already noted in this chapter, it is necessary to consider that not everybody whose rights are at stake in a political discussion is familiar with publically recognised sources. The lack of suitable cultural equipment pivotal to make effective use of such sources can hardly be a legitimate ground for exclusion in a multicultural society. Secondly, it is necessary to consider that real public cultures are often flavoured by a certain religious, ethical, or philosophical heritage. That heritage does not necessarily represent 'common' but 'contested' ground. It may have been regarded as legitimate in one particular period, but is no longer so in the light of changes in the cultural make-up of the population. The ability to criticise, protest, and dissent from this heritage is of crucial importance even if such criticisms are likely to be perceived as unreasonable from the standpoint of the cultural mainstream. Thus, apart from the fact that the criterion of reasonableness purporting to moderate disagreement is indeterminate as to whose claims and concerns should be excluded from consideration in conflict resolution, the idea of public reason seems to fail to appreciate the cultural and ideological heritage of public institutions and its immediate relevance to political discussion in societies that become more diverse.

While the political liberal idea is inclusive, it also acknowledges that any society is likely to include mad, unreasonable, and irrational views as well and that a theory of what the requirements of public justification involve must take this reality into account. According to the political liberal idea of public reason, a reasonable person assents to principles for co-operation that reflect what reasonable people might reasonably accept. When people put forward demands, counter-arguments, etc, in actual deliberations in the public forum, their actions are regarded as reasonable insofar as they are motivated with reference to the terms of co-operation. The terms of co-operation constitute the public reasons in discussions on matters of common concern. To reason publicly is to frame legislative proposals, objections, and

[90] M Tushnet, 'An Essay on Rights' (1984) 62 *Texas Law Review* 1363 at 1375. Tushnet holds that: 'Part of the argument for technical indeterminacy is that abstract rights get specified in particular legal contexts. The argument for fundamental indeterminacy is that rights get specified in particular social contexts.'

counter-arguments, always with a view to these terms. Thus, a crucial question for political liberals is how these terms are identified.

A focus on two ideas is critical for clarifying what is both distinct and problematic about the reasonable people thesis. The first idea refers to the claim about the centrality of the public culture of a state's institutional arrangement in articulating the repertoires of values, principles, and ideas that the subjects can legitimately rely upon in common discussions raising questions about justice and right. Thus, according to the reasonable people thesis, it is necessary to look to the public culture in search of principles that are accessible and agreeable to all, and thus, could possibly constitute the basic terms for social co-operation. The second idea refers to what it means to be treated as an equal. That idea has a tendency to reinforce ignorance of morally significant cultural difference (of primary concern in this book) among subjects whose rights and duties are affected by the political process.

The political liberal conception of public justification (or public reason) aspires to be a 'free-standing' view, to be 'political and not metaphysical'.[91] Instead of assuming that a set of fundamental claims are true, from the outset, we ought to search for principles and values embedded in the public culture when settling the issue about the fair terms of co-operation.[92] The more reasonable approach to what seem to be irreconcilable and incommensurable disagreements is to search for common ground. A political conception of justice is supposed to represent such common ground as it is developed on the basis of ideas and principles embedded in the public culture. As Rawls puts it, 'we turn instead to the fundamental ideas we seem to share through the public political culture.'[93] These ideas and principles form a shared or shareable conception of justice which is supposed to frame and inform common deliberations on matters of common concern. This idea warrants a set of comments from the standpoint of individual freedom.

The claim about the centrality of the public culture when thinking about right and justice for a given place may be problematic for several reasons. First of all, it seems to suggest that fundamental claims about liberty and equality are primarily accessible to subjects brought up in a place whose public institutions uphold and cherish these values.[94] It thereby downplays the possibility, indeed, the presupposition, that the accessibility of such values do not exclusively or primarily depend on learning capabilities, but on ability to reason, ie making use of intellectual and moral powers. The public culture approach to the question about the substance of public reason fails to consider the standpoint of people whose public culture (currently)

[91] See J Rawls, 'Justice as Fairness: Political not Metaphysical' (1985) 14 *Philosophy and Public Affairs* 223.

[92] J Rawls, *Political Liberalism*, above n 28, at 223.

[93] *Ibid*, at 150.

[94] For a general account of 'accessibility condition' see G Gaus, *Justificatory Liberalism*, above n 30, at 132 ff.

does not support values of liberty and equality. Their society might be classified as 'decently hierarchical.' As a consequence, they can not legitimately rely upon ideas, principles, or arguments collected in, say, a liberal (comprehensive) doctrine currently marginalised and excluded from the public sphere. Does Rawls support this conclusion?

In *The Law of Peoples*, Rawls focuses directly on the issue of legitimate recourse to differing substantive public reasons in different places. To this end, he distinguishes between liberal peoples and non-liberal peoples (also referred to as decent or hierarchical peoples). The former share a public reason consisting of a family of liberal conceptions of justice.[95] The latter, by contrast, are guided by a 'common good idea of justice', some of which have a 'common aim' while others have 'special priorities.'[96] As suggested in chapter five of this book, *The Law of Peoples* fails to appreciate the reality of human mobility and, above all, the permanence of this fact. It fails to consider the multicultural background to public institutions (both liberal and non-liberal ones) and the circumstances of political life, if not created then accentuated by this fact, including moral disagreement and communicative distance. These circumstances nevertheless indicate that a general theory of democratic politics must cope with the likelihood that there will be people in liberal societies with common good ideas of justice, as well as people with liberal conceptions of justice living in non-liberal societies.

In addition, if we take seriously the contention that people are capable of developing ideas about justice in a different direction from those currently dominating the official institutions in their place of birth and upbringing, it is furthermore necessary to account for the possibility of a deeper disagreement on a much broader range of issues not necessarily limited to regulatory matters (*adiaphora*) or to the socio-economic structure (the fair distribution of resources). On a political liberal account, it seems possible that those whose ideas, principles, or values are not familiar to all (ie not part of the public culture) may legitimately be regarded as unreasonable, even unintelligible, quite regardless of the substance of their claim. For example, demands for de-regulation of laws founded on religious predicament would be regarded as unreasonable in a place whose official institutions conduct their affairs according to a religious conception of justice.

In other words, whether a given demand is regarded as reasonable depends on what ideas, values, and principle are embedded in the public culture and, therefore, may count as public reasons. In a 'liberal' society, are these reasons limited to values of liberty and equality or do they comprise a broader range of values? It is a well-known fact that most societies that are characterised as 'liberal', in the sense of affirming a set of basic liberties,

[95] J Rawls, *The Law of Peoples* (Cambridge Mass, Harvard University Press, 1999), at 55–56.

[96] *Ibid*. For a fuller explanation of the idea of 'common aim', see 71 ff; and for an account of 'special priorities', see 75 ff.

often entertain predicaments that stand in need of reflection and revision as the cultural make-ups of the subjects change. The likelihood of legislative change largely depends on the role of the cultural and ideological heritage of a country for the spirit in which its inhabitants are expected to approach, assess, and examine questions of justice and right arising at any particular point in time.

While it is correct that the cultural and ideological heritage of a place influences the way in which most of its inhabitants approach these kinds of issues, it does not mean that this method should be endorsed as right. For example, a difference in terms of cultural and ideological heritage influences the way in which the United States and European states understand the multicultural problem itself. Steven Lukes and Christian Joppke note that, in the United States, the multicultural *problematique* is essentially about race while in Europe it is about foreigners. Their explanation of this difference is that:

> European nations are Christian in a way the United States, with its strict separation between Church and state, is not ... [As a consequence,] nationhood in Europe has strong cultural connotations that are absent in the United States.[97]

These differences explain why Rawls, for instance, defines cultural conflict as a conflict of race or status and does not seem to consider the full range of cultural conflicts occurring in Europe.[98] At the same time, however, attaching significance to this distinction makes us less aware of the racism that exists in Europe and less aware of the fact that a newcomer faces the same circumstance defined in terms of lacking cultural equipment wherever he or she happens to be, also in the United States.

Christian values appear to exert enduring influence upon the various Western political processes. As Yves Mény and Andrew Knapp point out,

> it may seem a paradoxical observation to make at a time when Christian religious practice is on the wane everywhere in the Western world, whether the branch of Christianity is Catholic, Anglican, Lutheran, or Calvinist. Yet the influence of religion endures, as if the values with it persisted and were directing political behavior despite the decline of religious practice and the weakening of institutional allegiances.[99]

This aspect of the cultural heritage of Europe is reflected in the various public cultures of states making up the European Union. It is reflected more

[97] S Lukes and C Joppke, 'Introduction' in S Lukes and C Joppke (eds), *Multicultural Questions* (Oxford, Oxford University Press, 1999), at 17.

[98] J Rawls, *Political Liberalism*, above n 28, at *lx*.

[99] Y Mény and A Knapp, *Government and Politics in Western Europe, Britain, France, Italy, Germany*, 3rd edn (New York, Oxford University Press, 1998), at 26.

obviously in, for example, the British and Italian blasphemy laws. It is furthermore reflected in the co-operative relationships (rather than separation) that exist between State and Church in some European states.[100] It is reflected in the firm insistence on the French principle of secularity once formulated in reaction to the power of the Catholic Church. It is also reflected in the Greek public culture and its declaration of Greek Orthodox Christianity as the official religion. It is obviously reflected in the European practice of Sunday as the day of rest. These are but few examples of dimensions of European public cultures necessary for understanding the source of some cultural conflicts in Europe today.

How are we to approach the cultural conflicts arising here and now that force us to reflect on these dimensions of the public culture? What does it mean to discuss such issues in the spirit of public reason? The central idea of public reason is that citizens ought to conduct their common affairs in a spirit of reciprocity and liberal values.[101] Rawls explains that the substantive content of public reason does not consist of one single conception of justice, but a family of such conceptions. A citizen is said to engage in public reason when he or she deliberates within a framework of what he or she sincerely regards as the most reasonable political conception. The distinguishing feature of such a conception is that it

> expresses political values that others, as free and equal citizens might also reasonably be expected to endorse. Each of us must have principles and guidelines to which we appeal in such a way that this criterion is satisfied.[102]

A participant is regarded as unreasonable if she affirms her position as true. She is likewise unreasonable if she simply seeks to impose her ideas, principles, or values, central to her own comprehensive doctrine, without consideration of pluralism.

Imagine we apply the idea of public reason to the controversy about the British blasphemy law, prohibiting blasphemous conduct in relation to Christian beliefs, which regained attention as a result of the *Salman Rushdie* affair.[103] One participant, *A*, who is agnostic on matters of religion, favours de-regulation and privatisation of matters of religious conscience given that Britain is a plural society. He seeks to justify his demand for de-regulation

[100] For an account of the relationship between the Church and the German State, see eg EA Moseley, 'Defining Religious Tolerance: German Policy Toward the Church of Scientology' (1997) 30 *Vanderbilt Journal of Transnational Law* 1129.

[101] J Rawls, *Political Liberalism*, above n 28. For the criterion of reciprocity, see *xliv* and 54; and for the content of public reason, 223 ff.

[102] *Ibid*, at 140.

[103] For a fuller account of the disagreement about the blasphemy law, see *Law, Blasphemy and the Multifaith Society*. Report of a seminar organised by the Commission for Racial Equality and the Interfaith Network of the United Kingdom (September 1989) (London, The Commission, 1990).

by appealing to the highly controversial principle of neutrality as well as to freedom of expression. Another participant, *B*, is a practising Christian. He believes that the law in question does not restrict freedom of expression in unreasonable ways. Above all, the law rightly prohibits conduct offensive to God, Jesus Christ, or the Bible. He thinks it is the case that people, such as Mr Wingrove, who tried to publish a pornographic video work entitled 'Visions of Ecstasy' where a Carmelite nun is experiencing 'powerful ecstatic visions of Jesus Christ' (ie erotic fantasies) commit a wrong and, as a consequence, should be punished.[104] A third participant, *C*, who is Muslim, agrees with B about the wrongs done in blasphemous conduct, but thinks it is grossly unfair that Islam is not similarly protected under the British blasphemy law in the same way as his Muslim fellows are protected under Italian law.[105]

How would their common discussion proceed if *A*, *B*, and *C* engaged in public reason when discussing the blasphemy law? *C* does not seem able to explain the deeper basis for his proposal about extending the protection accorded by the blasphemy law to Islam. Possibly, he could, as the Italian Constitutional Court has done, stress the principle of egalitarianism in advancing his proposal for legislative revision to the rest. Quite regardless of the substantive content of a particular protection, it ought to protect everyone and not merely a few. *A*, in contrast, is fundamentally opposed to the blasphemy law. He argues that he cannot appreciate the basis for that law and that all aspects of a legal system ought to be justifiable from the standpoint of public reason (narrowly defined). What this means, *A* affirms, is that all laws must be capable of being justified on grounds that do not presuppose a belief in God to make sense.

B really finds himself outside the ambit of acceptable lines of argumentation about maintaining the law as it is. He cannot reasonably find legitimate arguments from the standpoint of public reason (narrowly defined) unless he is able to draw upon the full repertoires of ideas, values, and principles stored in the British public culture legitimising the blasphemy law in the first place. After all, his concern derives from a belief in a culture-dependent conception of *malum in se* inasmuch as it does not exist in all cultures (although some account of offence or insult to persons might). *A* might nevertheless be

[104] *Wingrove v UK* no 17419/90 ECHR 1996–V 24 EHRR 1.

[105] See *Tutela penale del sentimento religioso. artt.* 402–406 e 724 *del codice penale*: *Sent.* N. 440 *del* 1995 (*Caianiello; Zagrebelsky*): Bestemmia (art 724 c.p.). '*In fatti, mentre la bestemmia contro la Divinità stessa a questa o a quella religione, di guisa che, già ora, risultano protetti dalle invettive e dalle espressioni oltraggiose tutti i credenti e tutte le fedi religiose, senza distinzioni o discriminazioni, la bestemmia contro i Simboli o le Persone venerati, di cui alla seconda parte della dispozione, si riferisce testualmente soltanto alla 'religione dello Stato', e cioè alla religione cattolica. Alla riconosciuta violazione del principio di eguaglianza, in presenza del divieto di decisioni additive, in materia penale, che preclude alle Corte l'estensione della norma alle fedi religiose escluse, consegue il suo annullamento per difetto di generalità*'; *Sent.* 329 *del* 1997 (*Granata; Zagrabelsky*): *Offese alla religione dello Stato mediante vilipendio di cose* (art 404, *primo comma*, c.p.).

able to argue that the cultural conflict ought to be excluded from the public forum on the basis that it involves discussing a topic that lies outside the domain of public reason. It necessarily involves moving in the direction of religion, and thus, irreconcilable issues, and that what they as citizens ought to do is to search for common ground. However, this strategy fails to be convincing since it involves transforming one 'issue' into a 'non-issue' in spite of the possibility of unreasonable restrictions upon individual rights. Possibly, *A* could use the support in *C*'s background beliefs about decent conduct and support *C*'s quest for universalisation and not insisting on the need for a shared basis for that law. In case of majority decision, then, the blasphemy law could prevail although in a modified version.

The idea of public reason frames a common discussion among individuals attached to different comprehensive doctrines by limiting the focus of their discussion regarding justice to values of liberty and equality (and, as the case may be, a broader range of values stored in the public culture). It is supposed to restrain *B* and *C* from invoking religious arguments in support of their respective demands. It also restrains *A* from arguing about the blasphemy law from the standpoint of his agnostic outlook on matters of religion. The political liberal idea thereby refuses to give weight and admit the full background of the cultural conflict in focus, ie the Christian cultural heritage of Britain as well as the diverse religious, ethical, and philosophical strands of thought co-existing in Britain today. Once in the public forum, each is to be treated as a free and equal citizen whose legitimate concerns are limited to those he shares with all others. *A* is not supposed to consider the religious identities of *B* and *C*. *B* and *C*, in turn, are not supposed to argue on the basis of their respective religious beliefs supporting their conviction that blasphemy is, after all, *malum in se* in their view.

Though *A* appears to be the only one able to argue for his proposal about de-regulation in what seems to be the true spirit of liberal public reason he might nevertheless fail to convince his audience about the reasonableness of his demands given their particular beliefs. Still, we may ask, are *A*, *B*, and *C* actually engaging in public reason in the example given? It has been suggested that the problem at stake has its source in differing and conflicting beliefs about decent conduct, different opinions, that is, about the reasons, if any, for regulating a certain field of action. The resolution of such conflict presupposes the need to reason about the basis for regulating action more generally. The idea of public reason is that the participants divest themselves from their own particular beliefs and move to common ground as they deliberate in the public forum. But is it is reasonable to suppose that the individual should distance himself from personal conditions on precisely the matter being discussed?

The political liberal approach risks assimilating cultural differences of moral significance (notably, difference on *adiaphora*) in unreasonable ways. One serious problem with the idea of public reason is its ignorance of the standpoint of conscientious objectors in relation to regulation associated with a scheme of social co-operation and discussed at length in chapter six. In highlighting the complications posed by this kind of case in a multicultural society, it becomes clear that the political liberal idea of reasonable political conduct does not require that the actor justify a law or regulation *to* those whose rights, interests, or duties are affected; instead, he or she is supposed to search for arguments that 'reasonable citizens might reasonably accept.' No attention is paid to cultural differences in terms of actual systems of beliefs and reasons in deliberations in the public forum.

In addition, what it means to act responsibly—what count as acceptable arguments, objections, counter-proposals, and so on—will depend, in part on the actual context as well as the content of the laws in force in one's place of residence. For example, as the analysis in this section indicates, in a Western European context, it is not unusual that activist, religiously inspired, Christian political parties attach more value to the public recognition of their religious norms than others. Consequently, many Western European political discussions are dominated by conflicting values of secularly and religiously inspired, mainly, Christian ideologies. Shadid and van Koningsveld suggest that, in the light of this background, actions on the part of Muslim groups aiming at the public recognition of some aspects of Islam in Western European states should be regarded, first and foremost, as legitimate forms of political participation, identical to those of other religiously-inspired actors active within the same communities.[106]

Though the acknowledgement of the relevance of context hardly settles the question as to what it means to act responsibly, it nevertheless indicates the difficulty of the question for the purposes of analysis. A conception of responsible (or, alternatively, reasonable) conduct must take seriously the importance of a right to disagree with, protest against, and dissent from laws, including laws legitimised by the public culture. That is to say, it must take seriously the point that the public culture approach upheld by political liberals offers no legitimate standpoint for those who differ in cultural terms to disagree about controversial components of the public culture itself.

While Rawls' criterion of reasonableness offers no determinate response to fair conflict-resolution involving people with differing cultural backgrounds and attachments, his account of public reason developed in the spirit of reasonableness may nevertheless indicate the need for some common principles to guide political discussions in multicultural settings. The idea of public reason seeks to formulate an account of what it means to use the right to participation in a responsible way. As this section demonstrates, there are obviously different understandings of what it means to reason publicly,

[106] See WAR Shadid and PS van Koningsveld, *Religious Freedom and the Position of Islam in Western Europe*, above n 59, at 61. Shadid and van Koningsveld distinguish between 'activistic' interpretations of religious doctrines and 'quiestistic' interpretations of religious doctrines. While the former comprise political aspirations the latter are individualistic in outlook.

that is, different conceptions of what is required for a legislative proposition to be considered publicly justified. However, at a more general level, it may be possible to consider the idea of public reason as asking everybody involved in political discussions to respect the requirements of public justification in the sense of seeking to reason with others on matters of common concern in a way that does not presuppose agreement. It also involves recognising that it is in the discussion with others that one might come to a better understanding of their claims and concerns, and the bases of those claims and concerns, and in this way arrive at a more informed judgement on conflicts involving rights compared to someone who has not taken part in that discussion. Nevertheless, there is no guarantee that others will agree with me that this is what public reason might minimally amount to in multicultural societies. Others might continue to insist on the need for a more substantive conception. The recognition of moral disagreement in political life involves coping with the fact that no value, idea, or principle is settled, once and for all, or even for now.

CONCLUSION

The account of fair conflict-resolution in multicultural societies developed in this chapter has offered little in the way of conclusive argument as to how the cultural conflicts outlined in the beginning of this chapter and also those alluded to later ought to be resolved. One reason for this silence is the contention that there may be no correct answers that we—as theorists of rights—are able to present as the final say on conflicts that occur between comprehensive conceptions of the good some of which concern matters of ultimate indifference and some of which are utterly complicated to resolve once the moral disagreement underpinning the rights in conflict has been taken seriously. As Gaus reminds us, however, moral disagreement is not necessarily 'indeterminate'; that is, it is not necessarily the case that we know there are no 'right' answers. More often disagreements may be 'inconclusive', an inconclusiveness that also explains why people continue to engage in these debates. As Gaus puts it:

> it is precisely because our moral disputes are not *typically* indeterminate that it makes sense to form opinions and keep arguing about them.[107]

I have sought to explain why it is nevertheless necessary to focus on cultural conflicts, and that doing so is not unfortunate in the light of a commitment to ensuring respect for individual freedom, but imperative because of that commitment. More specifically, since it is not unusual that cultural conflicts involve individual rights, the least to be expected is that those whose rights,

[107] G Gaus, *Justificatory Liberalism*, above n 30, at 154.

interests, and duties are affected have the right to take part in the political process expected to settle such conflicts. The affirmation of the right to equal participation is made on that basis. There are many forms of political participation, and so many ways of influencing the outcome of that process, not all of which are institutional and conventional (protests, demonstrations, civil disobedience). The use of these informal and unconventional avenues is expected to be more frequent in multicultural societies considering the many cultural barriers impeding access to the public forum for political discussion from the standpoint of those whose cultures are marginalised in that forum. At the same time, however, it must be noted that similar barriers, especially in terms of lack of suitable cultural equipment, pertain in the contest of the more informal and unconventional avenues as well. Nevertheless, reference to such barriers is not a legitimate ground for excluding conscientious dissent by marginalised cultures from the ambit of political life.

While an accommodation of cultural differences into the political process might complicate the deliberative part of that process, it does not necessarily render discussions on matters of common concern among people of differing cultural backgrounds and attachments unintelligible or unreasonable. In a multicultural society, it can hardly be required that everybody must limit the source of reason to that of the public culture; instead, it must be possible to use one's own cultural sources of reason when exercising the right to participation. At the same time, this is not to say that the exercise of that right is without restraint. The requirements of public justification involve at the very minimum that the holders of the right to participation recognise that there are others in society who may disagree on how conflicts are to be resolved given their differing conceptions of the good.

8

Cultural Ignorance of Law: An Excusing Condition?

DOES THE CIRCUMSTANCE characterised in terms of deficient suitable cultural equipment constitute an excusing condition in the event that a person has done (or not done) what is expected of him or her as a matter of law? Notwithstanding a commitment to securing suitable cultural equipment for all, instances of non-compliance with the law due to radical unfamiliarity with the cultural equipment in use by public institutions can (and do) occur. The question, then, is whether this sort of cultural difference could possibly count as valid excuse in case of non-compliance, based on the contention that punishing somebody for having done a thing he could not reasonably have known was illegal would be grossly unfair. Cases of non-compliance due to cultural ignorance may involve both criminal and administrative law. Thus, various sanctions are at stake. For example, apart from imprisonment, a person who fails to comply with a law due to cultural ignorance may not be provided a good that he or she is entitled to due to an inability to meet a deadline or to fill in a form correctly.

Against this background, this chapter focuses on the possibility of cases amounting to involuntary ignorance of laws in multicultural societies as a result of deficient suitable cultural equipment and how to respond to such cases in a way consistent with a minimum provision of respect for individual freedom. While the analysis pays special attention to the circumstance of newcomers (immigrants and refugees), the line of argument purports to be applicable to all cases exhibiting a similar circumstance, such as when a territory on which a people resides has been annexed to a foreign power and the inhabitants are suddenly expected to comply with a body of laws unfamiliar to them. What is decisive for my account of inadequate cultural equipment as a legitimate ground for excuse is whether a person can be expected to be familiar with the laws that apply to him by virtue of his territorial location in the light of his actual cultural equipment.

The analysis begins with an explanatory background to the supposition that an individual cannot reasonably be expected to be familiar with various bodies of rules under whose authority he may nevertheless be subsumed. It then explores how the reality of ignorance of law, primarily among ordinary people, has been approached assessed, and criticised by theorists of law.

The contributions made in this field frame the assessment of the question as to whether a person's cultural equipment, insufficient to access the law that claims authority over his conduct, should ever be considered as an excuse by law officials assigned to administrate and enforce that law in individual cases and, if so, under what conditions.

THE CIRCUMSTANCE OF NEWCOMERS

The multiculturalisation of local legal frameworks largely depends on an ever increasing human mobility across the surface of the earth in search for alternative places of settlement, work, or life and facilitated by global infrastructures of transportation and communication. Some are obviously familiar with the law of their destination. Indeed, they go to a place precisely because it permits what is forbidden elsewhere or to benefit from entitlements that are not provided for in their home country. Others whose travels are driven by necessity rather than business, pleasure, or rational calculation, cannot reasonably be expected to be familiar with the law of their host country. Unlike sex-tourists to Thailand, holiday drug-users to Amsterdam, or multinational industries in search of cheap labour forces, a vast number of people are unfamiliar with the law that claims authority over their conduct in their new place of residence. It is the acknowledgement of this fact that constitutes the starting point for this analysis.

POSITIVE LAWS DIFFER FROM PLACE TO PLACE

Why is it reasonable to assume that a notable number of newcomers are unfamiliar with the law in their new place? The surface of the earth is covered by a corresponding patchwork of local systems of law. The particular form and content of one such system differs from that of another. Sometimes only minor differences pertain; in other cases, the difference is radical. Though the inhabitants of one place can be said to share *general ideas* with all others elsewhere about what humans must never do to one another, the contours of their set of laws are likely to differ from those developed by others. In areas such as family law, immigration law, and criminal law, the difference can be most striking. The acknowledgement of differences between local systems of law is not intended as a *normative* claim. Thus, it is not suggested that we should care for such differences and seek to maintain them against any wave of assimilation. Particular laws can be seriously unjust and call for revision. In addition, diverse laws may need to be harmonised for the sake of efficacy in trade or other types of transnational interaction. For the purposes of the present argument, however, it is sufficient to note that such differences exist.

There are several explanations for legal differences. One is the result of differing authoritative settlements of ideological disagreements (discussed at length in the previous chapter in relation to disagreements about justice). A second explanation is a difference in terms of which substantive social norms flavour the spirit of interaction among the inhabitants clustered together in a given place. It obviously makes a difference for the shape and content of the law whether most of the inhabitants in a place conduct their affairs in a spirit of envy and vengeance or in a spirit of 'everyday Kantianism.' Thirdly, a difference in legal form and content may be the product of a range of possible solutions to various co-ordination problems (eg which side of the street to drive on, etc). Even if we accept the claim about the existence of independent moral norms, it may be necessary to also accept and consider this factor in a general explanation of variation among legal systems. In addition, as John Finnis, a contemporary natural law theorist explains, even if the legislative choice between driving on the left and driving on the right is a matter of ultimate indifference in the abstract, a concrete decision in any given place might not be perceived as such since people might already tend to drive on the left and already have adjusted their habits, vehicle construction, road design, and street furniture accordingly.[1]

A fourth explanation for legal difference in form and content that should also be mentioned is the difference explained as the product of 'path-dependence'. That is to say, in the words of Richard Posner:

> where you end up may depend on where you start out from, even if, were it not for having started where you did, a different end point would be better.[2]

The most notorious illustration of the economic concept of 'path-dependence' is that of the typewriter keyboard. Although we may contemplate better ways of organising the letters on the keyboard in order to type more effectively, the fact that so many are familiar with the current organisation renders any change in the foreseeable future highly unlikely. Legal institutions tend to frame their reasoning with a view of precedents as a vital source of law. A series of cases establishes a path that some believe takes on a life on its own. Possibly, a similar line of reasoning can be applied in relation to legislative work. Legislators seldom work out anew what the regulation of a given field of action ought to be without examining and considering the vocabulary, shape, and content of the present regulation, if it exists.

According to Posner, we expect to observe path-dependence when the transition cost is high relative to the benefit of change, and it tends to be high when transition requires a high degree of co-ordination. Thus, the difference need not be explained as a quasi-religious, mystical maintenance of ancient ways. Posner continues by noting that there is little doubt that path-dependence is an important phenomenon in law. Some evidence for this

1 J Finnis, *Natural Law and Natural Rights* (Oxford, Oxford University Press, 1980), at 287.
2 RA Posner, 'Past-Dependency, Pragmatism, and Critique of History in Adjudication and Legal Scholarship' (2000) 67 *University of Chicago Law Review* 573 at 583.

assertion is that the convergence of legal systems is much slower than the convergence of technology or economic institutions. For example, the laws and legal institutions of the different states of the United States vary more than the economic practices and institutions of the states do, and the variations are yet more significant and mysterious in a cross-country comparison, even when the comparison is limited to countries whose economic and political systems, and levels of education and income, are similar to those of the United States.[3] Legal theorists disagree as to why judges (and legislators) *ought* to look into the past when deciding about the present, and whether the past is best regarded as a storage of information or whether there is something valuable about looking into the past that goes beyond the mere search for relevant information.[4] For the purposes of the present analysis, however, it is not necessary to settle this issue. It is sufficient to note that path-dependence, whether it ought to be appreciated or not, is an important variable in explaining differences in laws and legal institutions.

Despite the variations that exist in terms of local laws and legal institutions new arrivals are expected to comply with the law in their new place by virtue of their territorial location. Since law is not the same everywhere, meeting this expectation can and often does require that new arrivals adjust themselves in terms of conduct. It may involve the abandonment of rituals thought necessary for a girl to become a woman or compromising certain clothing regarded as the only decent way of dress in social life. Since laws differ from place to place including laws on marriage, divorce, inheritance, business, child-rearing, speed limits, working hours, public health, rules protecting the environment and animals from suffering, access to land owned by others, and so on, it is evidently not sufficient to continue conducting one's affairs according to the laws of one's country of birth and upbringing in order to meet this expectation.

Expectations of adjustment to the law of the place of residence are not limited to laws already in force. The legislature in the recipient state may take legislative action so as to outlaw habits, rituals, or customs introduced by new arrivals and alien to the permanent population and deemed odd, harmful, or wicked by them. Notorious examples of laws enacted by several European legislatures as a result of human mobility and the consequent introduction of cultural practices include those relating to polygamy, arranged marriages, child marriages, and female circumcision. It must be noted that, although different cultural practices in these fields of action are real and significant from the standpoint of respecting individual freedom, the differences

[3] *Ibid*, at 584.

[4] For an account of the latter approach, see, for example, R Dworkin, *Law's Empire* (Cambridge Mass, The Belknapp Press of Harvard University Press, 1986), at 167. Dworkin states that 'the past must be allowed some special power of its own in court, contrary to the pragmatist's claim that it must not.' This is the principle of integrity in adjudication. See also L Kramer, 'Fidelity to History—and Through It' (1997) 65 *Fordham Law Review* 1627.

are often the result of disagreements about details as to how a general issue of common concern ought to be resolved. For example, while there is hardly any culture that is alien to the very idea of marriage, cultures differ in their understandings of the appropriate minimum age of marriage and with whom to marry. Of course, it should be pointed out that already established families—even if constituted in ways prohibited by European laws—are often protected from annulment or non-recognition upon arrival to the recipient state. A cosmopolitan legal regime purports to protect the stability of certain human relationships regardless of their particular location. For this reason, several European legal systems acknowledge polygamous marriages entered into prior to arrival. Even so, it is expected that newcomers conform to European laws on marriage, which are oriented towards ideas about romantic and monogamous love, should they stay. Thus, although family arrangements that are alien to the native-born are recognised upon arrival, newcomers must respect the law in force in their *future* dealings with one another and all other inhabitants. Given this expectation, their unfamiliarity becomes a direct concern for society as a whole.

This background explains the basis for the assumption about variation in terms of form and content among legal systems, and constitutes evidence for the contention that new arrivals are usually unfamiliar with the law in places other than that of their birth and upbringing. Is this conclusion correct? Some may come from a neighbouring country. Others may be comparative lawyers and have read virtually all there is to read about different legal systems. Others again may choose a destination whose inhabitants are known to conduct their social affairs in ways similar to theirs. At the same time, we know that, in spite of occasional exceptions, it can hardly be stated as an assumption that new arrivals would have sufficient knowledge of the laws of this or that place prior to arrival and for some period thereafter. In more general terms, social integration—or what is referred to in this book as the acquisition of suitable cultural equipment—is said to take time. This time lag has been acknowledged by the German Constitutional Court. It has pronounced that new arrivals are expected to have integrated socially and economically only after eight years.[5] Even so, they are expected to comply with German law right from the start. Leaving aside the spurious assertion by this court about a possible deadline for integration, how is the problem of 'legal integration' supposed to be approached?

Ignorance of Positive Law

Surprisingly enough, to find support for the claim about the circumstance of newcomers and its direct relevance for law and eventually for law-applying institutions in multicultural societies encountering individual cases of cultural ignorance in their daily operation, it seems necessary to resort to more

[5] BVerfGe 76, 1 (1987).

classical works in political theory such as Thomas Hobbes' *Leviathan*. Although the aim of the present chapter is not to assess simply what Hobbes had to say on the matter, much of his analysis continues to be relevant today. Therefore, the initial argument will be developed in the light of his understanding of what the circumstance of new arrivals consists of, and what sorts of questions in the field of law are relevant to that circumstance. Hobbes' account is confined to ignorance of criminal law. It obviously does not consider the growth of administrative law and the complications it gives rise to for newcomers and others who differ in cultural terms from the legal system in force. Nevertheless, his account constitutes a useful starting point for this analysis.

Hobbes did not expect that new arrivals would observe the law of a foreign place unless the sovereign declared to them what the law is. As a matter of fact, he thought that unfamiliarity or ignorance of new arrivals constitutes valid *excuse* in case of unlawful conduct. New arrivals were not to be held responsible for crimes according to the law until its commands and directives had been declared to them. In his words:

> Ignorance of the Civill Law, shall Excuse a man in a strange Country, till it be declared to him; because, till then no Civill Law is binding.[6]

Hobbes' remark must be read in the light of his account of legal validity. For him, the announcement of the law to newcomers is not a favour or a luxury, but necessary in order to bind them. This reading of Hobbes becomes clear in the light of his account of the significance of unfamiliarity or ignorance among the native-born. Unless the law has been sufficiently communicated, similarly to newcomers, the native-born are also excused in case of non-compliance:

> In the like manner, if the Civill Law of a mans own Country, be not so sufficiently declared, as he may know it if he will; nor the Action against the Law of Nature; the Ignorance is a good Excuse: In other cases Ignorance of the Civill Law, Excuseth not.[7]

Even if the present analysis focuses on unfamiliarity as a serious obstacle confronted by newcomers, this is not to deny that the native-born may also be confronted with similar trouble. Knowledge about the specific contents of a legal system is not secured simply by virtue of leading one's entire life in a certain town or country. Since law in the present is not necessarily what it was in yesteryear, without communication of what the law is here and now there is no guarantee whatsoever that it is known by any of its addressees. In this sense, ignorance can be understood as an issue that does

[6] T Hobbes, *Leviathan* (Cambridge, Cambridge University Press, 1997), at 203.
[7] *Ibid*.

not merely concern a few, but concerns everyone. In other words, Hobbes' account presupposes that there is a very direct connection between the issue of what law is (on the one hand) and what people actually know as law (on the other).

What people know as law may differ even among the subjects of the same legal system. In the United States, the notion of 'racial profiling' and its more colloquial cousin, 'driving while black' has become a way of explaining how members of minority groups feel about their relationships not only with the police, but also with the justice system as a whole.[8] For a long time, African-Americans and other minorities have found themselves subject to traffic stops in numbers that are far out of proportion with their presence on the road. These drivers know that these stops are not motivated by traffic enforcement, but about fishing for evidence of other crimes, in particular, drugs, even though they have done absolutely nothing suspicious. In this context, the notion of profiling also means that, once stopped, these drivers are treated differently, ie searched, often treated with less respect, and subjected to intrusive questioning more frequently than are white drivers. In effect, the notion of racial profiling supports the charge that blacks are singled out and treated differently from whites in numerous ways in the justice system, whether they are walking the streets as law-abiding pedestrians or being sentenced in trials as defendants.[9] Though the law is the same, formally speaking, for all to read, there are nevertheless seriously objectionable differences in terms of what real law is in the eyes of ordinary people due to outright discrimination in law enforcement practices.

Furthermore, Meir Dan-Cohen explains that a distinction between two sets of rules serves to indicate the possibility that the sovereign legislator might transmit two sets of messages, one to the general public and the other to officials. The message to the latter may involve a host of information, such as the degree of tolerance as regards law-breaking, if any, certain defences generally regarded as unacceptable before the courts, or as the above-mentioned case suggests, informal practices of 'profiling', etc. Partial acoustic separation is not unusual. It prevails when a normative message is likely to register with either the general public or the officials but not both. In effect, legal systems may take advantage of the benefits of acoustic separation by engaging in 'selective transmission'—that is, in the transmission of different normative messages to officials and to the general public, respectively.[10] Dan-Cohen states that the maxim 'ignorance of the law is no excuse' is well known among non-lawyers. However, in reality, it is a mere starting point for

[8] See KK Russell, '"Driving While Black": Corollary Phenomena and Collateral Consequences' (1999) 40 *British Columbia Law Review* 717 at 721.

[9] D Harris, 'Symposium: Law Enforcement's Stake in Coming to Grips with Racial Profiling' (2001) 3 *Rutger's Race and the Law Review* 9 at 9–10.

[10] M Dan-Cohen, 'Decision Rules and Conduct Rules: On Acoustic Separation in Criminal Law' (1984) 97 *Harvard Law Review* 625 at 635–636.

the development of complex conflicting standards and considerations that allow courts to avoid many of the harsh results that strict adherence to the maxim would entail.[11] The clear behavioural implication of the rule that 'ignorance of the law is no excuse' is that one had better know the law. The clarity and simplicity of this phrase make it a highly suitable form of communication to the legally untutored. At the same time, the complexity of the set of decisional variables that actually guides courts in this area is made obscure to the public, but not to courts.[12] Thus, selective transmissions de facto hide part of the law from the public, but in doing so might enhance the effectiveness of the law.

A similar comment on the inaccessibility of segments of modern legislation in the eyes of ordinary people is advanced by Edward Rubin. He criticises the modern legislature for its tendency to adopt 'standard less legislation', and thereby give away its power to implementation agencies, as well as for its 'vagueness'. This lapse, Rubin asserts, allows the implementation mechanism too much discretion and subjects the addressees to legal strictures that they cannot understand and to the uncontrolled, arbitrary power of the implementation mechanism.[13]

Apart from these factors influencing individual ability to access law, Hobbes alerts us to yet another source of cultural ignorance, namely, unfamiliarity with the sovereign legislator. Newcomers, and others who are similarly situated in cultural terms, may not know who enacts and communicates the law in their place of residence. In other words, besides being unfamiliar with the specific form and content of the legal system, they may also be unacquainted with the *source* of law. For Hobbes and other legal positivists, it is the *political authority* that is the proper source of law, but for other theorists, it may be a church of a religious denomination. This observation indicates that not only does the law differ from place to place, but so do settlements of who is the sovereign legislator. For example, some countries respond in a democratic manner that all the citizens who have attained the use of reason are legislators, and thus participate in the making of laws. In this case, it is the legislature that is the source of law. Other countries respond that it is the king who is the sovereign and so the one who authoritatively determines what the law is. Although Hobbes developed his argument some 350 years ago, this diversity remains relevant today.

This diversity and its impact on general ideas about individual familiarity with a given legal system call for more detailed comment. If a person moves between countries that have resolved the question of authority in similar ways, he cannot be said to be ignorant of the sovereign in any but a trivial sense. For example, a Swedish native-born can hardly be said to be unfamiliar with the

[11] *Ibid*, at 645–646.
[12] *Ibid*, at 648.
[13] EL Rubin, 'Law and Legislation in the Administrative State' (1989) 89 *Columbia Law Review* 369 at 397–398.

political arrangements of Spain or Norway, at least not as soon as he has been informed of their similarities. There may be some differences but they are not so great. Nevertheless, since democratic solutions are not the response provided to the question of authority everywhere (even if many of us believe that it *should* be and seek to take measures to revise this state of affairs), some attention must be paid to this diversity as well. If people come from a place where no democratic arrangements exist, it is a difference that has a direct bearing on a person's familiarity with the law of his host country. Thus, the circumstance of new arrivals may not be confined to ignorance of the law that applies to their conduct, but extend to ignorance of the source of that law. This reality influences their ability to find out what the law is. The recognition of diversity in terms of understandings of proper sources of law is not supposed to mean that democratic ideas would be inaccessible to those whose laws are enacted by a king or dictator. Indeed, democracy may be precisely what a person fought for in her place of birth and upbringing and which forced her to embark on her flight. Nevertheless, the day-to-day operation of democratic institutions in a given place may be unfamiliar to an outsider.

Hobbes acknowledged that ignorance of the sovereign legislator is not unique to new arrivals, but may be widespread among citizens with ordinary residence as well. However, unlike new arrivals, the possible ignorance of citizens with ordinary residence would not amount to a legitimate ground for excuse in the event that they should fail to pay attention to the will of the sovereign. It would be a logical contradiction since, according to the political theory of Hobbes, citizens are assumed to have consented to be ruled by their sovereign. In effect, the sovereign is supposed to be evident in any state because, in Hobbes' view, what has been constituted by the consent of everyone is obviously assumed to be sufficiently known. According to Hobbes:

> Ignorance of the Soveraign power, in the place of a mans ordinary residence, Excuseth him not; because he ought to take notice of the Power, by which he hath been protected there.[14]

All the same, Hobbes nevertheless recognised that since the permanent population may forget, the sovereign must take precautions to prevent a more widespread ignorance of its laws.[15]

It must be noted that Hobbes assumed that the law of a state is what its sovereign decides it is (and from now on this law will be referred to as *positive* law). His—or, as the case may be, their—commands and directives count as authoritative and binding insofar as they have been communicated to the

[14] T Hobbes, *Leviathan*, above n 6, at 203.
[15] *Ibid*, at 190.

addressees. Of course, the identification of law is not so clear in all places. Additionally, the criteria for identification are not the same everywhere. Hobbes develops a definition of law that does not acknowledge custom as an authoritative source of law unless it has been formally enacted and declared to be a rule by the sovereign legislator. However, other theorists contend that custom may be a more essential source of law. Indeed, most theorists in the common law tradition regard legislation as having less weight compared to other sources of law, above all, custom.[16]

The diffusion of law with lived practice is acknowledged and made central by HLA Hart in his account of law. He notes that in practice the criterion of identification of law is often unclear and that this is even more evident in modern legal systems. For a start, the question of how law is identified may be contested, and the rule for identification may not be explicitly stated, but must be studied by legal officials.[17] Thus, another factor influencing the accessibility of law is not merely a diversity of differing understandings of the proper criterion for its identification, but also that the actual criterion in use in a specific location is not always clear. Hart's elucidation of the uncertainty about the criterion that often prevails does not render the circumstance of newcomers, and others whose cultures differ from that informing the law that applies to them, less significant. In the event that this uncertainty pertains, the circumstance of these people is not overcome by a mere declaration of the sovereign legislator what the law is, since not all law that informs the decisions of the courts may be derived from a deliberate enactment by the political authority, but includes other sources, such as precedent, custom, and general principles of law. This background obviously complicates the development of an account of the nature of the circumstance imposed on people who can hardly be assumed to be familiar with the law that applies to them. Above all, it directs attention to the problem of legal uncertainty that inheres in many legal systems. It indicates that there is an advantage in the consistent application of the positivist legal thesis that law is law and, thus, binds its addressees if it has been enacted by the competent authority.[18] In this way, legal positivism provides a clear rule for the identification of the law that all inhabitants can confidently rely upon when legal controversies arise.

[16] See J Waldron, *The Dignity of Legislation* (Cambridge, Cambridge University Press, 1999). In this book, Waldron seeks to remedy the persistent ignorance of legal theorists of legislation as a significant source of law.

[17] HLA Hart, *The Concept of Law*, 2nd edn (Oxford, Oxford University Press, 1994), at 100. According to Hart, 'wherever ... a [secondary] rule of recognition is accepted, both private persons and officials are provided with authoritative criteria for identifying primary rules of obligation.' However, Hart also admits that 'there are certainly situations in which questions as to the precise content and scope of this kind of rule, and even as to its existence, may not admit of a clear or determinate answer' (at 109).

[18] For an account of legal positivism as a normative thesis, see J Waldron, 'Kant's Legal Positivism' (1996) 109 *Harvard Law Review* 1535.

The Limits to Unfamiliarity

According to Hobbes, then, unfamiliarity with the law is a serious problem. It is a sign that the law has not been communicated by the sovereign legislator and, if it has not, it is not valid law. It only binds those to whom it has been communicated. Thus, to the extent that the law has not been announced to the relevant addressees, they are not obliged to adjust their conduct to its specific rules and directives.

However, even if this seems to have been Hobbes' conclusion, he did not seem to have intended his claim to mean that people are free to do whatever they please in a remote place far away from their own, even though the law of that place has not been declared to them. That is to say, he did not suggest that people who move about in the world across local jurisdictions find themselves outside the bounds of legal systems in something like a state of nature situation in the absence of any communication as to what the law is. This would make the condition of the less mighty too severe. True, refugees, migrants, and others would not be held responsible for unlawful conduct in a foreign place; however, they would also lack access to justice in case of violence and harm done to them by their own cultural fellows. It would mean that new arrivals, due to their cultural difference, would stand—if not outside—then, at the margins of law's empire.

Hobbes did not believe that the mere fact of being in a 'strange country' is a licence to do whatever one pleases. There are universal limits to human conduct irrespective of territorial location and these limits are known by everybody irrespective of any announcement of what the law is in this or that place. Into whatever place a person may go, Hobbes proclaimed, he must respect the laws of nature. Knowledge of such laws does not depend on consultation of official sources, but is gained through the use of one's reason. An act contrary to these laws is thought to be a crime, regardless of whether it has been written down or declared by the sovereign. On Hobbes' account, the laws of nature are defined as the laws agreeable to the reason of everyone. The natural law is the only law that is such.[19] In this way, Hobbes seeks to find a basis for his claim about the existence of independent moral norms that are valid for everybody.

One example of such a norm is that which prohibits the use of violence. It is a norm that must be followed regardless of where you are. A second norm is that which prohibits actions that undermine the political conditions thought necessary for a political authority to reign. What these actions are cannot be determined once and for all, but changes over time. For Hobbes, one action believed to be essential for the preservation of stability is the acceptance of the dominant religion of a place. Thus, he argued, a man from the Indies should accept the religion in his new place of residence and not seek to change it. If he nevertheless attempts to impose his religion, or otherwise

[19] T Hobbes, *Leviathan*, above n 6, at 188.

acts in a way that tends to disobedience of the law of the host country, he commits a crime that he may justly be punished for.[20] While contemporary liberal scholars are also concerned with stability, they do not believe that it presupposes acceptance of the dominant religion. On the contrary, there is a general acceptance of the claim that stability requires acceptance of religious pluralism. This includes acceptance of new religions. Thus, more recent accounts of the necessary conditions for stability, the conditions that essentially led to the formulation of the rule about accepting the local religion, indicate that the Hobbesian fear of pluralism as the main cause of instability was exaggerated, if not entirely mistaken.

The changing understanding of what the conditions for political stability are does not necessarily mean that Hobbes was mistaken in his belief that the laws of nature prohibit actions that undermine such conditions. At the same time, since these understandings change, not merely across time, but also across places, it may be necessary to consult the legal sources of a particular place to find out what specific actions are believed to undermine those conditions, especially for people whose cultures differ from the public one in their place of residence. Thus, it is not sufficient to have recourse to one's own reason in deciding how to act in a given place so as not to undermine the conditions for political stability.

What about violence? Is violence an act that is so self-evident to everybody that no positive law is required to specify what it means? Is it reasonable to assume that, unlike, say the conditions for political stability, violence means the same at all times and in all places? Is it not still necessary to consult the legal sources in one's location to know what specific actions are violent and for this reason prohibited to be sure that one's actions are consistent with the law? The recognition of differences in understandings of which actions constitute violence does not necessarily undermine the claim about the existence of independent moral norms, but is better understood as conflicting and competing moral judgements about the correct interpretation and application of the norm against violence. As Bernard Williams argues, even if the insiders of one culture disagree with those of another about what their common laws ought to be, what matters is that it is *possible* for people of differing cultures to argue about matters of common concern. This fact demonstrates, states Williams, that there are already moral norms in place that are not in dispute and in the light of which our common deliberations continue.[21] However, it also indicates that nobody can confidently rely upon his own judgement as to which actions are contrary to the laws of nature to be sure that he acts in a way that is accepted everywhere when moving about in the world. The laws of nature simply do not constitute a sufficient source of legal knowledge.

[20] *Ibid*, at 202–203.
[21] B Williams, *Morality* (Cambridge, Cambridge University Press, 1993), at 19.

It is still a matter of dispute and controversy as to whether the laws of nature specify universal limits of human conduct, or instead refer to values (ideals) towards which our actions are oriented.[22] As liberals seem to contend, while humans disagree about substantive values, it is nevertheless necessary to insist upon the existence of moral norms that specify a minimum standard of universal conduct for individuals. This claim has been most forcefully articulated and formulated in the doctrine known as 'liberalism of fear'. This liberalism is not like a philosophy of life, but a political doctrine condemning cruelty absolutely and categorically. It is based on the idea that fear—especially systematic fear—renders freedom impossible:

> The fear we fear is of pain inflicted by others to kill and maim us, not the natural and healthy fear that merely warns us of avoidable pain. And when we think politically, we are afraid not only for ourselves but for our fellow citizens as well. We fear a society of fearful people ... If the prohibition of cruelty can be universalized and recognized as a necessary condition of the dignity of persons, then it can become a principle of political morality ... What liberalism requires is the possibility of making the evil of cruelty and fear the basic norm of its political practices and prescriptions.[23]

Judith Shklar continues by noting that the prohibition of cruelty is a basic norm that can be enforced in all places and upheld against all even if some fail to believe that it is the correct or honourable response in all situations.[24] On this account, then, at the very minimum, the laws of nature entail a prohibition against cruel acts (violent acts?) by any government. Once again, for our purposes, the argument does nothing but indicate the need to consult legal sources. To begin with, it does not entail any consideration of the permissibility of actions more generally. It only applies to governments. Secondly, instead of ruling out 'violence', it entails a prohibition against 'cruelty'. Whether violence and cruelty mean the same thing is unclear. The proliferation of terms indicates that the laws of nature are too general to be usefully applied by everybody without deciding on the legal authority of a specific interpretation.

Nevertheless, one dilemma is that people often believe that they already know the rules regulating their conduct, in particular, on matters of *adiaphora*. As discussed earlier on (in chapter six), it is not unusual that people's 'instructed' consciences are engaged on a wide range of issues and inform them about the rightful way of marriage, child-rearing, divorce, dress, animal slaughtering, and so on, regardless of location. All the same,

[22] For an account of the latter position, see eg J Finnis, *Natural Law and Natural Rights* above n 1, especially chapter 4.

[23] J Shklar, 'Liberalism of Fear' in N Rosenblum (ed), *Liberalism and the Moral Life* (Cambridge Mass, Harvard University Press, 1989), at 30–31.

[24] *Ibid.*

people cannot confidently rely upon their conscience as an authoritative source of rightful conduct in these fields of action. Even if these are actions of ultimate moral indifference from the standpoint of cosmopolitan law, they are often subject to intensive political debate and regulation. The demands of social justice have given rise to the establishment of several public non-political institutions assigned to distribute a range of goods, such as health care, social security, day care for children, elderly care, and so on. Each of these institutions has come to govern its affairs in accordance with specific rules regulating matters of *adiaphora*. Its rules may come into conflict with the ways people usually conduct their affairs, especially if they differ in cultural terms from the dominant one.

Furthermore, even if, from the standpoint of cosmopolitan moral law, humans may conduct their affairs in accordance with their conscience on matters of *adiaphora* because these are matters of ultimate moral indifference, their actual activities—also to the best of their ethical, religious, or philosophical knowledge—cannot be immune from legal restrictions. As noted in the previous chapter, people's activities in this realm of life tend to come into conflict with one another, especially in a multicultural society, not merely because of incompatibility between many actions that are ultimately indifferent, but also because people do not necessarily care solely for how they conduct their own affairs in this realm, but are equally involved in the way others conduct their affairs. For these reasons, the sovereign legislator must have legislative competence in this realm of life and impose legal restrictions insofar as they are warranted for the sake of well-being, security, safety, and so on. As noted in the earlier discussion on adequacy and *adiaphora* (chapter six), the recognition of this legislative competence is not a blanket right for the legislator to do what it likes as long as its actions are consistent with a concern for, say well-being, security, or safety. It is also necessary to be attentive to the way in which regulations may impose unjustifiable hardships on people who have cultural duties that come into conflict with those regulations. However, to consider any cultural difference as being non-negotiable would render the exercise of this legislative competence impossible.

Against this background, it is possible to consider, indeed, take seriously, the problem posed by unfamiliarity with the positive law of a given place, also from the standpoint of a natural law approach. There is no guarantee that all local legal systems rest on the same interpretation of independent moral norms or regulate matters of ultimate moral indifference in the same way.

IGNORANCE IN LEGAL THEORY

The circumstance of people whose cultures differ from the dominant one characterised in terms of unfamiliarity with the law that applies to them directs attention to an issue that has not been given more than marginal consideration by legal theorists, but which is believed to deserve a much more central place in theorising about law once the fact of multiculturalism and its adverse consequences on people's ability to comply with the law has been acknowledged. More precisely, it casts doubts on the assumption often made by contemporary theorists of law that whatever people seek to be and do in their lives, and irrespective of their opinions about right and justice, they are assumed to be familiar with the specific contents of the legal rules, directives, and prohibitions of their society, at least those regulations that affect their aims, and oppose or accord with their opinions. Such issues include home education, freedom of expression, working hours, hygiene, and much else. The circumstance of people attached to marginal cultures in terms of familiarity with the law of their location nevertheless undermines this assumption.

Contemporary theorists of law are not indifferent to unfamiliarity (or what they refer to as ignorance) and the potential trouble it poses for law, but tend to provide but a modest account of the relevance of unfamiliarity or ignorance for the validity of the law. For example, unlike the Hobbesian account of law, modern legal positivist approaches do not accord decisive significance to ignorance in their definition of law. At the same time, similarly to Hobbes, they are driven by a deeper concern about the need for authority that in an important sense presupposes communication. In order to find direct considerations of unfamiliarity—explicit rules on the topic—based on a concern with individual access to law as part of the definition of law, it is necessary to turn to earlier theoretical contributions and, more specifically, the contributions made by natural law theorists who took seriously the claim that the possibility of ignorance is a central issue for legal theory.

A Legal Positivist Approach

Theorists of law disagree about the way in which unfamiliarity becomes relevant for law and, more specifically, whether the issue of what counts as law ought to include a criterion concerning familiarity. A legal positivist approach assumes that law is identified by its institutional source. Its legal validity depends on whether it has been enacted by the competent authority. It is in this spirit that John Austin articulates a rule of identification stipulating that law is valid if it has been enacted by a competent authority. Hans Kelsen expresses a similar view. As he puts it:

> The mere fact that somebody commands something is no reason to regard the command as a 'valid' norm, a norm binding the individual at whom it is directed. Only a competent authority can create valid norms; and such competence can only be based on a norm that authorizes the issuing of norms.[25]

[25] H Kelsen, *The Pure Theory of Law* (Berkeley, University California Press, 1967), at 194.

One example of a more recent legal positivist account of law is that of Joseph Raz.[26] According to modern legal positivist accounts, the question 'what is law?' must be answered with reference to a formal criterion alone, and cannot be sensitive to questions such as whether the law is known by everybody expected to comply with it or simply by a few. It should be mentioned that the basic concern shared by legal positivists seems to be to clarify the relationship between law and morality and make the legal validity of the law independent of whether it accords with this or that particular view of morality. Still, to the extent that no allowance is made for the possibility of ignorance and its potential impact on law, legal positivists fail to consider the possibility of involuntary ignorance of law and how to respond to this condition in a way that is consistent with a minimum provision of respect for individual freedom.

Austin did pay some attention to unfamiliarity, though. According to him, total ignorance which is deemed inevitable, ie ignorance by all addressees that could not possibly be avoided by them, does challenge the validity of the law, regardless of whether or not the law has been issued by a competent authority. Thus, for example, Austin viewed retroactive law as a critical case in need of special consideration. This concession was heavily criticised by Hans Kelsen who articulated a legal positivist thesis about ignorance in more categorical terms. In his view, the rule about the irrelevance of ignorance is absolute; there is no exception to this rule, not even in the case of retroactive law. For this reason, an individual subject is legally obligated to observe a legal norm,

> even if the idea of this legal norm does not create any impulse toward the commanded behavior, even if he has no idea of the obligating legal norm at all, as long as the positive-legal principle prevails that ignorance of the law is no excuse.[27]

Thus, the legal positivist approach holds that law is valid regardless of whether its addressees, in fact, know what it requires of them in terms of conduct. Of course, in the absence of any consideration of ignorance whatsoever, the trouble posed by 'partial ignorance' also goes unnoticed.

Though Kelsen opposed the idea of a direct link between validity and ignorance, he acknowledged that ignorance might nevertheless raise issues about efficacy and, ultimately, about the validity of law. Kelsen maintains that it is necessary to distinguish between questions of the validity and of the efficacy of a particular law. According to him, a piece of legislation can be valid while, at the same time, ineffective. If it is valid, it means that the subjects *ought* to comply with it and will be punished if they do not. If a law

[26] J Raz, *The Authority of Law: Essays on Law and Morality* (Oxford, Clarendon Press, 1979), especially chapter 2 on 'Legal Positivism and the Sources of Law' (pp 37–52).

[27] H Kelsen, *The Pure Theory of Law*, above n 25, at 116.

is effective, in contrast, it means that its addressees actually behave in the way prescribed by it.[28] However, a widespread unfamiliarity with the law is likely to fuel processes of fragmentation which may lead to the dissolution of an entire positive legal system. In this way, unfamiliarity may eventually bring the validity of the law into question. As Kelsen affirms, no law is valid unless it belongs to a system of law that is, on the whole, efficacious.[29] In this sense, his argument about the irrelevance of ignorance for the validity of law presupposes a working legal order.

Kelsen addresses the question of the relationship between ignorance and efficacy separately. He contends that knowledge or awareness of a given law is insufficient to secure efficacy since it is not, in and of itself, a sufficient motive for compliance; instead, a system of sanctions is necessary. Kelsen's consideration of efficacy is similar to that of John Rawls. Rawls affirms that compliance with law must be secured by mutual assurance, ie assurance that others will comply as well. Sanctions secure such assurance.[30] Of course, whether a system of sanctions is effective depends on knowledge about it. A sanction can only perform its intended function if people know what they must do or not do in order to avoid being sanctioned. In this light, ignorance must nevertheless be considered as a legal positivist concern; though it may not cast doubt upon the validity of law (*pace* Austin's remark about retroactive law), ignorance is relevant insofar as it endangers the efficacy of the entire legal order.

However, what seems to be a remarkable indifference towards the possibility of ignorance and its relevance for law among legal positivists stands in need of further clarification. The legal positivist thesis must be understood in the light of the deeper concerns underlying its formulation. In an important sense, it represents the substantive response to a well-founded critique of customary law as being undeserving of the name of law when it is not expressed in words. If it is not, customary law is plainly inaccessible. As Jeremy Bentham notes,

> a great, perhaps the greatest, part of the business is done by way of *ex post facto* law. The decisions, being formed on grounds that were inaccessible to the party previous to the act for which he was made to suffer, carry with them a great part of the mischief of the *privilegia* against which Cicero inveighs with so much injustice.[31]

[28] H Kelsen, *General Theory of Law and State* (Cambridge, Mass, Harvard University Press, 1945), at 35 ff and 39 ff.

[29] *Ibid*, at 42. See also Kelsen's discussion of the relation between validity and effectiveness in H Kelsen, *The Pure Theory of Law*, n 25, at 211–214.

[30] J Rawls, *Theory of Justice* (Cambridge, Mass, Belknap Press of Harvard University Press, 1999), at 211.

[31] J Bentham, *Of Laws in General*, HLA Hart (ed) (London, Athlone Press, 1970), at 187. For a critique of the idea of customary law, see chapter V.

Evidently inspired by Bentham, Austin advanced a criticism against *judiciary* or customary law in favour of *statutory* or positive law. He was motivated precisely by a need to consider the serious and inescapable problem of ignorance of law inherent in customary law. A system of customary law, argues Austin,

> is nearly unknown to the bulk of the community, although they are bound to adjust their conduct to the rules or principles of which it consists. ... And as to the bulk of the community—the simple-minded laity (to whom, by reason of their simplicity, the law is so benign)—they might as well be subject to the mere *arbitrium* of the tribunals, as to a system of law made by judicial decisions.[32]

Austin continues by noting that some rules are simple, such as those related to certain crimes and to frequently used contracts. Nevertheless, the more complex portions of law not exemplified in practice on an everyday basis are usually utterly unknown by, and unknowable to, the mass of the legal community. Accordingly, customary law has the same mischievous effects as retroactive law. This is not to say that statute law cannot also be obscure and vague. Still, unlike customary law, statutory law has the potential to be compact and perspicuous, if constructed with care and skill.[33]

Furthermore, Joseph Raz' articulation of a 'service-conception' of law also seems to convey a recognition of the pervasive importance of securing effective channels of communication between the sovereign legislator and the legal subjects (even though they are not mentioned in the definition of law). Terms like command, order, or authority, associated with legal positivism, obviously presuppose not only that channels of communication are in place, but a kind of directness and immediacy between the law-giver and the relevant addressees that outmodes the likelihood of ignorance. In this sense, the idea that law is authoritative is inevitably bound up with efficacy considerations. Indeed, Raz' concern with effective channels of communication becomes clear in his analysis of the rule of law where he explains that the ideal rule of law requires, among other things, that the law is open, clearly stated, and publicised.[34] His concern with communication is implicit in his claim that 'the law must be capable of being obeyed', that is to say,

> *it must be capable of guiding the behavior of its subjects*. It must be such that they can find out what it is and act on it.[35]

[32] J Austin, *Lectures on Jurisprudence* R Campbell (ed), 3rd edn (London, John Murray, Albemarle Street, 1869), at 674.

[33] *Ibid*, at 674–676.

[34] J Raz, *The Authority of Law*, above n 26, at 214.

[35] *Ibid*, at 213–214 [emphasis in original].

As Meir Dan-Cohen notes, however, the availability of clear, generally applicable, and binding guidelines on how to conduct one's affairs is entirely compatible with selective transmission. According to him,

> the ability of decision rules to guide decisions effectively and thus to limit official discretion and arbitrariness does not depend on broad dissemination or easy accessibility of those rules to the general public. If anything, the opposite is true: the clarity and specificity of decision rules, and hence their effectiveness as guidelines, may be enhanced by the use of a technical, esoteric terminology that is incomprehensible to the public at large.[36]

Thus, Dan-Cohen takes seriously the distinction between primary and secondary rules and its relevance for the possibility of ignorance of the law. While primary rules refer to those rules regulating interaction among ordinary people and are addressed directly to them, secondary rules stipulate procedures for revising, interpreting, amending, and making new law and are addressed to public officials.[37] While the existence of secondary rules facilitates the management of a more complex society, it also renders the law, as a whole, vastly more inaccessible to the general public.

In a similar vein, Jeremy Waldron explains that it is possible that only officials accept and use the system's criteria of legal validity. Drawing upon the cynical underpinnings of Hart's view of law, he continues by noting that, while such a system would be appallingly sheep-like, and the sheep might finish in the slaughter-house, there is no reason for thinking that it could not exist or for not considering it as a legal system.[38] Hart did not make his account of law conditional on something like a minimum requirement of decency in relation to those it obliges. However, he did not do so, it seems, precisely because he wanted to convey the dangers inherent in the modern legal system, and direct attention to the importance of critical thinking about law. As Waldron articulates this thought, thus:

> We want people to respond to law not slavishly or mechanically, but critically, so that they will sometimes be willing (when it is morally appropriate) to resist law's demands.[39]

In other words, the legal positivist thesis makes a clear distinction between what law is and what it ought to be. This distinction makes it possible to argue that a legal system fails to meet the demands of the need for its laws to be accessible by its addressees.

[36] M Dan-Cohen, 'Decision Rules and Conduct Rules: On Acoustic Separation in Criminal Law' (1984) 97 *Harvard Law Review* 625 at 668.
[37] HLA Hart, *The Concept of Law*, above n 17, at 94.
[38] J Waldron, 'All We Like Sheep' (1999) 12 *Canadian Journal of Law and Jurisprudence* 169 at 169; see also HLA Hart, *The Concept of Law*, above n 17, at 117.
[39] *Ibid*, at 170.

A Natural Justice Approach

Depriving the concept of law of any kind of decency comes into deep conflict with the idea of 'law as something deserving of loyalty' and as supposedly representing a human achievement. As Waldron explains, 'it cannot be a simple fiat of power or a repetitive pattern discernible in the behaviour of state officials.'[40] This idea has influenced the approach to law advanced by natural justice theorists. According to them, it is not sufficient for law to count as valid on the mere basis that it has been enacted by a competent authority. Though law-applying public institutions do not seem well suited to meddling with questions concerning the validity of a given law, it may nevertheless be reasonable to require such institutions to examine whether the relevant law has been promulgated or not. To promulgate a law is to make it known to its addressees. It is an aspect of the Rule of Law stipulating that there is no offence without a law.[41] A law that has not been promulgated may not count as valid. As Lon Fuller states, an unpromulgated law does not qualify as valid law; if the competent authority fails to make its laws known to their addressees that authority has failed to make any law at all![42] Also Jeremy Bentham argued that promulgation is the least to be expected. According to him, it is of utmost importance to make the notoriety of every law as extensive as its binding force. Without promulgation, Bentham continues,

> the business of legislation is from the beginning to the end of it a cruel mockery, and every legislator without thinking about it a Caligula, or rather in this respect worse than a Caligula. Caligula published his laws in small characters, but still he published them: he hung them up high but still he hung them up.[43]

Of course, it should be noted that, in Roman times, laws were not considered binding until they were published, which might explain Caligula's promulgatory concerns. However, this acknowledgement does not invalidate Bentham's assertion about the unreasonableness of the claim that law can be valid as long as it remains only in the mind of the legislator.[44]

Broadly speaking, the rule is usually interpreted as requiring that the law-making institutions ensure that law is made known to all in the sense that it must be made available. Thus, the rule of promulgation is a general one; it does not specify the mode of communication once and for all. Though the term is associated with communication in the form of a written or published text, it may in principle be communicated orally as well.[45] John Austin notes

[40] *Ibid*, at 181–182.
[41] J Rawls, *Theory of Justice*, above n 30, at 209.
[42] L Fuller, *The Morality of Law* (New Haven, Yale University Press, 1969), at 39.
[43] J Bentham, *Of Laws In General*, above n 31, at 71.
[44] J Austin, *Lectures on Jurisprudence*, above n 32, at 543.
[45] *Ibid*, at 542–543.

that the meaning now annexed to the expression 'to promulge a law' is to publish a law already made, in order that those whom it binds may know its existence and content. However, according to the meaning originally annexed to the expression 'to promulge a law', it meant to submit a proposed law to the members of the legislature in order that they might know its contents and consider the expediency of passing it.[46] On Hobbes' account, the rule of promulgation calls for communication of law through the use of signs that are readily perceived by the addressees. Not only must the content of law be understood, but there must also be clear signs that it originates from the will of the competent authority.[47] Indeed, according to Austin, the term promulgation has close affiliations with law enacted by the sovereign legislator. Thus, according to him, promulgation does not merely indicate that law is made available, but it is also supposed to tell us something about its source. However, for the purpose of the present argument, it is not necessary to settle the question as to who may promulgate law. Instead, what is decisive is that an act of promulgation should be efficient in the sense that it is made known to those it is supposed to oblige; whether it is by word or writing or some other act depends on what is suitable for the relevant addressees.

The idea is that a law-making institution adapts its practice of communication to what are considered to be conventional methods of mass communication when promulgating laws. At the time of Hobbes' writings, it was suitable to set apart from the ordinary working hours of citizens some time in which they may attend those appointed to instruct them about laws and how they apply to their conduct. Hobbes argued that time should be allocated so as to make it possible for people to assemble together and hear the laws addressed to all read and expounded.[48] This mode of communication, Hobbes recognised, differs from that used in ancient times when laws were often put into verse in order to make them easily accessible to their addressees. Hobbes gave a range of examples of specific methods of making laws known in ways that take into account the specifics of society at any given time and place. To illustrate, he mentioned the laws which Moses gave to the people of Israel at the renewing of the covenant. Thus,

> he biddeth them to teach it their Children, by discoursing of it both at home, and upon the way; at going to bed, and at rising from bed; and to write it upon the posts, and dores of their houses; and to assemble the people, man, woman, and child, to heare it read.[49]

[46] J Austin, *Lectures on Jurisprudence*, above n 32, at 543–544.
[47] T Hobbes, *Leviathan*, above n 6, at 189. See also J Austin, *Lectures on Jurisprudence*, above n 32, at 36.
[48] T Hobbes, *Leviathan*, above n 6, at 234–235.
[49] *Ibid*, at 189.

Evidently, the invention of television, radio, the press, the web, and other means of mass communication together with a relatively homogeneous distribution of reading skills render the proposition about assembling all citizens in the main square outmoded. Indeed, as Charlotte Hoffman notes, whereas in the past human communication was profoundly affected by the invention of writing systems and then printing, the advent of computer-based data transmission and information technology constitutes a revolution that has had a more profound impact on human communication than any method preceding it. Without the traditional constraints of time and distance, individuals, at least in the developed world, can now have instant and world-wide access to information in various forms, written, graphic and in sound.[50] This development should make it all the easier for the law-making institutions to effectively promulgate their laws. Furthermore, since it may be in a law-making institution's own interest to make its laws readily accessible to their addressees, it is not unusual that it employs such tools as a complement to mere publication in official digests. If it wishes to address, say, private persons, such as dog-owners, parents, firms, and so on, it often does much better by informing the press about legislative changes that affect them. Such a strategy will in all likelihood be more effective in comparison to a mere publication in official digests. Even so, from the standpoint of a contemporary natural justice approach, the latter is sufficient for law to count as valid.

To conclude, even if contemporary natural justice theorists do not pay special attention to the possibility of unfamiliarity with law in spite of promulgation in the sense of publication in official digests, there seems to be ample space to do so once this issue has been brought to their attention. Their accounts of the need to be sensitive to the conventional methods of communication in society entails the recognition of cultural changes and their direct relevance for law. For this reason, their accounts constitute a starting point for advancing the claim about the need for a more careful assessment of the possibility of unfamiliarity when applying law in a multicultural environment.

IGNORANCE AND INDIVIDUAL FREEDOM

Far from all defences are valid in a case of non-compliance having its source in ignorance of law. One reason for considering the possibility of ignorance in spite of promulgation is its serious impact on individual freedom. As John Rawls notes, not knowing how to behave in order to avoid punishment has a serious impact on individual freedom. According to him,

[50] C Hoffman, 'Introduction' in C Hoffman (ed), *Language, Culture and Communication in Contemporary Europe* (Clevedon, WBC Book Manufacturers Ltd, 1996), at *x*.

> unless citizens are able to know what the law is and are given a fair opportunity to take its directives into account, penal sanctions should not apply to them.[51]

Rawls focuses his argument on the unreasonableness of punishing somebody for having done something that he did not know, and had not been given a fair opportunity to know, was illegal. Thus, his account is centered on ignorance of *criminal* law. However, involuntary ignorance of law poses other types of threats to individual freedom as well. A legal system may distribute entitlements and opportunities. In order to benefit from them, it is crucial for citizens to be acquainted with a variety of specific legal requirements regarding deadlines, application forms, conditions for eligibility, and so on. Meeting these requirements is not simply about taking advantage of the public institutions that have been established to provide a number of goods required by everybody given their critical importance to the enjoyment of individual freedom. To benefit from these goods is not a luxury, but necessary to be able to make use of that freedom.

It must be noted that this dimension is largely neglected in theoretical discussions about law and its impact on individual freedom. Edward Rubin explains this neglect as a result of a persistent focus on the judiciary. Theorists of law and justice have focused so heavily on the judiciary that there is no theory of law that is able to capture the significance of modern administrative agencies and their competences to administrate and enforce a wide range of regulations.[52] Because of this neglect, theorists of law and justice rarely focus on what sorts of vulnerabilities, obstacles, or difficulties individual citizens might be exposed to in relation to this field of law. Nevertheless, the absence of theory is hardly a reason for not considering the way in which ignorance of *administrative* law also has a direct impact on individual freedom.

Rawls claims that it is unreasonable to punish citizens who are involuntarily ignorant, leaving it an open question as to what may be the precise cause of their ignorance; what is decisive is that citizens were unable to know the law and had not been given a fair opportunity to take it into account. Could cultural difference be a legitimate cause of ignorance? If this is the case, can such ignorance be avoided? This depends on what is meant by inaccessible law in a multicultural society.

Several scholars define cultural difference in ideological terms.[53] The present study also considers ideological outlook (or conviction about justice and

[51] J Rawls, *Theory of Justice*, above n 30, at 211.

[52] EL Rubin, 'Law and Legislation in the Administrative State' (1989) 89 *Columbia Law Review* 369–426, at 369.

[53] See eg JB Thompson, *Ideology and Modern Culture: Critical Social Theory in the Era of Mass Communications* (Stanford Cal, Stanford University Press, 1990). Also feminist accounts of multiculturalism tend to define culture in ideological terms. See eg J Cohen, M Howard and MC Nussbaum (eds), S Okin Moller, *Is Multiculturalism Bad for Women?* (Princeton NJ, Princeton University Press, 1999).

right) to be a component of a person's culture. This conceptualisation of culture sometimes influences ideas of what is required for securing accessible laws in multicultural settings. From this standpoint, multiculturalism creates a distance between the law of society and its addressees that is understood as ideological opposition. As suggested in the previous chapter of this book, disagreement about justice and right with its source in cultural difference may be mediated by universal participation and influence in the legislative process. Encouraging participation in deliberations about common endeavours by people attached to different cultures is supposed to ensure that the distance experienced by law's addressees is less great than it would have been had they not participated at all. Above all, it is supposed to give the inhabitants an opportunity to shape and reshape the content of laws so as to better suit their convictions about right and justice.

One group of scholars argues that universal participation and deliberation transform diverse opinions and might eventually result in agreement and identification with the law.[54] On this account, if general involvement in deliberations preceded each and every law, it is natural to expect that all laws democratically enacted would not only be well known by all, but also be deemed as theirs. Drawing upon these ideas, some legal theorists imply that law is binding only if it is agreeable in this deep sense. According to them, for law to be accessible, it must be understood in a first-person and engaging sense by its addressees. It is not sufficient that the subjects are able to repeat what the law tells them to do. For example, RA Duff notes that subjects are supposed to be not merely familiar with the law and how it applies to their conduct for legal responsibility; above all, they should regard it as *their* law.[55] It must be noted that Duff focuses on communicative issues inside the court room. According to him, the *preconditions* of criminal liability are *conditions* of the legitimacy of the criminal trial. In his view, the defendant must be able to understand the values the law purports to protect. The values must be ones they could accept, as distinct from an alien imposition on them. The law must be accessible in first-person speech. It is a condition for criminal responsibility. Otherwise, the accused does not understand the charges against him. However, it does not require that defendants one-by-one, in fact, accept the law. Instead, it is to say that the law must be accessible to a defendant in the sense that it embodies values and demands which he could accept.[56] At the same time, Duff remarks that alienation does not render the law either conceptually or psychologically inaccessible.[57] However, apart from the fact that this understanding of what is

[54] See eg J Cohen, 'Democracy and Liberty' in J Elster (ed), *Deliberative Democracy* (New York, Cambridge University Press, 1998), at 185–231.

[55] RA Duff, 'Law, Language and Community: Some Preconditions of Criminal Liability' (1998) 18 *Oxford Journal of Legal Studies* 189, at 193–194.

[56] *Ibid*, at 199.

[57] *Ibid*, at 203.

meant by access to law seems far too demanding in a multicultural society, it also seems to legitimise the use of methods such as manipulation or even indoctrination.

Does access to law presuppose participation? If this is the case, a given law would fail to bind those who continue to disagree about the justice of its directives or commands even after deliberations. If deep identification with the law is required, a notable number of people would not be bound by it. However, it is hardly reasonable to require that all laws that bind us today have been enacted by us, or by our representatives, even if we believe that this is a real democratic aspiration. For one thing, as indicated in the previous chapter, democratic deliberations on matters of common concern, including matters of justice and right, do not begin with a clean slate. A significant portion of the legal system has not been enacted by us, but by our ancestors or by others elsewhere and then received or made part of the legal system a long time ago. The influence exerted by Roman law on European legal systems and on European ex-colonies is a standard example of reception practices without active democratic approval.[58] Nevertheless, it is unreasonable to hold that the law binds only those who took part in its making and design. In spite of our political involvement here and now, which informs us about some laws valid for the present, this engagement does not secure familiarity with laws enacted in the past. Still, laws bind us today because the authority of law does not rest on any absurdity such as that all addressees must participate in the making of a law prior to its enactment for it to be binding. This is so because law as a social institution is supposed to perform a range of crucial functions, including co-ordination of diverse pursuits, preventing violence from breaking out, securing the liberty and well-being of the subjects, etc.

Is there any other aspect of the relation between the individual and the law that might nevertheless be of direct relevance for determining what is meant by access to law? From the standpoint of individual subjects, access to law presupposes that law be communicated in a language and through the use of signs that are readily perceived by them. Furthermore, it presupposes familiarity with the official scheme of interpretation of law and fact in use by the law-applying institutions in one's location. Thus, unless a law is communicated with due regard to the culture(s) of the addressees, that is to say, with due regard to their cultural equipment, it can hardly be said to be accessible from their standpoint. As modest as this claim appears to be, it places notable burdens on the law-making institutions in multicultural societies. These institutions must be sensitive to the circumstance of people belonging to marginal cultures and their difficulties accessing law in their location and seek to ensure that their practices of promulgation accommodate difference in cultural equipment. This claim is motivated by a deeper

[58] The practice of reception of laws without active democratic approval continues in our times, notably, in Central and Eastern Europe after the collapse of communism.

concern with respect to securing a minimum provision of respect for individual freedom. One aspect of that provision is to make sure that everyone to whom the law applies knows about it and has been given a fair opportunity to take its directives into account.

THE POSSIBILITY OF EXCUSE

As noted earlier on in this chapter, legal positivists uphold the principle that ignorance of positive law excuses no one, quite regardless of whether their ignorance was involuntary and relates to particular law. According to them, ignorance, no matter how it came about, is not a valid excuse in cases of non-compliance.[59] This insensitive posture is best explained in the light of their account of law's validity. However, it also depends on the practical difficulties involved in the application of any other principle. Kelsen and Austin explain that their position on ignorance is the only one that is consistent with a functioning legal system. If offenders were allowed to submit evidence about ignorance, courts would be involved in issues that have the potential to undermine the entire legal system. According to Austin, the acknowledgement of involuntary ignorance as a possible basis for excuse would render the administration of justice next to impracticable.[60] Kelsen did not make any exceptions whatsoever. In his view, the irrelevance of ignorance is a fundamental principle of positive legal orders. The presupposition that ignorance is no excuse is an 'irrefutable assumption in the courtroom against which no evidence is permitted.'[61] Austin, by contrast, did make an exception for retroactive law since ignorance in this case would be possible to verify without having to examine evidence in individual cases.[62]

Thus, it is possible to avoid the practical difficulties involved in examining evidence in individual cases if excuse is decided on more principled grounds. Hobbes also discussed this possibility in relation to retroactive law. According to him:

> No law, made after a Fact done, can make it a Crime: because if the Fact be against the Law of nature, the Law was before the Fact, and a Positive law cannot be taken notice of, before it be made, and therefore cannot be obligatory.[63]

Unlike Austin, Hobbes argued that retroactive law is not a unique case in this respect, but that there are also other instances where ignorance is inevitable. What is decisive is not whether the individual actually knew

[59] See, for example, H Kelsen, *General Theory of Law and State*, above n 28, at 44.
[60] J Austin, *Lectures on Jurisprudence*, above n 32, at 498. For a comment on Austin's view, see H Kelsen, *General Theory of Law and State*, above n 28, at 74.
[61] H Kelsen, *General Theory of Law and State*, above n 28, at 44.
[62] J Austin, *Lectures on Jurisprudence*, above n 32, at 502.
[63] T Hobbes, *Leviathan*, above n 6, at 203–204.

about the existence and the specifics of the law, but whether it can be established that he had access to it, that is to say, whether the conditions for compliance were met in the first place. In Hobbes' view, whether a person can be said to have access to the law depends on whether it has been promulgated; however, it also depends on aspects—circumstances or characteristics—pertaining to the individual. For example, Hobbes thought that the 'infantile' and the 'imbecile' were excused on the basis of the supposition that they are incapable of unlawful intention or inadvertence at the time of the alleged wrong. However, he also acknowledged that this sort of incapacity is a matter of degree; thus, he argued that what is ultimately decisive is whether the individual is conscious of the unlawfulness of his conduct. If this is the case, he is no longer excused.[64]

On this account, then, the circumstance defined in terms of inability to access law does not cover ignorance that comes about as a result of the individual not having made the effort to learn about the laws that apply to his conduct. Even if the duty to secure channels of communication between the law and its addressees in principle falls, in great part, upon the law-making body, in practice, however, the addressees have rather extensive duties to find out about the laws regulating their activities. At the same time, however, this reminder about individual responsibility is not intended to imply 'any such absurdity that the dutiful citizen will sit down and read them all.'[65] What duties are incumbent on the general public, then? To quote Hobbes again:

> every man is obliged to doe his best endeavour, to informe himself of all written Lawes, that may concerne his own future actions.[66]

In particular, the individual is supposed to look for advice when he is *uncertain* about the law applicable to his future activities. There are several ways of informing oneself. One is to seek professional legal advice. Another possible source of advice may be the example of another whom one knows is better informed than oneself.[67]

Obviously, this responsibility may be more cumbersome for a new arrival. In a 'strange country', a migrant may even lack a *sense* of which actions are more strictly regulated than others are. The present study has argued that such a sense commonly extends to acts of violence. Even if cultures differ regarding the contours of what amount to universal wrongs, all cultures regulate such actions. However, cultures nevertheless differ in the extent to which they regulate actions in the field of *adiaphora* and what the specifics of such regulations are. These are actions that are part of ordinary

[64] T Hobbes, *Leviathan*, above n 6, at 187, 208.
[65] L Fuller, *The Morality of Law*, above n 42, at 51.
[66] T Hobbes, *Leviathan*, above n 6, at 190.
[67] L Fuller, *The Morality of Law*, above n 42, at 51.

life; part of what life is about for many people. In this field of action it is less clear whether everybody has a sense of whether or not their actions might be prohibited by law. Some cultures approximate to each other in this field of action; others differ in a more radical sense. In the latter case, it may nevertheless be necessary to 'sit down and read them all.' For example, if a European citizen plans to hire others for work or fire those workers, slaughter animals, sell real estate or exploit natural resources, build a house, marry or divorce, educate children at home, and so on, he is expected to consult official sources based on a rough idea as to when consultation is needed. In the case of newcomers from places with radically different public cultures, such a sense may not be a reliable measure for what a person should have done had he been sufficiently cautious or reasonable. This is so simply because by no means all local legal systems permit, say, the firing of people without reason or prior notice, or the ritual slaughtering of animals, or polygamous marriage, or home education of one's children after a certain age. Such a sense, common sense, is in a significant part acquired or learned. It fits one place or places with similar public cultures. It is not useful in all places.

The circumstance of new arrivals might be similar to the case singled out by Hobbes for special treatment, namely, where individuals are considered able to take notice of general laws, but unable to take notice of particular laws. According to Hobbes, such inability may excuse an action contrary to law. As Hobbes noted, some acts that seem to be crimes can prove to be none at all once attention is paid to this sort of circumstance of the defendant. As he puts it:

> That which totally Excuseth a Fact and takes away from it the nature of a Crime, can be none but that, which at the same time, taketh away the obligation of the Law.[68]

One such circumstance is the lack of means to know the law.[69] For example, inability to take notice of particular laws may depend on a lack of natural properties such as hearing or sight.

Hobbes did not consider that such means may be culture-specific. In fact, he stated that, insofar as the law has been declared to newcomers, they are no longer excused. One reason for this neglect might be that his argument is confined to a consideration of natural properties, such as hearing and sight. A person's culture, in contrast, refers to properties, such as skills, know-how, and tools, which are learned or acquired from childhood onwards. The absence of properties suitable for a given place is more difficult to verify. Nevertheless, what is significant is Hobbes' recognition that there are properties of some individuals that indicate their inability to access law

[68] T Hobbes, *Leviathan*, above n 6, at 207–208.
[69] *Ibid*, at 208.

despite promulgation. The recognition of this fact alerts us to the possibility of unintended non-compliance with law for reasons related to a circumstance which the individual cannot reasonably be held responsible for. The situation of newcomers and others who are similarly situated in cultural terms in relation to the law that applies to them amounts to such a circumstance.

An Objection to Group Exemptions

Is it possible to develop a more principled approach to the circumstance of people whose cultural difference radically undermines their ability to access law, an essential condition for abiding by it? The idea of a more principled stance on this issue must be treated with caution, in part, because cultural difference is a matter of degree and, in part, because it is not a permanent circumstance. For example, while a Swede may confront some difficulties in accessing Norwegian law until she is familiar with the culture of Norwegian public institutions, including its cultural equipment, she can hardly be said to lack access altogether. Furthermore, to announce that some group in society is incapable of accessing particular laws because of its culture can be an effective way of withholding the recognition of equal human capabilities for responsible conduct in civic life and, thus, amount to a deprivation of assistance to acquire the cultural equipment essential for such access. An anecdote from Roman law comes to mind. Roman law exempted certain groups of individuals from legal responsibility on the basis that their capabilities were not *adequate* for accessing particular laws (in Roman legal terminology, *Ius Civile*). Women, soldiers, and individuals under the age of 25 were exempted from legal responsibility as a matter of principle. The Roman decision to exempt these classes was founded on general characteristics, such as gender, age, or profession. Their exemption meant that their unlawful conduct in relation to particular laws was automatically excused.[70]

Indeed, the historical exemption of women from legal responsibility on matters pertaining to the family, including marriage, divorce, and child-rearing, or business-related matters is a painfully straightforward illustration of the serious discrimination involved in the withholding of the recognition of equal rights of women to play an autonomous and independent role in economic and social life. By excluding women from education in basic reading skills, the claim that women were unable to access particular laws was presented in a way that made sense. Similarly to the exemption of women from legal responsibility, a principled exemption for new arrivals is a morally dubious response to a circumstance that itself amounts to an injustice, at least if it persists over time since it seriously impedes an individual's ability to enjoy her freedom. The idea of a general exemption comes into conflict with the deeper claim about ensuring a minimum provision of respect for individual

[70] J Austin, *Lectures on Jurisprudence*, above n 32, at 500.

freedom. Whether a person's culture is a ground for excusing him for his actions contrary to particular law must be decided on a case-by-case basis. Such an approach increases the risk of arbitrariness and inconsistency in the way the law-applying institutions deal with cases of non-compliance with law. At the same time, a mere reference to this risk is hardly a sufficient reason for denying the relevance of my argument about the need for cultural equipment to access law. Such denial disregards the cultural conditions for being able to enjoy individual freedom. This commitment can give rise to policies of differential treatment on the basis of culture. However, it does not entail a policy that automatically exempts people from legal responsibility for reasons related to their culture. The circumstance of unfamiliarity with law caused by inadequate equipment is not a permanent one. Once it is clear that a cultural practice comes into conflict with the law, and that its observers are ignorant of that conflict, the most reasonable thing to do, it seems, is to inform them of this conflict and give them a fair opportunity to take the law into account.

An Individualised Condition

New arrivals often lack the cultural skills, know-how, and tools that are pivotal for gaining knowledge about the law in their host country. Evident as it is, anybody with deficient cultural equipment is unable to independently access the law. It is against this background that the possibility of non-compliance having its source in communicative interruptions between the law and its addressees becomes readily perceived. Such interruptions are caused by vast differences in terms of cultural equipment among the individual subjects, and the difficulties involved in attempts to be sensitive towards and accommodate a host of differing equipment into public practices of promulgation. The question arises as to whether ignorance caused by public neglect of diverse equipment should be given special consideration by courts and administrative agencies in their application of law.

Prior to examining the issue as to whether cultural difference could ever be a legitimate ground for excuse in case of non-compliance with law it is first necessary to discuss a related issue, that of different sorts of legal responsibility: absolute and fault responsibility, and their potential relevance to the issue at hand. To begin with, if liability is absolute, it is irrelevant *why* the defendant did not observe the law. In this case, no attention is paid to the intentions, motives, or beliefs behind his action. Instead, what is decisive is that his action brought about the effect declared as harmful and prohibited by law. The individual is seen as having acted in a negligent manner because he did not take the necessary measures of precaution; it is irrelevant why he did not do so.[71] This type of legal responsibility is common in cases of minor offences sanctioned by a fine. Temporary visitors do break such

[71] See generally H Kelsen, *General Theory of Law and State*, above n 28, at 65–67.

laws. One such case in point are Italian bus and train ticket rules. Most tourists to Italy do not know that tickets for trains must be stamped with a date before embarking on their trip. What is more, most temporary visitors do not know that bus tickets cannot be bought on the bus.[72] Since no consideration is given to the reasons, beliefs, or motives behind a person's nonobservance of the rules, tourists and other temporary visitors risk paying a fine despite their ignorance of the practices of Italian public transportation services. Is this reasonable?

Even if outsiders are unfamiliar with particular solutions for the financing of public transportation services, it is reasonable to assume that they know that such transportation is not free, at least if similar arrangements exist in their place of residence. Thus, it is part of their responsibility to learn from guides, information centres, bar tenders, and so on, what is required of them if they intend to use the transportation made available to all. In a like manner, it is reasonable to expect that tourists who intend to, say, camp in the Italian countryside, gather wood and make their own fire, hunt in the forest or fish in the water, should take the necessary precautions to find out about the relevant laws that apply to these sorts of activities. Although temporary visitors cannot reasonably be expected to know the particulars of Italian law, they are expected to know that most places do regulate such activities and on this basis make an effort to learn what the laws are. Besides, and more importantly for the present study, the cost for not complying with these kinds of regulations, a fine, seems too modest to be considered as having a significant impact on individual freedom.

However, this type of legal responsibility is also common in respect of the regulations of administrative agencies, whether in the field of social security, unemployment, or public health. The ability to respect these regulations does have a significant impact on individual freedom. They impose conditions for enjoying the goods they are set up to distribute. Indeed, as noted in chapter six of this book, at first sight, these regulations seem voluntary in the sense that one can avoid being subjected to them. However, a closer examination reveals that the intended beneficiaries are in a dependency relation with these agencies. For this reason, the regulations must be seen as coercive in the sense that they constitute a threat to individual freedom rather than an offer.[73] Nevertheless, such regulations can be difficult to access even for a person who possesses the cultural equipment of the culture dominating the public institutions in his location, since they regulate the behaviour of governmental agencies and not the conduct of private persons.

[72] Note that buses in Florence and Rome are exempted from this rule.

[73] R Nozick, 'Coercion' in S Morgenbesser and P Suppes (eds), *Philosophy: Science and Method* (New York, St Martin's Press, 1969), 440–472. For a more detailed discussion of the distinction between threat and offer see also *ibid*, ch 6, sec 3.4.

Indeed, there is a great deal of legislation of this kind.[74] If this is true, it must be even more difficult for people who lack the cultural equipment to access them. There is a constant risk of failing to respect deadlines, fill out application forms correctly, and meet other requirements. Thus, given the immediate impact of these regulations on individual freedom, it seems appropriate to consider the possibility of excuse in case of involuntary ignorance. One cause of involuntary ignorance is the lack of cultural equipment necessary to know about these regulations and take them into account. The possibility of excuse is limited to cases of non-compliance in which an individual would be deprived of basic goods, such as a minimum provision of welfare, as a result of his failure to observe a regulation due to involuntary ignorance. This possibility is warranted on the basis of a deeper concern with securing a minimum provision of respect for individual freedom. Part of what is required to ensure such a provision is to make sure that nobody is deprived of basic goods deemed essential for being able to enjoy this freedom. Thus, it does not cover cases of non-compliance amounting to a mere failure to take advantage of opportunities made available by public institutions. One example of such a failure would be a missed deadline for a job application.

A different sort of legal responsibility is that based on fault. Whether an individual is to be held responsible for his action turns on the reasons behind it. In legal terms, the determination of liability must consider a mental element (*mens rea*).[75] The requirement that law-applying institutions consider what a given individual knew, foresaw, or believed to be required of him, is common in more serious crimes that involve imprisonment. A consideration of the mental element is motivated by a deeper concern with individual freedom. To imprison somebody for having committed an action that he could not reasonably have known was criminalised in his location is a serious and unjustified intrusion on his freedom.

The requirement that the offender must have known what she has done does not mean that she must be *conscious* of wickedness or have malevolent intent.[76] Glanville Williams advances an approach whereby *mens rea* is not seen as requiring the existence of moral wrong, dishonest intent, or conscious guilt. A person may well believe that he has a good intention; still, he would be seen as committing a crime. Instead, *mens rea* means intention as to the elements constituting the *actus reus*. The criterion of intention refers not only to a desire for the consequence of action, but also knowledge of the surrounding fact. A person does not act intentionally if he is ignorant or mistaken about the surrounding circumstances.[77] In most instances, *mens*

[74] FA Hayek, *Law, Legislation and Liberty*: *Rules and Order*, vol 1 (Chicago, The University of Chicago Press, 1973), at 124–144.

[75] *Mens rea* is the Latin term for guilty mind.

[76] G Williams, *Criminal Law*: *The General Part*, 2nd edn (London, Stevens & Sons Limited, 1961), at para 14.

[77] *Ibid*, at para 52.

rea means only that the offender must know what she did and that her act was unlawful. However, in some cases, it is sufficient that she knows what she did and it is irrelevant whether she knew that her action was unlawful. In other words, liability to punishment for actions which constitute serious crimes according to law requires that the action must be accompanied by a certain state of mind. Otherwise, an individual must not be held responsible for her failure to observe a given law.[78]

It is consideration of *mens rea* that has resulted in the occasional use of 'cultural defence' in an attempt to protect people belonging to marginal cultures, and, in particular, immigrant cultures, from serious punishment in cases of unlawful action. For example, cultural defence cases have been successfully argued before domestic courts in the United States in relation to actions considered crimes in their respective jurisdictions.[79] However, most of these defence cases use cultural arguments not to excuse a person for something that he has done because of involuntary ignorance caused by his cultural difference; rather, culture is invoked as a mitigating condition for lowering a sentence.[80] Such cases must be dealt with separately since they are not so much about ignorance of law as about the idea that culture guides—at times, dictates—a certain course of action for its members when confronted with a problem, such as unfaithfulness. As noted in chapter six on *adiaphora*, the idea that culture has this power finds support in theories, not only about the human capacity for sociability, but also about the potential impact of instruction on the human conscience. In these cases, defendants seek to mitigate the seriousness of the violent actions, often murders, by referring to the existence of duties to perform such actions, duties internal to their cultures, in response to the wrongdoing of others. Unlike these cases, then, which focus on the justificatory potential of a unlawful and violent action, the cases in focus in the present study focus on circumstances that explain a person's unlawful behaviour.[81] As George Fletcher explains, justificatory reasons are essentially preoccupied with the act as such; excusing reasons, in contrast, refer to the circumstance or, possibly, the character of the individual.[82] The question remains as to whether a person could be excused for having acted contrary to criminal law due to involuntary ignorance explained by his cultural difference.

[78] A Kenny, *Freewill and Responsibility* (London, Routledge & Kegan Paul, 1978), at 1–2, 5.

[79] See generally NA Wanderer and CR Connors, 'Culture and Crime: Kargar (State v Kargar, 679 A. 2d 81 (Me. 1996)) and the Existing Framework for a Cultural Defence' (1999) 47 *Buffalo Law Review* 829.

[80] See eg DL Coleman, 'Individualizing Justice Through Multiculturalism: The Liberals' Dilemma' (1996) 96 *Columbia Law Review* 1093.

[81] For a distinction between different sorts of reasons, see J Gardner, 'Justifications and Reasons' in AP Simester and ATH Smith (eds), *Harm and Culpability* (Oxford, Clarendon Press, 1996), 103–129 at 103.

[82] GP Fletcher, 'The Individualization of Excusing Conditions' (1974) 47 *Southern California Law Review* 1269 at 1271.

Even if a law has been promulgated to all its addressees, there is no guarantee that they will apply it correctly, that is, in the way it would be applied by the courts and other law-applying institutions. If the problematic circumstance of newcomers and others whose cultures differ from the one dominating the public institutions in their location could be resolved through translation of the law into all the languages spoken in society, the communicative trouble that multiculturalism gives rise to would not be so significant, at least not from a theoretical standpoint. However, in addition to having *linguistic* access to a law, so to speak, it is also necessary to be familiar with, and be able to use, the official scheme of interpretation of law and fact. Of course, some terms are plain and do not call for interpretation; others nevertheless tend to house diverse meanings. Similarly to other elements of cultural equipment, the precise meaning of a term is learned from others in one's territorial proximity and, at least to some extent, from the educational institutions of one's state. Such interpretative schemes differ from place to place and change over time. Thus, the precise meaning is not something that one learns once and for all. Unlike new arrivals, the native-born citizens are expected to be familiar with the official scheme in use, and accustomed with the conventional ways of keeping themselves up to date with changes. For this reason, native-born citizens are believed to be better equipped to fully appreciate what is required of them as a matter of law. Unfamiliarity with an interpretative scheme increases the likelihood of mistakes and misunderstandings of what the law in a foreign place forbids us to do there, or requires us to do in order to benefit from a co-operative scheme, and so on.

The circumstance amounting to unfamiliarity with the official scheme of interpretation is more difficult to overcome than, say, a lack of language skills. The occurrence of mistakes and misunderstandings of law seems inevitable if its interpretative scheme is unknown or unfamiliar to its addressees. Herein is a possibility of communicative interruptions between the law-making institutions and the legal subjects that differs from an interruption brought about by deficient language skills. Even if a positive law has been enacted and declared with due consideration to linguistic diversity, the possibility of communicative interruptions remain.

One illustration of the circumstance of unfamiliarity with an official scheme of interpretation and its impact on the ability to observe the law is the *Kargar* case in which an Afghani refugee was charged with gross sexual assault due to his unfamiliarity with the official scheme of interpretation governing the law of the state of Maine in the United States.[83] At the time of arrest, Kargar had lived with his family in the United States for almost four years. His youngest son, Rahmadan, was born in America. Kargar was held responsible for two counts of gross sexual assault under Maine law for having

[83] *State v Kargar*, 679 A. 2d 81 (Me. 1996).

kissed his son's penis. One count related to a photo allegedly showing him kissing the penis when the child was approximately nine months old. The second count related to an incident in which he allegedly kissed the child's penis while undressing the child to go to bed when the child was approximately 15 months old. Maine's gross sexual assault statute prohibits any contact between an adult's mouth and a child's penis. No intent or sexual gratification is required. When Kargar admitted that he had kissed his son's penis, it was concluded by the lower court of Maine that he had violated the statute. No consideration was given to Kargar's motives, reasons, or beliefs behind his action. He was sentenced to concurrent terms of 18 months in prison on both counts, the terms were suspended, and he was placed on probation for three years with the condition that he must learn English.[84] Kargar's convictions also exposed him to the risk of deportation under federal law.[85]

Kargar appealed to the Supreme Court of Maine to have the conviction against him quashed. He argued that he did not know about the existence of the statute, and that his conduct was consistent with the law of Afghanistan which prohibits sexual abuse and, in fact, punishes such an act with death penalty. In support of his appeal to be excused for his action he submitted cultural evidence that his conduct was regarded as neither wrong nor sexual under Islamic law; according to that law, his conduct was not only deemed innocent, but even considered appropriate. A professor at the University of Arizona and the Director of the Afghan Mujahideen Information Bureau, verified this evidence. A caseworker from the Maine Department of Human Services (DHS), who had investigated the incident after the arrest, also testified. Kargar himself explained that, consistent with Islamic Afghan culture, by kissing Rahmadan's penis—a body part that is 'not the holiest or cleanest'—he was showing how much he truly loved his son. The submitted evidence was also supported by an Ahman, or priest, in the Maine Muslim community who stated that the conduct for which Kargar had been convicted was deemed innocent, non-sexual, and appropriate in Islamic Afghan culture. The Supreme Court of Maine reversed the outcome and the case against Kargar was dismissed. It found that the court below had erroneously concluded that the defendant's cultural background was irrelevant in determining whether the charge for gross sexual assault against him should have been dismissed. Unlike the lower court, the Supreme Court held that it is necessary to take account of the intention of the defendant as well as whether any harm was caused by his conduct. The

[84] See Appellant's Brief at 15–16, Kargar (No 7719, CUM-95–300), cited by N Wanderer and CR Connors, 'Culture and Crime: Kargar (State v Kargar, 679 A. 2d 81 (Me. 1996)) and the Existing Framework for a Cultural Defence', above n 79, at 840 footnote 41.

[85] Pursuant to current US deportation statutes, an alien is deportable if he is convicted for two 'crimes involving moral turpitude, not arising out of a single scheme of criminal misconduct' even if no prison sentence is imposed. See 8 USC 1227 (a)(2)(A)(ii) (Supp 1998) (originally enacted as 1251 (a)(2)(A)(ii)(1994), cited *ibid*, at 840 footnote 45.

basis for the dismissal was that Kargar was ignorant of the statute; in addition, he lacked intent to harm his son either physically or mentally. Indeed, the Afghani culture does not stigmatise this conduct, but understands it as an expression of love.[86]

Kargar seems to have believed that sexual abuse is a crime wherever he goes. In other words, sexual abuse would be contrary to what Hobbes declared to be prohibitions against the laws of nature. Therefore, such prohibitions do not presuppose any act of declaration by the legislative authority to be seen as valid. However, as noted earlier on in this chapter, it is still possible, likely even, that the specific understanding of what counts as sexual abuse in a given place is not necessarily the same as in other places. In contrast to the courts of Maine, Kargar applied an Islamic scheme of interpretation that accommodated Afghani practices. Thus, without any specific act of declaration by the legislative authority of Maine about its understanding of sexual abuse in a language that he understands (Kargar obviously did not know English), and in the absence of any 'intuitive' sense that his way of showing love for his son might be criminalised in his new place of residence, his cultural background should, and did, excuse him for his action.

The Limits to Excuse

Hobbes' claim that new arrivals are excused in cases of conduct contrary to the laws of their host country due to ignorance was not intended as a plea for absolute tolerance of the behaviour of newcomers. His claim was confined to what he defined as 'particular laws' as opposed to 'general or natural laws'. The latter restrain human conduct regardless of location. Since the laws of nature are agreeable to all they need no specific act of declaration in order to be valid. Instead, knowledge of these laws is gained through the use of one's reason.[87] Actions contrary to such laws are never excused since everybody knows that they constitute universal wrongs. William Blackstone articulates a similar claim when commenting on the principle that, unlike *mala prohibita*, natural duties and *mala in se* are binding upon men's consciences. As he puts it:

> So also in regard to *natural duties*, and such offenses as are *mala in se*: here we are bound in conscience, because we are bound by superior laws, before those human laws were in being, to perform the one and abstain from the other. But in relation to those laws which enjoin only *positive duties* and forbid only such things as are not *mala in se* but *mala prohibita* merely, without any intermixture of moral guilt, annexing a penalty to non-compliance, here I apprehend conscience is no farther concerned, than by directing a submission to the penalty, in case of our breach of those laws.[88]

[86] See generally *ibid*.
[87] T Hobbes, *Leviathan*, above n 6, at 188.
[88] W Blackstone, *Commentaries on the Laws of England*: *Book the First* G Tucker (ed) (Philadelphia, William Young Birch and Abraham Small, 1803), §57.

Nevertheless, though it may be possible to appeal to human conscience as indicating the outer limits to excusing somebody for having done something contrary to the laws in his location, the human conscience is nothing but a rough guide to the specific prohibitions of the laws of nature. The Kargar case illustrates how reliance on one's conscience is insufficient to act in a way that is agreeable to everybody regardless of location. This is so since the laws of nature must be given specific contents by way of interpretation. The difficulty of such interpretation is explained by John Rawls as having its source in the burdens of judgement. These burdens also explain the possibility of differing and conflicting judgements, not only with respect to the specific contents of the laws of nature, but also as to how to apply these laws to concrete cases. Thus, even if everybody agrees that violence is contrary to the laws of nature, the specific contents of that prohibition, its range of application, and the possibility of exceptions are disputed. In other words, there may be no safe standards of conduct to rely upon besides the many laws that have been enacted by the various law-making institutions that exist in the world today and which are believed to give content to something like the laws of nature.

The development of international criminal law, in particular, the recent establishment of a permanent international tribunal, the International Criminal Court, with jurisdiction to interpret international criminal law, represents a serious effort to respond to the need, not only to punish acts contrary to the laws of nature, but also to give specific content to those laws, through international codification and jurisprudence. The Rome Statute of the International Criminal Court (1998)[89] defines acts that constitute 'genocide' as well as 'crimes against humanity,' among them, widespread or systematic murder, extermination, rape, enslavement, apartheid, and torture.[90] These are considered as 'the most serious crimes of concern for the international community as a whole [which] must not go unpunished.'[91] It must be noted that the Rome Statute of the International Criminal Court builds on earlier efforts of international codification, notably the Genocide Convention (1948).[92] Also the Statute of the International Tribunal for the Former Yugoslavia (1993)[93] and the Statute of the International Tribunal for Rwanda (1994)[94] are noteworthy in this respect. Though the

[89] Rome Statute of the International Criminal Court, 17 July 1998, UN Doc A/CONF 183/9 (1998) (entered into force on 1 July 2002) [hereinafter the 'Rome Statute'].

[90] Rome Statute, Arts 6 and 7.

[91] Rome Statute, preamble, para 4.

[92] Convention on the Prevention and Punishment of the Crime of Genocide, GA Res 260 A (III), 9 Dec 1948, 78 UNTS 277.

[93] United Nations Security Council Resolution 827 on Establishing an International Tribunal for the Prosecution of Persons Responsible for Serious Violations of International Humanitarian Law Committed in the Territory of the Former Yugoslavia, SC Res 827, UN SCOR, 48th Sess, 3217th mtg at 1, UN Doc S/RES/827 (1993) [hereinafter 'ICTY Statute'], Arts 2 and 3.

[94] United Nations Security Resolution 955 Establishing the International Tribunal for Rwanda, SC Res 955, UN SCOR, 49th Sess, 3452d mtg, at 15, UN Doc S/RES/955 (1994) [hereinafter ICTR Statute], Arts 2 and 3.

competence of these international criminal tribunals is *ad hoc* and limited to crimes committed in armed conflicts in Rwanda and in former Yugoslavia, their establishment manifests the need to hold the individuals involved in these crimes accountable for their actions irrespective of whether the laws of their respective states were ineffective or in some way legitimised those actions at the time of their commission, as well as the need for international codification and interpretation of the laws of nature with respect to especially serious crimes. At the same time, at present, international criminal law seems clearly unsatisfactory as a guide to human conduct regardless of location. It disregards rape, abuse, murder, torture, etc, if the acts are not of such magnitude that they deserve international attention and an international response. The acts in question must be 'part of a widespread or systematic attack directed against any civilian population.'[95] If international criminal law were to be understood as defining the laws of nature, the occasional acts of murder, rape, and torture, etc, of newcomers would go unpunished.

Thus, international criminal law fails to offer a satisfactory guide in the adjudication of cases involving different cultural understandings between immigrants and the domestic courts of the United States about the permissibility of the use of violence. At present, there is a discernible pattern of differential treatment of offenders prosecuted for rape and murder because of their different cultural backgrounds. This differentiation has been severely criticised in academic circles in the United States. The critical issue is that culture is not considered as a ground for total excuse, but as a mitigating factor that lowers the punishment for the crime.[96] The offenders were immigrants and the crimes were committed against family members. The academic debate has centred not so much on how to cope with differing cultural understandings of the permissibility of violence as it has on the problem of balancing the legal right of offenders with the legal right to protection from crime. Most of the participants in these debates affirm that the balance must be struck in favour of the victims. The American courts can safely ignore the reality of different cultural understandings of the precise contours of a general prohibition of violence and enforce the criminal statutes without differentiation for the sake of securing equal protection to victims of crimes regardless of cultural attachment.

[95] Rome Statute, Art 7(1).

[96] These cases have been discussed because they raise pertinent issues about the moral accuracy of cultural defence. See eg DL Coleman, 'Individualizing Justice Through Multiculturalism: The Liberals' Dilemma', above n 80. Lambelet refers to three cases of critical importance in the debates surrounding cultural defence. The first case is about a Chinese man in New York who beat his wife to death some weeks after she had told him that she had been unfaithful. Her husband explained that his conduct comported with a Chinese custom that allows husbands to dispel their shame in this way when their wives have been unfaithful. He was acquitted of murder charges (*People v Chen*. No 87–774 (NY Sup Ct Dec 2, 1988)). The second case is a Japanese-American woman who drowned her two young children in Santa Monica and then attempted to kill herself because her husband had been unfaithful to her. She spent only one year in jail, the year she was on trial (*People v Kimura*. Record of Court

What should be done in cases such as these? How should courts deal with actions considered contrary to the laws of nature in their jurisdiction, yet permitted in others? How should cases involving offenders whose cultures encourage the occasional use of violence be dealt with? The universal seriousness of violence is indicated by the fact that all cultures regulate this activity. Indeed, all cultures prohibit the use of violence and punish those who breach that prohibition. The difference lies in the way some cultures permit violence as a form of punishment for somebody who has done something contrary to the conduct rules of these cultures. Such punishment is intolerable from the standpoint of a culture whose members uphold a universal categorical prohibition against violence. From such a standpoint there is obviously nothing wrong in enforcing the prohibition of violence, regardless of people's particular opinions about it. Indeed, a consistent enforcement of the prohibition is a method of curbing violence in the name of culture. At the same time, the fact that violence is part of some cultures remains. Violence may be considered not only as acceptable, but as an appropriate form of punishment. In other words, violence has a justificatory potential from the standpoint of the person whose culture it is.

The balancing of the right of offenders with the right to equal protection before the law takes place against this background. To settle this balancing it will be necessary to take sides. Having said that, whether it is reasonable for a court to settle a case with due regard for the justificatory potential of the violent act from the standpoint of the offender's culture is uncertain. It allows defences of unlawful actions inside the courtroom whose justificatory potential in the sense of substantive argument (for example, 'I must kill my wife if she has been unfaithful to me') is not agreeable to everybody in society. In the face of disagreement, the argument is up for grabs and, although it is embedded in a particular culture, it is not immune from criticism or disrespect. Indeed, the law may have been enacted precisely to protect unfaithful women from outraged and dishonoured husbands. What is at stake in these cases is not involuntary ignorance of a particular law caused by the circumstance of unfamiliarity, but a conflict or disagreement about the limits to tolerable forms of human behaviour. The law of a state represents the authoritative settlement of such disagreement among its citizens.

Nevertheless, there is a possibility that a new arrival will be unfamiliar with the law of his host state concerning the particulars of universal wrongs, at least for a period of time. Thus, the question arises as to whether non-compliance with such law could ever be excused if it depends on involuntary

Proceedings, No A–091133 (Super Ct LA County Nov 21, 1985)). The third case is about a Laotian-American woman who was abducted from her place of work at Fresno State University and forced to have sexual intercourse against her will. Her Hmong immigrant assailant explained that, among his tribe, such behaviour is not only accepted, but expected: it is the customary way to choose a bride. He was sentenced to 120 days in jail, and his victim received $900 in reparations (*People v Moua*. Record of Court Proceedings, No 315972-0 (Super Ct Fresno County, Feb 7, 1985)).

ignorance caused by deficient cultural equipment. In one sense, the account advanced in the present study seems to support the possibility that, although the justificatory potential of cultural defence is undermined in multicultural societies in the light of conflict and disagreement, a person could be excused for his action on the basis of the circumstance of unfamiliarity. Indeed, on this account, unfamiliarity seems to extend to unfamiliarity with the prevailing interpretation of universal wrongs. However, though it has been recognised that cultures may differ in their understandings of the particulars of universal wrongs, such as violence, this is not to say that straightforward acts of violence, whether physical or psychological, such as murders, torture, inhuman or degrading treatment, could ever be excused. The protection of individuals from abuse, and fear of abuse, whether committed by states, corporations, international organisations, or private persons, is the essence of what it means to ensure a minimum provision of respect for individual freedom. To excuse such conduct on the basis of unfamiliarity is to negate the very basis for which individual freedom ought to be respected, namely a human capacity to exercise that freedom in responsible ways with due regard for the capacity of others to do the same.

CONCLUSION

The critical importance of suitable cultural equipment for being able to access law is the background to my claim about the possibility of excuse in individual cases for reasons related to culture in multicultural societies. The widespread lack of suitable cultural equipment is an issue that is appropriately responded to by legislative authorities offering educational opportunities for newcomers and others who are similarly situated in cultural terms. However, as this chapter also suggests, insofar as the lack of suitable cultural equipment is an inevitable circumstance for newcomers, at least for a period of time, the possibility of excuse is an issue that inevitably crops up in the day-to-day administration and enforcement of law. For this reason, it is an unavoidable issue for the courts as well as administrative agencies assigned to distribute goods deemed essential for effective individual freedom.

In summary, the claim advanced in this chapter is that deficient cultural equipment can result in unintentional failures to observe the law due to the inability to access the law. Whether it is a valid ground for excuse depends, first of all, on the nature of the law in question. It must be a particular law, ie a law that regulates actions that are morally indifferent. Excuse is not allowed in relation to a general law, ie a law that specifies the particulars of universal wrongs, unless there was, in effect, no abuse, harm, or violence caused by the unlawful action. Secondly, the failure to observe the law must have a serious impact on individual freedom, such as imprisonment, deportation, or deprivation of basic goods. Finally, a person must be willing to comply with the law once he knows about it and has been given a fair opportunity to take it into account. If, by contrast, a person fails to observe a law for reasons related to his cultural duties or the worth he attaches to a cultural practice, his non-observance amounts to conscientious refusal or civil disobedience and, thus, must be dealt with as such.

9

An International Human Rights Agenda on Culture

THIS BOOK HAS advanced an account of the relationship between culture and respect for human rights according to which culture is best understood as a property possessed by the individual, with direct influence on her ability to enjoy the rights and freedoms as recognised in international human rights law. It indicates that the issue of culture cannot be treated in an isolated fashion, but is critical to just about every area of human rights.

A closer examination of international human rights law reveals several understandings of the link between culture and human rights. At present, culture is depicted not merely as something that everybody has a right to participate in, but also as hampering and debilitating, possibly violating the right to enjoy the rights and freedoms guaranteed in international human rights law. Nevertheless, to the extent that culture has received attention in the international human rights context, it is mainly perceived as referring to community and as warranting the strengthening of the right to enjoy one's own culture or community by recognising a right to cultural identity. Other notions of culture and their significance to the advancement of human rights are left in the background.

At the level of international law and policy, what is suggested is not the introduction of new or additional rights, but a more detailed account of the meaning of the rights already at hand, (not merely first and second generation cultural rights, but also other rights), and their relationship to the cultural dimension of the individual. Such an account must explain what actions a right to culture reasonably protects, who may enjoy it, under which conditions it may be exercised, and what the absolute limits upon such exercise are. In addition, it is essential to clarify what duties and responsibilities are generated by a right to culture and to whom they are (to be) addressed. For these and similar questions, it is necessary to articulate the ultimate purpose for which everybody needs and wants a right to culture, namely to enjoy individual freedom. It is this purpose that must shape and inform the core content of an international human rights agenda on culture.

First of all, the right to culture is meant to secure individual access to the cultural framework dominating the public institutions that have the authority to deliberate, interpret, and enforce international human rights law in one's place of residence. This is made possible through the acquisition of suitable cultural equipment. Such acquisition is a precondition for the exercise of the right to cultural participation as well as a range of other individual rights and freedoms similarly recognised in international human rights law. In other words, suitable cultural equipment is not an end in itself, but is essential to the effective enjoyment of international human rights in general. A focus on culture directs attention to the fundamental importance of possessing the set of tools, skills, and know-how necessary to access laws and legal institutions as well as for participating in economic and political life. For most people, political, economic, and legal participation are the main avenues available for protecting particular interests and securing a fair share of income and wealth. Nevertheless, without any suitable cultural equipment on hand, the individual is incapable of utilising any of them. An international human rights agenda devoted to culture must pay due regard to this fact.

Secondly, an international human rights agenda on culture must consider the critical importance of the cultural infrastructure that organises and informs ordinary life issues, such as modes of dress, prayer, and diet, in the field of *adiaphora*. The various rules and norms that we follow to facilitate day-to-day activities are not necessarily part of our definition of the good life; rather, they constitute the very infrastructure that makes thought and reflection about the good life possible. However, suggesting that there is a basis for an individual right to enjoy one's own culture does not necessarily mean that the pursuit of culture is an end in itself or should be encouraged to be perceived as such. The politics of recognition and of difference are signs that the cultural infrastructure is at risk of collapse or else felt (mistakenly or not) to be so. Public ignorance towards an individual's conscientious objection to changing his ways on matters of *adiaphora*—that is, on matters that ultimately are irrelevant from the standpoint of cosmopolitan moral law—may similarly serve to make the pursuit of culture a goal in itself. Nevertheless, these are unfortunate developments that can be avoided if due regard is given to the reality of diverse cultural infrastructures and the significance of such structures for the enjoyment of individual freedom.

The present study distances itself from an interpretation of the right to enjoy one's own culture as primarily motivated by community-oriented interests and concerns. Instead, it advocates an understanding of that right as a freedom of the individual to go about his own business on matters of *adiaphora* to the extent that this is possible and to the extent that it does not harm anybody else. This seems to be a very modest claim; all the same, in contemporary deliberations about law and policy, especially related to public health, security, and safety, major international human rights institutions do not pay sufficient attention to the reasons for which everybody needs and wants to protect his own cultural infrastructure. For example, as we have seen, the European Court of Human Rights fails to recognise the direct relevance of cultural infrastructures in securing enjoyment of the rights and freedoms under the European Convention on Human Rights. Nevertheless, an international human rights agenda on culture must consider how the civic freedoms already on hand, notably, freedom of religion, thought, and belief, may be interpreted so as to accommodate this human rights concern.

Thirdly, the risk of politicisation of culture is real and significant; it is experienced in many multicultural societies. It induces a sense of culture as passionate and irrational and, at times, as posing irresolvable conflicts and disagreements in political life. This is so because culture is not only about practices, but also encompasses doctrines—religious, ethical, and philosophical—seeking to provide right answers to deep and eternal questions about the ultimate purpose of human life. Still, historical experience indicates that there is room for negotiation, compromise, and adjustment of doctrines for the sake of peace and justice when societies become more diverse. An international human rights agenda must emphasise the possibility of mutual adjustment and not present the fact of multiculturalism as non-negotiable. More importantly, international human rights institutions must be willing to risk putting their own agenda up for grabs, to argue for it, and to allow others to disagree about its specific contents. Even if dissenters to international human rights law may be misinformed or inauthentic, it is by no means certain that there is nothing that dissenters may contribute that could further improve this law and its implementation. Widespread participation would also enhance the legitimacy of any specific international human rights agenda at any given point in time.

Fourthly, there is a need to articulate a universal prohibition against practices of violence in the name of culture. As things stand, the formal recognition of the wrongs of practices of violence regardless of cultural sources (notably, female genital circumcision) is currently confined to African human rights law and focuses on children and women. Even so, cultural legitimisation of violence is not a regional, but an international phenomenon. However, at present, there is no international human rights instrument that absolutely and categorically prohibits and punishes violence regardless of source or perpetrator. Disagreement on the precise contours of a general prohibition of violence is to be expected. Even so, the development of international criminal law and the recent establishment of an International Criminal Court are critical steps toward the realisation of a universal notion of the outer limits of acceptable human conduct. At the same time, it must be noted that violence in the name of culture is more difficult to erase precisely because it is legitimised by culture-specific rules and norms. It indicates that a formal prohibition is not enough and that much more needs to be done by international human rights institutions in terms of direct involvement, education, and information. Still, such a prohibition would constitute a legal basis for international debate, discussion, and activities focusing on absolute limits to cultural difference that is not confined to certain places or groups.

Finally, a human rights agenda on culture must specify the duties and responsibilities generated by a right to culture in all its facets and to whom these duties and responsibilities are addressed. It is suggested that a right to culture as a right to access culture places duties on states, in particular, legislative authorities, to facilitate the acquisition of suitable cultural equipment for everybody. However, the effective acquisition of suitable equipment presupposes that the individual is willing to learn; otherwise, his acquisition is likely to take time and perhaps never happen. Thus, some burdens of responsibility are placed on the individual in this respect. In addition, courts must consider the possibility of excusing involuntary ignorance due to deficient cultural equipment in cases of non-compliance with laws and regulations. In a similar fashion, the right to enjoy one's own culture generates duties for states—legislative authorities, administrative authorities, and courts—to address and respond to cases of conscientious objection on matters of *adiaphora* in the form of cultural accommodation, including legislative revisions and exemptions, when such accommodations are possible and do not legitimise violence or harm anybody. At the same time, the fact of multiculturalism presupposes a certain human willingness to adjust culture-specific rules and norms to make them fit others. While any idea of human responsibility should be treated with caution, especially in the context of international human rights law, it is important to bear in mind that the very recognition of individual freedom assumes that humans are capable of acting responsibly in exercising their rights and freedoms.

More generally, an international human rights agenda on culture must reaffirm the universal and overarching importance of culture in advancing respect for human rights and seek to rebalance the present agenda dominated by a right to cultural identity with an urgent emphasis on the fundamental importance of cultural equipment and cultural infrastructure to individual freedom, as well as the need to address and specify the absolute limits to cultural difference. In so doing, the international human rights community is more likely to achieve its objective of securing a universal minimum provision of respect for persons. By taking seriously the circumstances of those who currently stand, because of their cultural difference, if not outside, then at the margins of the society in which they live, the international human rights community will thereby allow them to nevertheless profit—alongside all others—from their status as equal bearers of human rights.

Bibliography

Literature

Addis A, 'On Human Diversity and the Limits of Toleration' in I Shapiro and W Kymlicka (eds), *Ethnicity and Group Rights* (New York, New York University Press, 1997).

Albrecht H-J, 'Ethnic Minorities: Crime and Criminal justice in Europe' in F Heidensohn and M Farrell (eds), *Crimes in Europe* (London, Routledge, 1991).

Alston P, 'A Third Generation of Solidarity Rights: Progressive Development or Obfuscation of International Human Rights Law?' (1982) 29 *Netherlands International Law Review* 307.

—— 'Conjuring up New Human Rights: A Proposal for Quality Control' (1984) 78 *American Journal of International Law* 607.

—— (ed), *People's Rights* (New York, Oxford University Press, 2002).

American Anthropological Association, 'Statement on Human Rights' (1947) 48 *American Anthropologist* 539.

Anderson B, *Imagined Communities: Reflections on the Origins and Spread of Nationalism* (New York, Verso, 1991).

Arendt H, *Origins of Totalitarianism* (New York, Harcourt Brace Jovanovich, 1951).

—— 'Civil Disobedience' in H Arendt (ed), *Crises of the Republic* (New York, Harcourt Brace Jovanovich, 1972).

Arneson RJ, 'Equality and Equal Opportunity for Welfare' in L Pojman and R Westmoreland (eds), *Ideas of Equality. Selected Readings* (New York, Oxford University Press, 1997).

Austin J, *Lectures on Jurisprudence,* R Campbell (rev ed), 3rd edn (London, John Murray, Albemarle Street, 1869).

Axelrod R, 'The Dissemination of Culture. A Model with Local Convergence and Global Polarization' (1997) 41 *Journal of Conflict Resolution* 203.

Bahm A, 'Theories of Conscience' (1965) *Ethics* 128.

Barry B, *Justice as Impartiality* (New York, Oxford University Press, 1995).

—— 'The Limits of Cultural Politics' (1998) 24 *Review of International Studies* 307.

—— *Culture and Equality* (Oxford, Polity Press, 2001).

Bauböck R, 'Changing the Boundaries of Citizenship. The Inclusion of Immigrants in Democratic Polities' in R Bauböck, *From Aliens to Citizens. Redefining the Status of Migrants in Europe* (Aldershot, Avebury, 1994).

Beitz C, *Political Theory and International Relations*, 2nd edn (Princeton, Princeton University Press, 1999).

Bentham J, *Of Laws in General,* HLA Hart (ed) (London, University of London, Athlone Press, 1970).

Berlin I, 'Equality as an Ideal' in FA Olafson (ed), *Justice and Social Policy* (Englewood Cliffs, NJ, Prentice Hall, 1961).

—— *Four Essays on Liberty* (Oxford, Oxford University Press, 1969).

—— 'Benjamin Disraeli, Karl Marx and the Search for Identity' in I Berlin and H Harder (eds), *Against the Current. Essays in the History of Ideas* (London, Hogarth Press, 1979).

BLACKSTONE W, *Commentaries on the Laws of England: Book the First,* G Tucker (ed) (Philadelphia, William Young Birch and Abraham Small, 1803).

BÖCKENFÖRDE E-W, '"Kopftuchstreit" auf dem richtigen Weg?' (2001) 3 *Neue Juristische Wochenschrift* 723.

BOURDIEU P, *Distinction: A Social Critique of the Judgement of Taste* (Cambridge, MA, Harvard University Press, 1998).

—— *The State Nobility: Elite Schools in the Field of Power* (Cambridge, Polity Press, 1996).

BOYLE K and J Sheen (eds), *Freedom of Religion and Belief: A World Report* (London, Routledge, 1997).

BROWNLIE I, *Principles of Public International Law*, 4th edn (New York, Oxford University Press, 1990).

CANEY S, 'Diversity and the Lexical Priority of the Right to Equal Freedom' (1997) 17 *Oxford Journal of Legal Studies* 147.

CAPOTORTI F, *Study on the Rights of Persons Belonging to Ethnic, Religious and Linguistic Minorities* (New York, UN Publications, 1979).

CAROTHERS T, *Aiding Democracy Abroad: The Learning Curve* (Washington DC, Carnegie Endowment for International Peace, 1999).

CARTER SL, *The Dissent of the Governed: A Meditation on Law, Religion, and Loyalty* (Cambridge, MA, Harvard University Press, 1998).

CASSESE A, *Self-determination of Peoples: A Legal Reappraisal* (Cambridge, Cambridge University Press, 1995).

CASTIGLIONE D and McKinnon C (eds), *The Culture of Toleration in Diverse Societies: Reasonable Tolerance* (Manchester, Manchester University Press, 2003).

CHILDRESS JF, 'Appeals to Conscience' (1979) *Ethics* 315.

COHEN J, 'Deliberation and Democratic Legitimacy' in A Hamlin and P Pettit (eds), *The Good Polity: Normative Analysis of the State* (Oxford, Basil Blackwell, 1989).

—— (ed), Martha Nussbaum with respondents, *For Love of Country. Debating the Limits of Patriotism* (Boston, Beacon Press, 1996).

—— 'Democracy and Liberty' in J Elster (ed), *Deliberative Democracy* (New York, Cambridge University Press, 1998).

COHEN J, Howard M and Nussbaum MC (eds), S Moller Okin with respondents, *Is Multiculturalism Bad for Women? Susan Moller Okin with Respondents* (Princeton, Princeton University Press, 1999).

COLEMAN DL, 'Individualizing Justice Through Multiculturalism: The Liberals' Dilemma' (1996) 96 *Columbia Law Review* 1093.

COVER RM, 'Nomos and Narrative' (1983) 97 *Harvard Law Review* 4.

CRAWFORD J, *The Creation of States in International Law* (New York, Oxford University Press, 1979).

DAN-COHEN M, 'Decision Rules and Conduct Rules: On Acoustic Separation in Criminal Law' (1984) 97 *Harvard Law Review* 625.

DARWELL SL, 'Two Kinds of Respect' (1977) 88 *Ethics* 36.

DAS V, 'Cultural Rights and the Definition of Community' in O Mendelsohn and U Baxi (eds), *The Rights of Subordinated Peoples* (Bombay, Oxford University Press, 1994).

DONNELLY J, 'Human Rights, Individual Rights and Collective Rights' in J Berting *et al* (eds), *Human Rights in a Pluralistic World: Individuals and Collectivities* (Westport, Meckler Corporation, 1990).

DWORKIN R, *Taking Rights Seriously* (Cambridge, MA, Harvard University Press, 1978).

—— *A Matter of Principle* (Cambridge, MA, Harvard University Press, 1985).

—— *Law's Empire* (London, Fontana Press, 1986).

—— *Life's Dominion: An Argument about Abortion, Euthanasia, and Individual Freedom* (New York, Knopf, 1993).

—— *Sovereign Virtue* (Cambridge, MA, Harvard University Press, 2000).

DUFF RA, 'Law, Language and Community: Some Preconditions of Criminal Liability' (1998) 18 *Oxford Journal of Legal Studies* 189.

DUSTMANN C and Fabbri F, 'Language Proficiency and Labour Market Performance of Immigrants in the UK' (2000) *Centre for Economic Policy Research. Discussion Paper Series*, no 2487.

ELDEN Å, 'The Killing Seemed to Be Necessary: Arab Cultural Affiliation as an Extenuating Circumstance in a Swedish Verdict' (1998) 6 *NORA* 89.

ELSTER J, *Sour Grapes: Studies in the Subversion of Rationality* (New York, Cambridge University Press, 1983).

—— *Nuts and Bolts for the Social Sciences* (New York, Cambridge University Press, 1989).

—— *The Cement of Society: A Study of Social Order* (New York, Cambridge University Press, 1989).

—— 'Rationality and Social Norms' (1991) 32 *Archive Européene Sociologique* 109.

—— *Alchemies of the Mind: Rationality and the Emotions* (New York, Cambridge University Press, 1991).

ELY JH, *Democracy and Distrust: A Theory of Judicial Review* (Cambridge, MA, Harvard University Press, 1980).

EVANS MD, *Religious Liberty and International Law in Europe* (Cambridge, Cambridge University Press, 1997).

FAVELL A, 'The Europeanisation of Immigration Politics' (1998) 2 *European Integration Online Papers* [available at: <http:/eiop.or.at/eiop/texte/1998-010a.htm>]. Last visited on 23 October 1999.

FINNIS J, *Natural Law and Natural Rights* (Oxford, Oxford University Press, 1980).

—— 'The Authority of Law in the Predicament of Contemporary Social Thought' (1984) 1 *Journal of Ethics and Public Policy* 115.

—— 'Natural Law and Legal Reasoning' (1990) 38 *Cleveland State Law Review* 1.

FITZMAURICE, D, 'Autonomy as a Good: Liberalism, Autonomy and Toleration' (1993) 1 *The Journal of Philosophy* 1.

FLETCHER G, 'The Individualization of Excusing Conditions' (1974) 47 *Southern California Law Review* 1269.

FØLLESDAL A, 'Indigenous Minorities and the Shadow of Injustice Past' (1998) *Oslo ARENA Working Papers* 98/7.

FRANCK, TM, 'Postmodern Tribalism and the Right to Secession' in C Brölman, R Lefeber, and M Zeick (eds), *Peoples and Minorities in International Law*, (Dordrecht, Martinus Nijhoff Publishers, 1993).

FRANKFURT H, 'Equality and Respect' (1997) 64 *Social Research* 3.

FRASER N, 'Recognition or Redistribution? A Critical Reading of Iris Young's Justice and the Politics of Difference' (1995) 3 *The Journal of Political Philosophy* 166.

—— *Justice Interruptus: Critical Reflections on the 'Postsocialist' Condition* (London, Routledge, 1997).
FULLER LL, *The Morality of Law* (New Haven, Yale University Press, 1964).
GARDNER J, 'Justifications and Reasons' in AP Simester and ATH Smith (eds), *Harm and Culpability* (Oxford, Clarendon Press, 1996).
GAUS GF, *Value and Justification: The Foundations of Liberal Theory* (New York, Cambridge University Press, 1990).
—— *Justificatory Liberalism: An Essay on Epistemology and Political Theory* (New York, Oxford University Press, 1996).
—— *Social Philosophy* (New York, ME Sharpe Inc, Armonk, 1999).
GEE JP, *The Social Mind: Language, Ideology and Social Practice* (New York, Bergin and Garvey, 1992).
GEERTZ C, *The Interpretation of Cultures: Selected Essays* (New York, Basic Books, 1973).
—— *After the Fact: Two Countries, Four Decades, One Anthropologist* (Cambridge, MA, Harvard University Press, 1995).
GLEAVE R, 'Elements of Religious Discrimination in Europe: The Position of Muslim Minorities' in Stratos V Konstadinidis (ed), *A People's Europe: Turning a Concept into Content* (Aldershot, Dartmouth, 1999).
GLENDON MA, *A World Made New: Eleanor Roosevelt and the Universal Declaration of Human Rights* (New York, Random House, 2001).
GOODWIN-GILL GS, *The Refugee in International Law*, 2nd edn (New York, Oxford University Press, 1996).
GRUNDMANN R and Mantziaris C, 'Habermas, Rawls, and the Paradox of Impartiality' (1990) *EUI Working Paper SPS* no 90/1.
GUTMANN A and Thompson D, *Democracy and Disagreement* (Cambridge, MA, The Belknap Press of Harvard University Press, 1996).
HABERMAS J, 'Civil Disobedience: Litmus Test for the Democratic Constitutional State' (1985) 30 *Berkeley Journal of Sociology* 95.
HAGNER C, 'Flickförtryck i Traditionens Namn' (2001) 5 *Barn. Tidningen om Barns Rättigheter.*
HAMPTON J, *The Authority of Reason,* R Healey (ed) (New York, Cambridge University Press, 1998).
HARRIS D, 'Symposium: Law Enforcement's Stake in Coming to Grips with Racial Profiling' (2001) 3 *Rutger's Race and the Law Review* 9.
HART HLA, *Punishment and Responsibility. Essays in the Philosophy of Law* (Oxford, Oxford University Press, 1968).
—— *The Concept of Law*, 2nd edn (Oxford, Oxford University Press, 1994).
—— 'Rawls on Liberty and its Priority' in N Daniels (ed), *Reading Rawls* (Stanford, Stanford University Press, 1989).
HARTLEY TC, *Constitutional Problems of the European Union* (Oxford, Hart Publishing, 1999).
HAYEK FA, *Law, Legislation and Liberty: Rules and Order* (Chicago, The University of Chicago Press, 1973).
HEARN PM and Button DF (eds), *Language Industries Atlas* (Brussels and Luxembourg, Amsterdam IOS Press for CEC, 1994).
HEIDENSOHN F and Farrell M, *Crime in Europe* (London, Routledge. 1991).
HERNANDEZ DJ and Charney E (eds), *From Generation to Generation: The Health and Well-being of Children in Immigrant Families.* The Committee on the Health

and Adjustment of Immigrant Children and Families, Board on Children, Youth and Families, National Research Council, Institute of Medicine (Washington, National Academy Press, 1998).

HERZOG D, *Happy Slaves: A Critique of Consent Theory* (Chicago, University of Chicago Press, 1980).

HOBBES T, *Leviathan,* R Tuck (ed) (Cambridge, Cambridge University Press, 1991).

HOFFMAN C (ed), *Language, Culture and Communication in Contemporary Europe* (Clevedon Avon, WBC Book Manufacturers Ltd, 1996).

HOHFELD WN, *Fundamental Legal Conceptions* (New Haven, Yale University Press, 1923).

HOLMES S, *Passions and Constraint: On the Theory of Liberal Democracy* (Chicago, University of Chicago Press, 1995).

—— and Sunstein CR, *The Cost of Rights: Why Liberty Depends on Taxes* (New York, WW Norton & Company, 1999).

HUGHES R, *Culture of Complaint: The Fraying of America* (New York, Oxford University Press, 1993).

HÖFFE O, 'Moral Reasons for an Intercultural Criminal Law. A Philosophical Attempt' (1998) 11 *Ratio Juris* 206.

IGNATIEFF M, *The Needs of Strangers: An Essay on Privacy, Solidarity, and the Politics of Being Human* (New York, Elisabeth Sifton Books, Viking, 1984).

—— 'Whose Universal Values? The Crisis in Human Rights' *Praemium Erasmianum Essay* (The Hague, Foundation Horizon, 1999).

JENKINS CN, Tao L, McPhee SJ and Ngoc TH, 'Health Care Access and Preventive Care Among Vietnamese Immigrants: Do Traditional Beliefs and Practices Pose Barriers?' (1996) 43 *Social Science and Medicine* 1049.

JENKINS I, 'The Significance of Conscience' (1954) *Ethics* 261.

JOLY D, *Britannia's Crescent: Making a Place for Muslims in British Society* (Aldershot, Ashgate Publishing Ltd, 1995).

—— *Haven or Hell? Asylum Policies and Refugees in Europe* (New York, St Martin's Press, 1996).

JONES P, 'The Ideal of the Neutral State' in RE Goodin and A Reeve (eds), *Liberal Neutrality* (New York, Routledge, 1989).

JOPPKE C, 'Immigration Challenges the Nation-State' in C Joppke (ed), *Challenge to the Nation-State* (New York, Oxford University Press, 1998).

—— and Lukes S (eds), *Multicultural Questions* (New York, Oxford University Press, 1999).

KANT I, *The Metaphysical Elements of Justice,* J Ladd (trans) (Indianapolis, Bobbs-Merrill, 1965).

—— 'To Perpetual Peace. A Philosophical Sketch (1795)' in *Perpetual Peace and Other Essays,* T Humphrey (trans) (Indianapolis, Hackett Publishing Company, 1983).

—— *Metaphysics of Morals,* M Gregor (trans) (Cambridge, Cambridge University Press, 1991).

—— *Lectures on Ethics,* P Heath and JB Schneewind (eds), P Heath (trans) (Cambridge, Cambridge University Press, 1997).

KATEB G, *Hannah Arendt: Politics, Conscience, Evil* (Totowa, NJ, Rowman & Allanheld Publishers, 1984).

KELSEN H, *General Theory of Law and State,* A Wedberg (trans) (Cambridge, MA, Harvard University Press, 1945).

—— *The Pure Theory of Law,* M Knight (trans) (Berkeley, University California Press, 1967).

KENNY A, *Freewill and Responsibility* (London, Routledge & Kegan Paul, 1978).

KING M (ed), *God's Law Versus State Law: The Construction of an Islamic Identity in Western Europe* (London, Grey Seal, 1995).

KOSKENNIEMI M, *From Apology to Utopia: The Structure of International Legal Argument* (Helsinki, Lakismiesliiton Kustannus, 1989).

—— 'National Self-Determination Today: Problems of Legal Theory and Practice' (1994) 43 *International and Comparative Law Quarterly* 241.

KRAMER L, 'Fidelity to History—and Through It' (1997) 65 *Fordham Law Review* 1627.

KYMLICKA W, *Liberalism, Community and Culture* (New York, Oxford University Press, 1989).

—— *Multicultural Citizenship* (New York, Oxford University Press, 1995).

KYMLICKA W and Wayne N (eds), *Citizenship in Diverse Societies* (New York, Oxford University Press, 2000).

LAUTERPACHT H, *An International Bill of Rights* (New York, Columbia University Press, 1945).

LAVER J and Roukens J, 'The Global Information Society and Europe's Linguistic and Cultural Heritage' in C Hoffman (ed), *Language, Culture and Communication in Contemporary Europe* (Clevedon, Avon, WBC Book Manufacturers Ltd, 1996).

LEVY J, 'Classifying Cultural Rights' in W Kymlicka and I Shapiro (eds), *Ethnicity and Group Rights* (New York, New York University Press, 1997).

—— *Multiculturalism of Fear* (New York, Oxford University Press, 2001).

LOCKE J, *Two Treaties of Government,* P Laslett (ed), (Cambridge, Cambridge University Press, 1988).

—— 'An Essay on Toleration' in M Goldie (ed), *Political Essays: Cambridge Texts in the History of Political Thought* (Cambridge, Cambridge University Press, 1997).

LOVIBOND S, *Realism and Imagination in Ethics* (Minneapolis, University of Minnesota Press, 1983).

LUKES S, *Individualism* (Oxford, Basil Blackwell, 1973).

—— 'The Rationality of Social Norms' (1991) 32 *Archive Européene Sociologique* 142.

—— 'Toleration and Recognition' (1997) 10 *Ratio Juris* 213.

—— 'Humiliation and the Politics of Identity' (1997) *Social Research* 36.

MACEDO S, *Liberal Virtues: Citizenship, Virtue, and Community in Liberal Constitutionalism* (New York, Oxford University Press, 1990).

MALHAIC J-P, 'The Formulation of Translation Strategies for Cultural References' in C Hoffman (ed), *Language, Culture and Communication in Contemporary Europe* (Clevedon, Avon, WBC Book Manufacturers Ltd, 1996).

MARGALIT A and Raz J, 'National Self-determination' (1990) 87 *The Journal of Philosophy* 439.

MAYER AE, *Islam and Human Rights: Tradition and Politics* (Boulder, Westview Press, 1999).

MILL JS, *On Liberty,* S Colloni (ed) (Cambridge, Cambridge University Press, 1989).

—— *Utilitarianism,* G Sheer (ed) (Indianapolis, Hackett Publishing Company, 1979).

MOADDEL M, 'Diversities and Discontinuities in the Islamic Response to Modernity' in M Cousineau (ed), *Religion in a Changing World. Comparative Studies in Sociology* (Westport, Conn, Praeger, 1998).
MORUZZI NC, 'A Problem with Headscarves: Contemporary Complexities of Political and Social Identity' (1994) 22 *Political Theory* 653.
MRAZEK P and Haggerty RJ (eds), *Reducing Risks for Mental Disorders: Frontiers for Preventive Intervention Research.* Committee on Prevention of Mental Disorders, Division of Biobehavioral Sciences and Mental Disorders, Institute of Medicine (Washington DC, National Academy Press, 1994).
NIELSEN JS, *Muslims in Western Europe* (Edinburgh, Edinburgh University Press, 1992).
—— *Towards a European Islam* (London, Macmillan Press Limited, 1999).
NORMAN R, *Free and Equal: A Philosophical Examination of Political Values* (Oxford, Oxford University Press, 1987).
NOZICK R, 'Coercion' in S Morgenbesser and P Suppes (eds), *Philosophy, Science and Method* (New York, St Martin's Press, 1969).
—— *Anarchy, State, and Utopia* (Oxford, Basil Blackwell, 1974).
NUSSBAUM M and O'Neill O, 'Justice, Gender, and International Boundaries' in M Nussbaum and A Sen (eds), *The Quality of Life* (New York, Oxford University Press, 1993).
OFFE C, 'Challenging the Boundaries of Institutional Politics: Social Movements since the 1960s' in C Mayer (ed), *Changing the Boundaries of the Political: Essays on the Evolving Balance between the State and Society, Public and Private in Europe* (New York, Cambridge University Press, 1987).
—— 'Homogeneity and Constitutional Democracy: Coping with Identity Conflicts through Group Rights' (1998) 6 *The Journal of Political Philosophy* 113.
O'KEEFE R, 'The "Right to Take Part in Cultural Life" under Article 15 of the ICESCR' (1998) *International and Comparative Law Quarterly* 904.
ORTNER SB, 'Theory of Anthropology since the Sixties' in NB Dirks, G Eley and SB Ortner (eds), *Culture/Power/History: A Reader in Contemporary Social Theory* (Princeton, Princeton University Press, 1994).
PAREKH B, 'Equality in a Multiracial Society' in J Franklin (ed), *Equality* (London, Institute for Public Policy Research, 1997).
—— *Rethinking Multiculturalism. Cultural Diversity and Political Theory* (Cambridge, MA, Harvard University Press, 2000).
PETERS FE, *Greek Philosophical Terms. A Historical Lexicon* (New York, New York University Press, 1967).
POGGE T, *Realizing Rawls* (Ithaca, Cornell University Press, 1989).
—— 'Cosmopolitanism and Sovereignty' (1992) 103 *Ethics* 48.
—— 'An Egalitarian Law of Peoples' (1994) 23 *Philosophy & Public Affairs* 195.
—— 'The Global Resources Dividend' in DA Crocker and T Linden (eds), *Ethics of Consumption: The Good Life, Justice and Global Stewardship* (Lanham, MD, Rowman & Littlefield, 1998).
—— 'Human Flourishing and Universal Justice' (1999) 16 *Social Philosophy* 333.
POSNER RA, 'Past-Dependency, Pragmatism, and Critique of History in Adjudication and Legal Scholarship' (2000) 67 *University of Chicago Law Review* 573.
POULTER S, 'Ethnic Minority Customs, English Law and Human Rights' (1987) 36 *International and Comparative Law Quarterly* 589.

—— 'Muslim Headscarves in School: Contrasting Legal Approaches in England and France' (1997) 17 *Oxford Journal of Legal Studies* 43.
—— *Ethnicity, Law and Human Rights. The English Experience* (Oxford, Clarendon Press, 1998).
PRZEWORSKI A *et al*, *Sustainable Democracy* (New York, Cambridge University Press, 1995).
—— 'Deliberation and Ideological Domination' in J Elster (ed), *Deliberative Democracy* (New York, Cambridge University Press, 1998).
PUTNAM RD, *Making Democracy Work: Civic Traditions in Modern Italy* (Princeton, Princeton University Press, 1993).
RAMSEY P, *Teaching and Learning in a Diverse World: Multicultural Education for Young Children* (New York, Teachers College, Columbia University, 1987).
—— 'Caring for Children in a Diverse World' in B Spodek and ON Saracho (eds), *Issues in Child Care. Yearbook in Early Childhood Education*, vol 3 (New York, Teachers College Press, 1992).
RATZLAFF C, Matsumoto D, Kouznetsova N, Raroque J, and Ray R, 'Individual Psychological Culture and Subjective Well-being' in E Diener and EM Suh (eds), *Culture and Subjective Well-being* (Cambridge, MA, MIT Press, 2000).
RAWLS J, 'Social Unity and Primary Goods' in B Williams and A Sen (eds), *Utilitarianism and Beyond* (Cambridge, Cambridge University Press, 1982).
—— 'Justice as Fairness: Political not Metaphysical' (1985) 14 *Philosophy and Public Affairs* 223.
—— *Political Liberalism* (New York, Columbia University Press, 1995).
—— 'Public Reason Revisited' (1997) 64 *University of Chicago Law Review* 765.
—— *A Theory of Justice*, 2nd rev edn (Cambridge, MA, Harvard University Press, 1999).
—— *The Law of Peoples* (Cambridge, MA, Harvard University Press, 1999).
RAZ J, *The Authority of Law* (Oxford, Clarendon Press, 1979).
—— *The Morality of Freedom* (Oxford, Clarendon Press, 1986).
—— *Ethics in the Public Domain: Essays in the Morality of Law and Politics* (New York, Oxford University Press, 1994).
RORTY R, 'Human Rights, Rationality, and Sentimentality' in S Shute and S Hurley (eds), *On Human Rights. The Oxford Amnesty Lectures 1993* (New York, Harper Collins Publishers, 1993).
ROSEBURY A, Mcintyre E, and González N (eds) *Classroom Diversity: Connecting Curriculum to Students' Lives* (Portsmouth, NH, Heinemann, 2001).
RUBIN EL, 'Law and Legislation in the Administrative State' (1989) 89 *Columbia Law Review* 369.
RUSSELL KK, '"Driving While Black": Corollary Phenomena and Collateral Consequences' (1999) 40 *British Columbia Law Review* 717.
SAMUELSSON J, *Islam i Sverige. Nutid och Framtid* (Stockholm, Natur och Kultur, 1999).
SANTA CRUZ ROBLES MJ, 'Refugees from South-East Asia in Spain: The Challenge of Hope' in D Joly and R Cohen (eds), *Reluctant Hosts: Europe and Its Refugees* (Aldershot, Avebury, 1989).
SCANLON T, 'The Difficulty of Tolerance' in D Heyd (ed), *Toleration. An Elusive Virtue* (Princeton, Princeton University Press, 1996).
SEN A, 'Equality of What?' in A Sen, *Choice, Welfare and Measurement* (Cambridge, Cambridge University Press, 1982).

—— 'Rights and Capabilities' in A Sen, *Resources, Values and Development* (Oxford, Basil Blackwell Publishers, 1984).
—— *Commodities and Capabilities* (Amsterdam, North-Holland, 1985).
—— 'Well-being, Agency and Freedom' (1985) 82 *The Journal of Philosophy* 169.
—— 'Justice: Means versus Freedoms' (1990) 19 *Philosophy & Public Affairs* 111.
SHADID WAR and van Koningsveld PS, *Religious Freedom and the Position of Islam in Western Europe. Opportunities and Obstacles in the Acquisition of Equal Rights* (Kampen, Kok Pharos Publishing House, 1995).
SHAIN BA, 'Individualism' in R Wuthnow (ed), *The Encyclopedia of Politics and Religion* (Washington, DC, Congressional Quarterly, 1998).
SHACHAR A, 'The Puzzle of Interlocking Power Hierarchies: Sharing the Pieces of Jurisdictional Authority' (2000) 35 *Harvard Civil Rights-Civil Liberties Law Review* 385.
SHKLAR J, 'The Liberalism of Fear' in N Rosenblum (ed), *Liberalism and the Moral Life* (Cambridge, Harvard University Press, 1989).
SOYSAL Y, *Limits of Citizenship: Migrants and Postnational Membership in Europe* (Chicago, Chicago University Press, 1994).
—— 'Changing Parameters of Citizenship and Claims-Making: Organized Islam in European Public Spheres' (1996) *EUI Working Paper. EUF* no 96/4.
SPIRO ME, 'Some Reflections on Cultural Determinism and Relativism with Special Reference to Emotion and Reason' in RA Shweder and RA LeVine (eds), *Culture Theory: Essays on Mind, Self and Emotion* (New York, Cambridge University Press, 1984).
STAVROS S, 'Freedom of Religion and Claims for Exemption from Generally-applicable, Neutral Laws: Lessons from Across the Pond?' in Council of Europe, *Religion and the Integration of Immigrants* (Strasbourg, Council of Europe, 1999).
SULTANHUSSEIN T, *A Muslim Commentary on the Universal Declaration of Human Rights* (Guildford, FJ Goulding, 1970).
SWIDLER A, 'Culture in Action: Symbols and Strategies' (1986) 51 *American Sociological Review* 273.
STEINER H, *An Essay on Rights* (Oxford, Blackwell Publishers, 1994).
TAMIR Y, *Liberal Nationalism* (Princeton, Princeton University Press, 1993).
TAYLOR C, *Sources of the Self: The Making of the Modern Identity* (Cambridge, MA, Harvard University Press, 1989).
—— 'The Politics of Recognition' in A Gutmann (ed), *Multiculturalism: Examining the Politics of Recognition* (Princeton, Princeton University Press, 1994).
—— 'To Follow a Rule' in Charles Taylor (ed), *Philosophical Arguments* (Cambridge, MA, Harvard University Press, 1995).
—— 'Conditions of an Unforced Consensus on Human Rights' in JR Bauer and DA Bell (eds), *The East Asian Challenge for Human Rights* (New York, Cambridge University Press, 1999).
—— 'Democratic Exclusion (and Its Remedies?). The John Ambrose Stack Memorial Lecture' in AC Cairns *et al* (eds), *Citizenship, Diversity, and Pluralism. Canadian and Comparative Perspectives* (Montreal, McGill-Queen's University Press, 1999).
THOMPSON EP, *The Poverty of Theory and Other Essays* (New York, Monthly Review Press, 1979).
THOMPSON JB, *Ideology and Modern Culture: Critical Social Theory in the Era of Mass Communications* (Stanford, Cal, Stanford University Press, 1990).

THOREAU H, 'Resistance to Civil Government (Civil Disobedience)' in N Rosenblum (ed), *Henry Thoreau: Political Writings* (Cambridge, Cambridge University Press, 1996).

THORNBERRY P, *International Law and the Rights of Minorities* (Oxford, Oxford University Press, 1991).

TUCK R, *Natural Rights Theories* (New York, Cambridge University Press, 1995).

—— 'Scepticism and Toleration in the Seventeenth Century' in S Mendus (ed), *Justifying Toleration: Conceptual and Historical Perspectives* (New York, Cambridge University Press, 1988).

TUSHNET M, 'An Essay on Rights' (1984) 62 *Texas Law Review* 1363.

—— *Taking the Constitution Away from the Courts* (Princeton NJ, Princeton University Press, 1999).

—— 'Questioning the Value of Accommodating Religion' in SM Feldman (ed), *Law and Religion. A Critical Anthology* (New York, New York University Press, 2000).

TYLOR E, *Primitive Culture* (New York, Harper & Row, Publishers, 1958).

VAN DIJK P and van Hoof GJH, *Theory and Practice of the European Convention on Human Rights* (The Hague, Kluwer Law International, 1998).

VÉLEZ-IBÁÑEZ C and Greenberg J, 'Formation and Transformation of Funds of Knowledge Among US Mexican Housholds' (1993) 23 *Anthropology and Education Quarterly* 313.

VERMEULEN H (ed), *Immigration Policy for a Multicultural Society: A Comparative Study of Integration, Language and Religious Policy in Five Western European Countries* (Brussels, Migration Policy Group, 1997).

VOLL JO, 'Islam' in R Wuthnow (ed), *The Encyclopedia of Politics and Religion* (Washington DC, Congressional Quarterly, 1998).

WALDRON J, *Theories of Rights* (New York, Oxford University Press, 1984).

—— 'Nonsense Upon Stilts? A Reply' in J Waldron, *Nonsense Upon Stilts: Bentham, Burke and Marx on the Rights of Man* (New York, Meutheu, 1987).

—— 'Superseding Historic Injustices' (1992) 103 *Ethics* 4.

—— 'Minority Cultures and the Cosmopolitan Alternative' (1992) 24 *University of Michigan Journal of Law Reform* 751.

—— 'Spécial Ties and Natural Duties' (1993) 22 *Philosophy and Public Affairs* 3.

—— *Liberal Rights: Collected Papers (1981–1991)* (New York, Cambridge University Press, 1993).

—— 'A Right-Based Critique of Constitutional Rights' (1993) 13 *Oxford Journal of Legal Studies* 18.

—— 'Rights' in RE Goodin and P Pettit (eds), *A Companion to Contemporary Political Philosophy* (Oxford, Blackwell, 1993).

—— 'Rights and Needs—The Myth of Disjunction' in A Sarat and TR Kearns (eds), *Legal Rights: Historical and Philosophical Perspectives* (Ann Arbor, University of Michigan Press, 1996).

—— 'Kant's Legal Positivism' (1996) 109 *Harvard Law Review* 1535.

—— *The Dignity of Legislation* (Cambridge, Cambridge University Press, 1999).

—— *Law and Disagreement* (Oxford, Clarendon Press, 1999).

—— 'All We Like Sheep' (1999) 25 *Canadian Journal of Law and Jurisprudence* 169.

—— 'Cultural Identity and Civic Responsibility' in W Kymlicka and W Norman (eds), *Citizenship in Diverse Societies* (New York, Oxford University Press, 2000).

—— 'What is Cosmopolitan?' (2000) 8 *The Journal of Political Philosophy* 227.

—— 'Redressing Historic Injustice' (2000) 52 *University of Toronto Law Journal* 135.

—— 'One Law for All? The Logic of Cultural Accommodation' (2000) 59 *Washington Lee Law Review* 3.

—— 'Toleration and Reasonableness' in D Castiglione and C McKinnon (eds), *The Culture of Toleration in Diverse Societies: Reasonable Tolerance* (Manchester, Manchester University Press, 2003).

WALZER M, *Obligations: Essays on Disobedience, War, and Citizenship* (Cambridge, MA, Harvard University Press, 1970).

WANDERER NA and Connors CR, 'Culture and Crime: Kargar (*State v Kargar*, 679 A 2d 81 (Me 1996)) and the Existing Framework for a Cultural Defence' (1999) 47 *Buffalo Law Review* 829.

WEITHMAN P, 'Introduction: Religion and the Liberalism of Reasoned Respect' in P Weithman (ed), *Religion and Contemporary Liberalism* (Indianapolis, University of Notre Dame Press, 1997).

WILLIAMS B, *Morality*, 2nd edn (Cambridge, Cambridge University Press, 1993).

WILLIAMS G, *Criminal Law: The General Part*, 2nd edn (London, Stevens & Sons Limited, 1961).

WUTHNOW R, *Meaning and Moral Order: Explorations in Cultural Analysis* (Berkeley, University of California Press, 1987).

WRONG D, 'The Oversocialized Conception of Man in Modern Sociology' in D Wrong, *Skeptical Sociology* (London, Columbia University Press, 1977).

YOUNG IM, *Justice and the Politics of Difference* (Princeton, Princeton University Press, 1990).

International Documents

Legal

Convention on the Prevention and Punishment of the Crime of Genocide. Approved by the General Assembly of the United Nations by its resolution 260 A (III) of 9 December 1948.

Convention Relating to the Status of Refugees. Adopted on 28 July 1951 by the United Nations Conference of Plenipotentiaries on the Status of Refugees and Stateless Persons convened under General Assembly resolution 429 (V) of 14 December 1950.

International Convention on the Elimination of All Forms of Racial Discrimination. Adopted by the General Assembly of the United Nations by its resolution 2106A (XX) of 21 December 1965.

International Covenant on Economic, Social and Cultural Rights. Adopted by the General Assembly of the United Nations by its resolution 2200 (XXI) of 16 December 1966.

International Covenant on Civil and Political Rights. Adopted by the General Assembly of the United Nations by its resolution 2200 (XXI) of 16 December 1966.

Convention on the Elimination of All Forms of Discrimination against Women. Adopted by the General Assembly of the United Nations by its resolution 34/180 of 18 December 1979.

African Charter on Human and Peoples' Rights. Adopted by the Organisation of African Unity at the 18th Conference of Heads of State and Government on 17 June 1981.

Additional Protocol to the American Convention on Human Rights in the Area of Economic, Social and Cultural Rights, "Protocol of San Salvador". Adopted by the Organisation of American States on 17 November 1988.

Convention Concerning Indigenous and Tribal Peoples in Independent Countries. Adopted by the General Conference of the International Labour Organization at its seventy-sixth session on 27 June 1989.

Convention on the Rights of the Child. Adopted by the General Assembly of the United Nations by its resolution 44/25 of 20 November 1989.

International Convention on the Protection of the Rights of All Migrant Workers and Members of Their Families. Adopted by the General Assembly of the United Nations by its resolution 45/158 of 18 December 1990.

African Charter on the Rights and Welfare of the Child. Adopted by the Organisation of African Unity on 11 July 1990.

Inter-American Convention on the Prevention, Punishment and Eradication of Violence against Women, "Convention of Belem Do Para". Adopted at the twenty-fourth regular session of the General Assembly of the Organisation of American States on 9 June 1994.

The Statute of the International Tribunal for the Former Yugoslavia. Adopted by the Security Council by its resolution 808 (1993) on 25 May 1993.

The Statute of the International Tribunal for Rwanda. Adopted by the Security Council by its resolution 955 (1994) on 8 November 1994.

The Framework Convention for the Protection of National Minorities. Adopted by the Committee of the Council of Europe on 10 November 1994.

Optional Protocol to the Convention on the Elimination of All Forms of Discrimination against Women. Adopted by the General Assembly of the United Nations by its resolution 54/4 of 15 October 1999.

Charter of Fundamental Rights of the European Union. Signed and proclaimed by the Presidents of the European Parliament, the Council and the Commission at the European Council meeting in Nice on 7 December 2000.

Declarations, etc

American Declaration on the Rights and Duties of Man. Adopted by the Ninth International Conference of American States by OAS resolution XXX of 2 May 1948.

Universal Declaration of Human Rights. Adopted by the General Assembly of the United Nations by its resolution 217 (III) of 10 December 1948.

Helsinki Final Act. Adopted by the Conference for Security and Co-operation in Europe on 1 August 1975.

Declaration on the Right to Development. Adopted by the General Assembly of the United Nations by its resolution 41/128 of 4 December 1986.

Document of the Copenhagen Meeting of the Conference on the Human Dimension of the CSCE. Adopted by the Conference for Security and Co-operation in Europe on 29 June 1990.
Charter of Paris for a New Europe. Adopted by the Conference on Security and Co-operation in Europe on 21 November 1990.
Cairo Declaration on Human Rights in Islam. Issued by the Organisation of the Islamic Conference on 5 August 1990.
Tunis Declaration on Human Rights. Adopted by the Regional Meeting of Africa of the World Conference on Human Rights on 6 November 1992.
UN Declaration of the Rights of Persons belonging to National or Ethnic, Religious or Linguistic Minorities. Adopted by the General Assembly of the United Nations by its resolution 47/135 of 18 December 1992.
San José Declaration on Human Rights. Adopted by the Regional Meeting for Latin America and the Caribbean of the World Conference on Human Rights on 22 January 1993.
Bangkok Declaration on Human Rights. Adopted by the Regional Meeting for Asia of the World Conference on Human Rights on 2 April 1993.
Vienna Declaration and Programme of Action. Adopted by the United Nations World Conference on Human Rights on 25 June 1993.
Declaration on the Elimination of Violence against Women. Adopted by the General Assembly of the United Nations by its resolution 48/104 of 20 December 1993.
Beijing Declaration and Platform of Action. Adopted by the Fourth World Conference on Women on 15 September 1995.
Charter for European Security. Adopted by the Organization for Security and Co-operation on 19 November 1999.

Other

General Comment No 23 (50) on Article 27/ Minority Rights. Adopted by the Human Rights Committee of the International Covenant on Civil and Political Rights at its 1314th meeting (fiftieth session) on 6 April 1994. Doc. CCPR/C/21/Rev1/Add5. Reproduced in *Human Rights Law Journal*, vol 15 No 4–6 (1994) (234–236).
Draft Declaration on the Rights of Indigenous Peoples. Adopted by the UN Sub-Commission on Prevention of Discrimination and Protection of Minorities by its resolution 1994/45 at its 36th meeting on 26 August 1994.
Draft Code of Crimes against the Peace and Security of Mankind. Adopted by the International Law Commission at its 48th session of 31 May 1996.
UNESCO Report "Our Cultural Diversity". Drafted by the World Commission on Culture and Development and submitted to UNESCO and the United Nations in November 1995 (Paris, UNESCO, 1998).
Draft Protocol to the African Charter on Human and Peoples' Rights on the Rights of Women in Africa. Adopted by the Organisation of African Unity on 13 September 2000.
Proposal for a Council Directive on minimum standards on procedures in Member States for granting and withdrawing refugee status. The Commission of the European Communities (Brussels, 20 September 2000).
*Statistical Survey of Individual Complaints Under the Procedure Governed by Article 14 of the International Convention on the Elimination of All Forms of Racial

Discrimination, 31 March 2004 [available at: <http://www.unhchr.ch/html/menu2/8/stat4.htm>]. Last visited on 4 January 2005.
Compilation of General Comments and General Recommendations adopted by Human Rights Treaty Bodies, 12 May 2004 (HRI/GEN/1/Rev 7).
Human Development Report 2004. Cultural Liberty in Today's Diverse World (New York, United Nations Development Programme, 2004).

Case Law

European Court of Human Rights

Relating to Certain Aspects of the Laws on the Use of Languages in Education in Belgium Series A no 6 (1968).
Kokkinakis v Greece Series A no 260–A (1993) 17 EHRR 397.
Wingrove v UK no 17419/90 ECHR 1996–V 24 EHRR 1.
Sidiropolous and Others v Greece no 26695/95 ECHR 1998–IV.
Buscarini and Others v San Marino no 24645/94 ECHR 1999–I.
Gorzelik and Others v Poland, no 44158/98, judgment of 17 February 2004.
Zeynep Tekin v Turkey, no 41556/98, judgment of 29 June 2004.
Leyla Sahin v Turkey, no 44774/98, judgment of 29 June 2004.

European Commission of Human Rights

Appl 1753/63, *X v Austria*, Yearbook VIII (1965), 174.
Appl 7992/77, *X v the United Kingdom*, D&R 14 (1979), 234.
Appl 8231/78, *X v the United Kingdom*, D&R 28 (1982), 5.
Appl 11579/85, *Khan v the United Kingdom*, D&R 48 (1986), 253.

European Court of Justice

Case 29/69 *Stauder v City of Ulm* [1969] ECR 419.
Case 55/87*Moksel v BALM* [1988] ECR 3845.

Inter-American Court of Human Rights

Mayagna (Sumo) Awas Tingni Community v Nicaragua, judgment of 31 August 2001, IACHR Series C no 66 (2000).

German Federal Constitutional Court

BVerfGe 76, 1 (1987).
BVerfGe 16.05.1995–1BvR 1087/91 *Neue Juristische Wochenschrift* Ausgabe 38/1995 at 2477.

German Administrative Court

VG Lüneburg Urt v 16. 10. 2000–1 A 98/00 (NJW 2001, 767).

Italian Constitutional Court

Sent N 440 *Caianiello; Zagrebelsky* (1995).
Sent N 329 *Granata; Zagrabelsky* (1997).

French Conseil d'Etat

Avis No 346893 du 27 November 1989. *Assemblée générale plénière* (1990). *L'actualité juridique—Droit administratif* (AJDA) 39 (1990).

Human Rights Committee of the United Nations

Mahuika et al v New Zealand (547/1993), ICC PR, A/56/40 Vol II (27 October 2000).

United States Federal Supreme Court

Braunfeld v Brown, 366 US 599 (1961).
Sherbert v Verner, 374 US 398 (1963).
Wisconsin v Yoder, 406 US 205 (1972).
Thomas v Review Board of Indiana Employment Security Division, 450 US 707 (1981).
Estate of Thornton v Caldor Inc, 472 US 703 (1985).
Goldman v Weinberger, 475 US 503 (1986).
Bowen v Roy, 476 US 693 (1986).
Hobbie v Unemployment Appeals Commission of Florida, 480 US 136 (1987).
O'Lone v Estate of Shabazz, 482 US 342 (1987).
Employment Division v Smith, 494 US 872 (1990).
City of Borne v Flores, 521 US 507 (1997).

United States Lower Courts

People v Moua Record of Court Proceedings, No 315972-0 (Super Ct Fresno County, Feb 7 1985).
People v Kimura Record of Court Proceedings, No A–091133 (Super Ct LA Country Nov 21 1985).
People v Chen Record of Court Proceedings, No 87–774 (NY Sup Ct Dec 2 1988).
*You Vang Yang Is Kue Yang v William Q Sturne*r (750 F Supp 558) (Nov 9 1990).
State v Kargar, 679 A. 2d 81 (Me 1996).

Other Documents

Law, Blasphemy and the Multifaith Society. Report of a Seminar organised by the Commission for Racial Equality and the Interfaith Network of the United Kingdom (September, 1989) (London, The Commission, 1990).
Religious Freedom Restoration Act of 1993. Enacted by US Congress. 107 stat. 1488 public law 103–141–nov 16 1993.
The Muslim Parliament. Building a better future for Muslims in Britain. London, May, 1995 [available at: <http://ummah.net/mp/mp-doc.htm>]. Last visited on 27 January 2000.
Committee on Economic, Social and Cultural Rights *Statement on Globalization and Economic, Social and Cultural Rights*: *11/05/98*, 18th session, 27 April–15 May 1998, Geneva [available at: <http://www.unhchr.ch/tbs/doc.nsf/0/adc44375895aa10d8025668f003cc06e?Opendocument>]. Last visited on 4 January 2005.
Fact Sheet No 16 (Rev 1), The Committee on Economic, Social and Cultural Rights [available at: <http://193.194.138.190/html/menu6/2/fs16.htm#4>]. Last visited on 4 January 2005.

Turkey Country Report on Human Rights Practices for 1997. Released by the Bureau of Democracy, Human Rights and Labor, US Department of State, January 30, 1998.

Comments to the Swedish government proposition 1998/99:70: Female Circumcision—abolishment of the requirement on double criminal liability. Amendment to the Swedish law (1982:316) prohibiting circumcision of women.

Loi no 2004–228 *du* 15–3–2004 (JO du 17-3-2004) *Texte adressé aux rectrices et recteurs d'académie; aux inspectrices et inspecteurs d'académie, directeurs et directrices des services départementaux de l'éducation nationale* (2004) 21 *Bulletin Officiel* 1043.

Index

www.ingramcontent.com/pod-product-compliance
Ingram Content Group UK Ltd.
Pitfield, Milton Keynes, MK11 3LW, UK
UKHW020832290926
15470UKWH00009B/1860/J

9 781841 135069